MW00358375

Eugene "Pineapple" Jackson : His Own Story

EUGENE "Pineapple" JACKSON

His Own Story

by Eugene W. Jackson II
with Gwendolyn Sides St. Julian

with a foreword by ZAIID LEFLORE

McFarland & Company, Inc., Publishers
Jefferson, North Carolina, and London

COVER: *Jackson as he appeared in the 1924* Our Gang *comedies.*
FRONTISPIECE: *Jackson as Isaiah tries on the outfit of his hero, Yancey Cravat (Richard Dix), in the 1931 film* Cimarron.

British Library Cataloguing-in-Publication data are available

Library of Congress Cataloguing-in-Publication Data

Jackson, Eugene W., 1916–
    Eugene "Pineapple" Jackson : his own story / by Eugene W. Jackson II with Gwendolyn Sides St. Julian ; with a foreword by Zaiid Leflore.
        p.   cm.
    Filmography: p.
    Includes bibliographical references and index.
    ISBN 0-7864-0533-3 (case binding : 50# alkaline paper) ∞
    1. Jackson, Eugene W., 1916–   . 2. Afro-American entertainers — Biography.   I. St. Julian, Gwendolyn Sides.
II. Title.
PN2287.J26A3   1999
791'.092 — dc21
    [B]   98-38734
                                                              CIP

Manufactured in the United States of America

McFarland & Company, Inc., Publishers
  Box 611, Jefferson, North Carolina 28640

EUGENE W. JACKSON II

To Sue, my beloved wife

In loving memory of my mother, Lillie B. Foster

To the memory of the best brother
a man could have, Freddie Baker

To my children, Eugene Jackson III, Hazel, Sue Carol

To all of the *Our Gang* comedy cast and crew

To my grandchildren, Simone, Garrett, Rashaan,
Kareem, Sueandra and Malvin IV

To my nieces, Jeanette, Rosina, Ferdie and Lorraine

GWENDOLYN SIDES ST. JULIAN

To Dedrick James Julian, Sr. and Jr.

To my mother, Alberta Spicer Kemp

Table of Contents

Acknowledgments
by Gwendolyn Sides St. Julian

I'd like to thank Eugene Jackson for asking me to help put his fascinating life story into words, and for sharing photographs from his private collection. His wife, Sue, is a supportive, wonderful lady, and she and Eugene have been like parents to me. They have three beautiful, talented children: Eugene III, Hazel and Sue Carol.

I must also thank my son, Dedrick James Julian, Jr., who allowed me to work many hours both in the library and at home. He has always been excited about and involved in this project. When he was a young tyke, he and I would sit for hours on the floor of our living room, organizing pieces of paper from different books. He worked diligently by my side, traveling with me daily to the library and sitting attentively in the children's section reading every book he could find. This is part of the reason why he writes and reads so well today.

Thanks also to my mother, Alberta Spicer Kemp, who taught me to stick with a task no matter how difficult.

When a person takes on as large a task as this one, there is always a need for spiritual guidance. I would like to thank two pastors and their congregations for prayer, support and positive words of encouragement while I worked on this monumental project. Many times I wouldn't know which path to follow, but the prayers of the pastors and members of these great institutions would show me the way. I was always able to pick up the phone and have prayer with any of them. I am sincerely grateful for the Rev. Dr. Bobby T. Newman, pastor of Citizen of Zion Missionary Baptist Church of Compton, California, and the Rev. Dr. Alvin J. Wesley, pastor of Hermon Baptist Church of Chicago, Illinois. Eugene and I worked on this project for over 17 years. There is no way I could have mastered each goal without prayer from these people.

From the onset of this book, I wrote around the United States for assistance. I would like to thank the following organizations for responding with phone calls, letters, magazines and brochures: the National Association for the Advancement of Colored People (NAACP); the Academy of Arts and Sciences; the Cultural Affairs Department of Los Angeles; the National Council of Jewish

Women; Women in Community Services; and members of the Pen American Center, the National League of American Pen Women, the Illinois Arts Council, the Illinois Humanities Council, the Screen Actors Guild, and the American Federation of Television and Radio Artists.

Special thanks go to my typists: Regina Payton, Rukeesha Keys, Rosetta Tetteh, Princess Parker, and the Blake and Crawford families. Thanks go also to the Laurem Business Center for their professional service, and to entertainment attorney Matthew Rosenberger for his expertise in the legal aspects of publishing, in addition to his encouragement and counseling. I am grateful to Dr. Mack Morant for guidance, words of advice, and knowledge of the publishing industry.

I do not know what I would have done without the world renowned educator Marva Collins, founder of Westside Preparatory School in Chicago, Illinois. By educating Dedrick Jr., she provided me (through him) with all the wonderful black history facts for documentation of the inventions and patents of Africans and African Americans; these facts enhanced our book. The Our Authors Study Club of Los Angeles provided a 1992 bus tour of all the black historical locations of Los Angeles. This tour proved very beneficial to me, for one of the riders on the bus was Amelia Morrison, sister of *Our Gang* actor "Sunshine Sammy." She and others gave wonderful stories of how prosperous some black communities were in the early 1900s. I was also fortunate to attend two reading clubs sponsored by Charlsie Pollard and Edna Johnson. These clubs presented oral interpretations of African American literature at its best, and their discussions were valuable to me when I began to express and write about our African American heritage. Mayme Clayton, curator and archivist of the Black Western State Research Archive and the Black American Cinema Society of Independent Filmmakers, found old, lost and almost destroyed films of African Americans from the past. She single-handedly searched, catalogued and restored films from the 1920s to the present. I give my thanks to this librarian and historian for the preservation of black life in films and art. Walid Khaldi of Golden Moon Films of Allen, Texas, provided documentation on the *Amos 'n' Andy* series. The Dusable Museum of African American History and the Chicago Historical Society had exhibits on the lifestyle of African Americans in the twenties in Chicago. These exhibits validated Eugene Jackson's oral history.

Gwendolyn Brooks, poet laureate and director of the Gwendolyn Brooks Center at Chicago State University, took the time from her busy schedule to read some of my information on Eugene Jackson and offer suggestions. I attended her writer's workshop, which was very enjoyable and helpful.

Thanks to Mr. Bob Sloane, dance librarian of Chicago's Harold Washington Library Center, for all the reference books. I was a regular on the eighth floor in the film and dance department. All the staff members of the Chicago Public Library and libraries across the United States were most helpful. I'd like to say thank you to the regular patrons of the Chicago Public Library for their interest and involvement in this project. They often brought information to add to my book. I don't know them all by name, but I am very appreciative of their kind gestures.

I had some wonderful people on the West Coast who helped me with research: Antoinette and Michelle Newson, Rheba Smith, Dedrick Julian, Sr., and Minnie E. Miller. Thanks to Frank "Junior" Coghlan and Diana Serra Cary, better known as "Baby Peggy" from the comedies. Both provided much-needed information on the *Century*, *Buster Brown*, and *Mary Jane* comedies.

Special thanks to the following organizations, which sponsored writing workshops and services and helped me learn the business aspects of writing: the National Council of Negro Women; the Association of Black Filmmakers of Chicago; California Lawyers for the Arts; Lawyers for the Creative Arts; Chicago Women in Publishing; and the National Writers Union. Thanks also go to four professional business women who have been mentors to me over the years: Inez Barnes, Sue Jamison Browning, Martha Wheeler-Fair and Rosie Bean.

I wouldn't be anything without my extended family — Carolyn Smith, Alice Mason, David Sides, Gina Eanes, the twins Steve and Stephanie Taylor, Joy Jackson Lee, Estelena Cooksey, Joyce Givens and Paul Banks. My sister, Phyllis Sides, who writes for a newspaper, spelled every word quickly when I would wake her at odd hours. I could always rely on my smart older sister! From the bottom of my heart I am grateful to all of them; each helped in his or her unique way.

Thanks to the telephone operators and directory assistance people, who provided me with correct spellings of cities and streets around the United States. Their quick access into their computer databases saved me many hours of library research.

Thanks are also due to two people who no longer walk the face of this earth, but whose spirits are among us, watching and guiding to make sure the story is represented accurately. They are Lillie B. Foster Baker and Freddie Baker. These two people kept albums full of newspaper clippings and photos of Eugene from his early days in film as a child star, which made documentation easy.

I say thank you to all unmentioned friends. Time, space and paper won't permit me to mention you. You know who you are and what you contributed to this book. You're in my heart, which is where it counts.

GWENDOLYN SIDES ST. JULIAN
November 1998

Foreword

by Zaiid Leflore

(former student of Eugene "Pineapple" Jackson)

For a black history assignment, I had to write about a famous person. I immediately thought of Mr. Jackson, who has helped me over the years to become a great tapper. He and I have a special relationship that no one can tear apart. I just thank God that my grandparents thought enough of me to take me to the best in the field of tap. Mr. Jackson is the "grandmaster of tap" — believe me when I say that no one has anything on him when it comes to tap. His style, grace and manner are all his own. I felt he would be great to write about because many of the students and maybe even my teacher may not have heard of Mr. Jackson, a fact that would make my report stand out above all the others. My report would be different, one that would stick in the minds of everyone, because Mr. Jackson lived right here in Compton, where I live, in a city that is almost always negatively portrayed. Mr. Jackson has high values and high expectations of himself and his students. He is a positive force throughout his life and travels all around the United States. He brings joy to the hearts of people wherever he is. I told myself that Mr. Jackson is someone that we could all touch. He didn't live far away in Beverly Hills; he lived right here in Compton with us. He was part of the community, he was part of us, and I was proud. Here is what I wrote on November 25, 1992, for my class. I wrote this report with pride in my heart. He was a part of me, and I was a part of him:

> My character is Eugene Jackson, an all around entertainer. He is a short, bald man with the biggest clownlike smile you ever saw. He has heavy eyebrows, chubby cheeks and a big round mole on his cheek. Mr. Jackson has humorous facial expressions. When he talks, he uses lots of hand actions. Mr. Jackson is very hyperactive and has a very bubbly personality. Mr. Jackson has acquired many special abilities and talents in his seventy years. Mr. Jackson can play the drums, bass guitar, saxophone, piano, ukulele, trumpet, violin and cello. He is also an excellent tap dancer and actor.

1

Mr. Jackson has experienced almost everything an entertainer could be and do in his life. He was at Pearl Harbor at the time of the bombing during World War II, was in vaudeville and was one of the original *Our Gang* characters. He worked the radio circuit. He appeared in the old silent films with Mary Pickford and was in the new *Addams Family* movie. His most recent commercial is for GTE.

One never knows what Mr. Jackson can and will do. Once at a restaurant in Las Vegas while waiting for his food, he started to play his ukulele. He had everybody in line singing "Tiny Bubbles." His daughters were embarrassed, but he said, "I just like to make people happy." He's a true entertainer from his heart.

When his children were young, he taught them how to tap dance. Later he started his own tap dance school, The New Stage Workshop in Compton, California. His daughters now run the school. I am Mr. Jackson's young protégé. His grandson and I have started a duo called "LeBlack." From all the routines Mr. Jackson has taught us, we have won many tap competitions in Las Vegas and appeared in a Paula Abdul video. We have performed at many banquets and parties.

Mr. Jackson is a person all of us can look up to. At the present time, he is in the process of having his biography written. Right now he is a little under the weather. I hope he gets well soon because I love him very much. I want him to get well soon so he can teach me more tap steps.

This foreword is just one testimonial of a life that Mr. Jackson has touched. He has touched so many people's lives that if you ask him, "Hey, Mr. J., didn't you teach that student?" he may respond with "I can't remember." But to the surprise of Mr. J., his students always remember him because he touched their lives. Their lives will never be the same because of his kindness and care. It took a lot of patience to work with children, youth and adults, but he did it all because he had a love for the art, a respect for dance and mankind.

He's a man with vision and insight into the hearts of people. He believes sincerely that if he can lift the spirit of a person for just one moment, his mission has been accomplished. Mr. Jackson truly loves people and the arts. He's always on a mission to create a dance and a challenging routine to take it to its highest level. Once the zenith has been reached, his goal has been accomplished. In entertaining, no mission is impossible for Mr. Jackson. He's going to climb that ladder until the crowd begs for more. When he hears the laughter and remarks, and sees the smiles on the faces and feels the smiles in the hearts of the public, he is content. He has lit the hearts of so many by lifting their spirits. He's the showman of all shows.

Prologue

I never had a day of professional training in dancing or acting. My gift from God was a flair for entertaining. I've been interviewed, discussed, and written about in newspapers, but never has my life story been turned into a book. I want my spot in the history books. I want to leave my mark so that everyone will know that I was here. I want the children to be able to go to the library, look up my name, and know that Eugene Jackson was involved with the shaping of the arts. As a child, I didn't realize how important it was to keep history, but as an adult I understand the value. My mother knew all the time, for she kept good records of our life in the business. She kept every newspaper clipping, social program and billboard she could find in the towns that we toured.

I recall that I had rickets as a child. The doctor told my mother that I would never walk. But my mother had a strong belief in God. When I was at the age that normal children walked, she would bathe me outside in a big iron tub with dishwater. She did this every day all through the day for nine months. To the surprise of the doctor and the entire family, I walked and ran like any other child. At the age of three, I began dancing at my grandfather's barber shop in Houston, Texas. By the age of six, I was picking up nickels and dimes for dancing on Los Angeles street corners. When I was seven, my mother and I — encouraged by friends — boarded the W Yellow Street Car for Thomas Ince Studios.

I've been ignored and forgotten about for too long. Now it's my time to tell my story. It won't bore you; it will excite you. It will show you how we made it in a business that is tough. I cherish my past. My thoughts have been within me for years. My coauthor, Gwendolyn Sides St. Julian, has vividly captured the stories that flowed clearly from my mind and my lips. I did not have to search for a thought, for these are memories from my heart, mind and soul. They are special and dear to me, a part of me that is alive. My past prances and dances around in my head. When I speak of these events, my heart and entire body are energized, and my voice relates my enthusiasm.

My life can be compared with two amusement park rides: as exciting as the roller coaster, and as relaxing as the Ferris wheel. It has never been dull. It's always been full of challenges, which I eagerly met without hesitation. I met fear face to face and conquered it. I've had my share of sorrow, pain,

3

humiliation and joy. However, the story has never left my mouth. It is now a fitting time for my story to be told, and I must release it from my heart. My memories have been nurtured with love and respect for my past. Don't try to ignore me, forget me or become embarrassed because of the roles I played, but embrace me and be glad I came along to help tame the situation and calm the waves for you. Acknowledge me, accept me, learn from me and be proud of me.

I created dance steps and strides naturally — nobody taught me. Yes, I danced for nickels and dimes and made less than you. I've performed in places you've never been to or heard of. At times, I would be hurting inside from ridicule or unkind words. I've smiled while I cried inside from incidents that I had no control over. I've had to gaze at things so as not to show an emotion on my face. We had to be smart, wise and clever to make it. I carry on with pride while entertaining. I've ridden in cars, buses and trains, and I've walked many miles — all for the love of show biz.

I love, respect and admire the artists and technologies of today. I've sung my song and done my dance to pay my dues. I just want to be recognized — I don't believe that's asking too much. I want the entertainment business and the children to know about me. I'm your bridge, your link to your past and present. I'm extending my hand. Catch it! Hold it tight to form a chain to your past. Remember, before there was you, there was me.

EUGENE "PINEAPPLE" JACKSON

He's a forgotten child star who opened the doors for African Americans to follow. He has never received his rightful place in history; and unlike many overlooked stars of his era, he has yet to be given his much deserved star on the Hollywood Walk of Fame. His family heritage is African American, Cherokee Indian, German, Irish and Jewish. I'm speaking of Eugene Jackson II, "Pineapple" in the 1924 *Our Gang* comedy series. He wanted to write this book to show what people were made of back then. He had perseverance, guts and determination — and still does. He is loved and respected by all.

Jackson's story is an important and historic one. He traveled a road of joy, pleasure, and at times humiliation, but the show had to go on. He was an entertainer with heart, and he worked with such entertainment giants as Gene Autry, Richard Dix, Irene Dunne, Bill "Bojangles" Robinson, George Peppard, John Wayne, Sammy Davis, Jr., Clark Gable, Judy Garland, Dorothy Dandridge, Gene Kelly, Eddie "Rochester" Anderson, Clarence Muse, Madame Sul Te Wan, Rex Ingram, A.C. Billbrew, Fayard Nicholas, Liza Minnelli, Lincoln Perry (Stepin' Fetchit), Al Jolson, Elvis Presley, and Gregory Hines, just to name a few. Many, like Dorothy Dandridge, were showcased in his revues and later became stars. Some have forgotten to return their thanks. It wasn't an easy road, but it was one he would travel over and over again out of love for the entertainment industry.

He's a man with stamina and courage, a jovial and kind person who is happiest when bringing pleasure to people. Through the pages of this book you will travel from his childhood days with the *Our Gang, Buster Brown, Mary Jane*, and Mack Sennett comedies. He worked steadily through the silent film era of the twenties, and talked his way into the talkies that followed soon after. He galloped into the cowboy scene as Gene Autry's film sidekick, "Eightball." He toured 89 cities and 16 states in his personal vaudeville tour of 1932. Times were rough, but he began to manage his acts and incorporate dancing girls, performing in beer joints and nightclubs in 1938.

He worked throughout the United States, and when the opportunity arose he sailed for the beautiful, clear waters of Honolulu in 1941. However, the waves were churned into a storm by the bombing of Pearl Harbor. He felt trapped on a beautiful island until he was released to return to his home soil. His love and patriotism for his country were displayed when he did defense work and joined the army. While in the army he was fortunate enough to be in special services and to be trained with the famous Buffalo Soldiers (for whom a postal stamp has been issued honoring their contributions).

His marriage to a wonderful lady named Sue Watt produced three lovely and talented children. With his brother and friends, he formed the Jackson Trio and traveled all around the United States. His family was always his nucleus: his dedicated wife, wise Mama and beloved handsome brother. He was an excellent provider for his family, caring for his mother until she departed from this world. He introduced his children, grandchildren and countless other people's children to the world of dance. He's an actor, comic, singer, dancer and musician all wrapped up in one.

The contribution of the African American is now being documented in all areas, and the film industry is no exception. The tap dancing of Eugene Jackson and his brother Freddie was used in the 1941 Disney movie *Dumbo*; artists copied the style in order to animate the dancing crows. His contributions are valued by dignitaries, as demonstrated by the awards received for his fiftieth wedding anniversary from the president of the United States, the governor of California and various city mayors (such as Los Angeles and Compton). His golden years of life tell of his commitment to his wife, children and the world. He followed his talents and dreams, which many people aren't able to do. His life has been full of rousing adventures that will captivate readers. He deserves to see his name on the cover of a book; he deserves his applause and accolades. He was a trailblazer in the motion picture industry, becoming in *Hearts in Dixie* the first African American child star in sound films. He is a living legend.

In this book, the words "colored" and "Negro" are used by Mr. Jackson. Mr. Jackson came of age during a time when African Americans, as well as others, used these words to refer to Americans of African descent.

GWENDOLYN SIDES ST. JULIAN

1
My Childhood and Early Career

I was born in New York on December 25, 1916, to Eugene Jackson and Lillie B. Foster. My father met my mother in Houston, Texas. They had a big wedding, and moved to Buffalo to live. My mother stayed with my father for one year after finding out that he was a playboy working on the railroad. Before leaving him, she thought about her large fancy wedding. But she quickly realized that she had a lot of pride and self respect, so back to Houston, Texas, she went. She lived with her father, Joe Foster, her sister, Hazel, her brothers Freddie and Cuney, and half-sister Josephine Foster. Three years after her divorce from my father, she married Clemmark Baker. They had a son, Freddie Baker, but the marriage lasted only a short while.

My maternal grandfather was a prosperous barber who also owned a drug store. Because my grandfather was well off, he was afforded the opportunity to purchase items for his family that many American families, especially colored, were not able to buy — such as an Indian motorcycle for his son, Joe, and a player piano for my mother and her sister. But gloom overtook our family for a short while. Every family experiences problems, and we were no different. My uncle Joe got into trouble in Dallas. My grandfather lost everything trying to save Joe. However, sadness never stayed with our family long because we had a tradition of strength.

My grandfather had a daughter from a previous marriage. Her name was Josephine Foster, and she moved to Los Angeles in 1921. Auntie Hazel, as I so affectionately called her, would receive letters from Aunt Joe trying to lure her to beautiful, sunny California. It worked. Baby sister Hazel caught the bait and relocated to California. We came from a family of hard work and self-determination, so it was no surprise to the family back in Texas to hear that Hazel had a good job. She was married to a man named Leon Hubert. They both had successful employment at the Broadway department store downtown. Aunt Hazel had tested the western waves first and proved successful. Because she had done extraordinarily well, she encouraged us to venture west.

A young, energetic Eugene Jackson preaching his first "sermon": "Don't do as I do—do as I tell you."

She had a friend named Stella Williams, and they urged us to take the Southern Pacific train to Los Angeles. It took a lot of guts to uproot the family and leave friends, but we were a visionary family. We knew greener pasture lay ahead.

I was five years old when I boarded that locomotive, and I can still remember the excitement in my heart. Riding on a "choo-choo" was a big adventure for me. I recall the lavish basket of food Mama prepared for the trip to eat on the train because we had little funds. We were met by Aunt Hazel and Uncle Leon at the Los Angeles Union Station on Fifth and Central. The train station looked gigantic to Freddie and me. The large columns and high ceilings were like a Greek arena. All our belongings, in suitcases and two old trunks, were put in a 1923 Model "T" Ford. Uncle Leon drove down Central to Twelfth Street pointing out the sites to the family. We saw the *California Eagle* newspaper, the Rosebud and Florence Mills theaters, the Dunbar Hotel, YMCA, Second Baptist Church and the oldest and second oldest black fire stations.

This was the "Black Belt" of Los Angeles. It was a Broadway. I had never seen so many colored people in my life. I was like a windmill, turning my head and twirling my body so as not to miss a scene. We rented a room on Twelfth Street, and the following day we visited the barber shop of George and Stella Williams. Because I was a quick-witted kid, I immediately noticed the hair on the floor. When I asked if I could sweep up the hair, Mr. Williams told me that I had just landed myself a job. (He also employed my grandfather.)

I would sweep and dance up and down the shop for tips, amazing the customers with my skillful style. Onlookers in the shop would grin and comment that I was a natural born dancer. They would say that I was going to make something of myself. Hearing those positive remarks would make me glide in fancy steps across the floor. A crowd would gather, clapping their hands and stomping their feet. I was given money, along with praise and advice such as "save this money, boy."

Before I could comment, Mr. Williams would continue cutting hair in the last chair and holler, "Oh, the boy knows what to do with his money. He saves. He's a thrifty li'l fella. He helps his mama." The customers would nod their heads in approval, and I would smile and say "thank you." From there I began dancing on the street corners, making up steps and perfecting my style. People would throw money at me, which would pump more energy into my tiny, quick feet. I was only five at the time, having begun dancing at age three in my grandfather's barber shop back in Houston.

In California, I would bring home the money for groceries. I was a daring young entrepreneur, promoting myself without fully knowing my own power and strength. I would dance my way from Twelfth Street on down to Main Street. A casting office for colored people, run by Jimmy Smith and Charles Butler, was located on Twelfth and Central. I still hadn't made my debut in the movies, but directors and producers would come to Twelfth and Central to pick different types for their films. After Smith and Butler stopped casting blacks for Central Casting, Jasper Weldon picked it up. He ran the business from his apartment on Fifty-Second Street between Hooper and Central. Many colored plantation movies were being produced at that time.

We moved from Twelfth and Central to a two-story rooming house on Seventeenth Street. Our landlords were Mr. and Mrs. Thomas, an interracial couple with four girls and one boy. It was great having more children to play with even though they were older than we were. The girls were nice, but somewhat promiscuous: They would try to coax Freddie and me into kissing and playing house with them. At times we would play willingly. Freddie wouldn't mind playing if they were playing spin the bottle. He would get to choose which one he wanted to kiss if the bottle pointed toward him. One of the daughters had a crush on him, and was always bugging Freddie to play with her. He pretended he didn't like it, but deep down inside I believe he enjoyed all the extra attention.

Freddie was smooth with the female species, except with Mama. She made him walk a straight chalk line; he lived by her rules. Mama would have no nonsense. She loved her boys equally, and we were treated the same. Freddie wasn't able to sweet-talk her into getting out of anything. He carried his weight in life in our family.

We were quite a distance from our initial neighbors, but this area proved just as exciting and thrilling as our old one, for on Eighteenth and Central was a colored musicians' local union, 767. In this area was the colored-owned Clark Hotel. Across the street was the Jewish-owned Gold Furniture Store.

School was enjoyable for me. My first school was Twentieth Street, between Central and Naomi streets. I was active in the Glee Club. I was too busy to be a bad child, but just mischievous enough to require a few visits to the principal's office. Mr. Peterson would administer a few swats on the hand or behind, which quickly brought me back to my senses of proper behavior.

I would wait for Freddie after school, and we would walk to Twentieth and

Central where my grandfather worked as a barber. We would sometimes ride our homemade skate scooters to and from school. Freddie and I were always close. Wherever I would go, he would go. Mother always dressed us alike. My auntie would buy us the same items. She always bought our shoes from the top-quality Baker Shoe Store. This still didn't stop me from having flat feet.

Like all cities, there were wayward boys and gangs. They would imitate the bad guys from the movies like Edward G. Robinson in the movie *Little Caesar*, James Cagney and George Raft. These boys only beat me up once. They respected me, and I was friendly with them. However, they would beat the heck out of other guys.

There was a Twenty-Second Street playground that had a big swimming pool where all the kids could learn to swim. Because so many black children swam there, it was known as the "ink hole." You had to pay to get in, but the lessons were free. I would take lessons, but I did not pick up swimming as fast as some of the other kids. I would fight the water. I was involved in a host of extracurricular activities, such as selling *Collier's* magazines and running my newspaper route. As I became older and started appearing in movies, I didn't have time to attend the pool regularly.

To pay our rent, Mama worked as a maid in Hollywood apartments and private homes. When Mama would return from work, it was a joy to see her get off the street car: It would take her a few minutes to get off because her employers had loaded her down with food and goodies. Our mouths would be watering with excitement upon sight of her. Freddie and I would scamper to meet her, both of us pulling at the bags to help relieve her. We wanted to peek in the bags to see what was inside, but Mama had rules that nothing should be opened on the street. So, we had to restrain ourselves until we arrived home.

Our family was crazy about the movies, and my grandfather would take us to see them. There was a theater on Twentieth and Central called the Rosebud, managed by Mr. Wolf. Saturday matinees would star such screen giants as Tom Mix, Hoot Gibson, and Harry and William Desmond. Every Saturday night there were amateur shows, and on Sunday they would give free candy bars to all the kids who attended. I was only seven, and Freddie was four, but we would run down to the front seats for some hugging and kissing with the girls. My grandfather would have to beckon us from the front of the theater when it was time to leave. We would be having so much fun with the other children that we hated to leave.

I believe I received some of my acting ability from watching some of the silent stars at the Rosebud. For hours I would sit and watch Clara Bow, Charles Gilpin, Pola Negri, Norma Shearer, William S. Hart, Greta Garbo, Douglas Fairbanks, Sr., Mary Pickford, Irene Rich, Rudolph Valentino, Henry B. Walthall, John Gilbert, Richard Dix, Buster Keaton, Harold Lloyd, Bert Lytell, Lon Chaney, Paul Robeson, Wallace Beery and John Barrymore. I borrowed some of my dancing technique from a well-known dancing shimmy star named Clara Bow. Some of my acting abilities may have come from my father's sister, Aunt Lula. Her name was Catherine Jackson Ayres, and she was in the New York stage production of *Porgy and Bess*.

My acting began at the Rosebud, where every Saturday night Mr. Wolf would have an amateur night contest. The contest would consist of singing and dancing, and the first prize was a big box of groceries. I entered the contest and danced away with first prize, doing the Shimmy and singing "You Got to See Your Mama Every Night or You Can't See Your Mama at All." We had enough groceries for a week. I went back the following week and won first prize again. Still only seven years old, I won so many times that I was named the "Shimmy King."

One Saturday I did not show up

One of Jackson's earliest acting influences, Aunt Lula (Catherine Jackson Ayres), who appeared in the New York stage production of *Porgy and Bess*.

at the Rosebud because I was sick. Mr. Wolf called my house to see what had happened to me, and my mother told him I was ill. He told my mother that he and others had been discussing me. He told her that I had natural talent and that she should put me in the movies. So when I was seven, Mama and I boarded the W Yellow Street Car for Thomas Ince Studios, on Washington Boulevard in Culver City, for a part in *Her Reputation*, a silent movie starring May McAvoy. A little boy was needed to fall in a fish pond. The child was to be knocked into the pond by mistake at a big wedding fiesta fight. The pond looked like an ocean to me, and I was scared. The pay was five dollars, but I did such an excellent job of showing fear with my big eyes that I was paid $7.50.

There were Charleston contests going on all over the city. At the Shrine Auditorium, there were two kid favorites. One was a cute little talented girl named Hyson Lark. The other was the rich Clark boy, whose father owned the Clark Hotel. Dressed like a million dollars, he had on white pants and a blue suit jacket. I had on a gingham shirt, which was worn but clean, and my pants were faded from being washed so much. I had been picking up the Charleston and the Black Bottom. While dancing I fell, but I did not stop. Instead, I continued to dance by doing a "scoot, scoot, scoot" on my behind like I was rowing a boat. That move stole the show — it was all over. The crowd went mad, and I came away with second prize. Hyson Lark came in first place. The Clark kid came in third, shocked that a poor little kid practically dressed in rags had beat him. (A word to the wise: Remember, there is always someone better than you. Learn from that person. Don't be jealous of anyone. Practice hard and always be open for changes.)

When I was growing up, I stayed busy and constructive. Even after I started working in the movies, I stayed active. When I wasn't acting, I worked as a page boy at the Criterion Theatre. When *The Patent Leather Kid* (one of the first war movies starring Richard Barthelmess) was showing at the Criterion, a patent leather suit was made for me. I opened the door for such stars as Al Jolson, who starred in Warner Bros.' first vitaphone talking movie, *The Jazz Singer*.

If I wasn't working as a page boy at the Criterion Theatre, I was laboring at something. I would cut grass and clean up back yards for twenty cents, fifty cents and a dollar. I would sell *Collier's* magazines to the studios. I had thriving paper routes (about 60 customers) for *The Herald* and *The Examiner*. I was one of their top salesmen: The *Herald* gave me a bike, and the *Examiner* gave me a wagon. I had a dog named Jack that would go with me on my paper route and would ride on my bike to protect my papers. With the wagon, Freddie and I would go to the big market on Eighth Street to pick up slightly bruised fruit and vegetables that had been discarded into a barrel. We would take them home to wash and then sell to senior citizens. We were little entrepreneurs, always trying to make money because we knew Mama was doing all she could for us financially.

Hollywood had a certain style of child they wanted: one with a dark complexion, big lips, and kinky hair. Though many children fit that bill, they didn't have the acting ability that I did. This made a lot of people envious of me. When I would go for auditions, both children and their parents would make comments like, "Oh, here comes Jackson," or "You know he'll get the job." I was only perfecting a God-given talent, doing a job that I loved dearly.

On Saturdays, my mother cleaned house for a lady named Gladys Boggs, a music and drama teacher who lived in Hollywood off of North Gardner. She taught me my first dramatic act, one I would use in vaudeville and would prove beneficial to me all of my life. In fact, today I still teach this act to my students. The act was titled "Mary Had a Little Lamb," and it had three parts: the song and dance, the Shakespearean bit, and the Hollywood vamp. (A vamp is a musical passage of two or four measures often repeated several times, before a solo, between verses.)

When we moved from Seventeenth Street, we went to Nevin Elementary School on Thirty-Second and Nevin. We lived right in front of the school, across the street in a rear house. I would be almost late for school every day. I would have to run to school. We only lived on Thirty-Second Street for about two or three years, but I will never forget the near-fatal accident that happened to me. It was cold one morning, and I had on my flannel pajamas. I had gotten too close to our little gas burner to warm myself, and my pajamas caught fire. It was a good thing that I didn't run because I would have been burnt severely. Somehow, I grabbed my leg and managed to put out the fire. I had third degree burns on my thighs. I still have the scar for memories.

Just around the corner on Thirty-Third Street lived Ernest Morrison, Sunshine Sammy of *Our Gang*. I would see him when he would come in from his tour. I knew his family, and I had worked with his sister, Dorothy Morrison, in *Hearts in Dixie* (she played my sweetheart, Amelia). Sammy was such a big shot. He was an established star. When he arrived home, the entire neighborhood would come out to see him. He had a great big limousine a mile long. His dad would take him on the road to perform, while his mom was home raising the children.

When I was around 10 or 11 years old, I worked with Loretta Butler, who had the Kiddie Minstrel Show at the Philharmonic Theater. From there I went to Alma Hightower, where I got a good start in show business. Her top dancers were Dorothy and Vivian Webster, Roy Presley and Little Minnie, who was related to Mrs. Hightower. I remember Minnie to this day as being small and cute. She could really dance. One could tell that Mrs. Hightower spent a lot of time with her. Willie and Red, who played music, were also her students. Freddie and I began lessons in the front living room of her small apartment. For the first three days, Freddie didn't do well. Mrs. Hightower sent a message home by me to tell my mother that she was wasting her money on Freddie.

I picked up tap dancing and the beginning routine in one week. I told Mama what Mrs. Hightower said, and Mama told us that Freddie was going to learn to tap. She sat us down and explained to Freddie, "Gene is feeding the family. You must learn to do something productive." He was told that he had to carry his own weight. I began working with him after school. He would cry, and Mama would hit his little legs with a strap. I was also allowed to tap his small legs. After two weeks of that, he picked up tapping and loved it. He would dance all day and night. All throughout the house, he would dance here and there, on this and that. Had the ceiling been available, he would have danced on it. Mama and I stood in the wing smiling with approval. He had now acquired a love for tapping. It was in his walk and talk. We were now a team. I was very advanced by this time. Mrs. Hightower promoted me to her top dancing group. We would perform at clubs: We entertained at the Elks Lodge, American Legion, Masonic Lodge and social clubs. During this time, I was still teaching Freddie at home.

I got ready for adult theater work at the Gaiety Theater on Twenty-Third and Central Avenue, across from the Lincoln. The Gaiety, which was owned by a Japanese man, would have vaudeville shows on Saturday and Sunday. The producers were all teenagers. Happy Mitchell and Eddie Redman were tap dancers, and Happy did all the directing. Billy Tucker was our emcee and comedian. The musicians in our band were Lorenzo Flenory on piano, his brother Otis on drums, Big Six on sax, and Jack Trainer on trumpet, Marguerite Thompson (sister of famous champ fighter Jack Thompson) and Marguerite Jones were singers. The comedians were Sketes and Lost Motion. I was the youngest member in the show, doing short skits and singing songs like "Mammy," "Singing in the Rain," "Baby Face," "Ain't She Sweet," "Happy Days," "Five Foot Two," "Shine" and "That's My Weakness." The chorus dancers were Emma Priestly, Juanita Moore and Lucille Battle. Our male singer was Wilbur Johnson, whose nickname was "Street Singer Wilbur." He was able to do anything. He had a velvet sounding voice and played the ukulele, which enhanced everything he did. By working with this talented group, I was really getting a taste of show business.

A friend of Happy Mitchell, entertainer Diamond Tooth Billy Tucker booked our entire show in Long Beach at the Pike. A big tent was pitched for us to entertain the people. At the end of the first week, when it came time to be paid, the shyster ran off with our money — I haven't seen him since. After that bad deal, I told Mama that Freddie and I were going to form our own dance team. Freddie had developed an outstanding romantic voice. I was still involved in movies. When I was around ten or eleven, to promote my movies or tours I would appear on the radio to sing and dance. After my musical performance on the radio, an interview would follow. When I was in Los Angeles, the show would be sponsored by Don Cadillac on KFI. This type of promotional work was done throughout the United States on my traveling route.

Mama met a man by the name of General White, a colored World War I hero. He was nicely built, an attractive man about 5'8" and around 40 years of age. He was bald in front with hair on the side. He was brown skinned, wore a mustache and smoked cigarettes. Mama invited him over for a delicious dinner to hear his business proposal. When he visited our home, he showcased himself by wearing his uniform with his purple and blue heart medals from Germany. He was smooth with his pitch. He halted one of his stories by saying he didn't want to bore us any longer with his war adventures. We tried to assure him that we were interested. He stated it was getting late. He had to be on his way. When he rose from his chair, his movements were exact and precise. He walked swift and erect with his head high as if he were still in the military. Freddie and I moved quickly with him to the door, looking up to him with awe and respect in our eyes. He and Mama shook hands on his business deal. He had convinced us to put together a Kiddie Revue, to be called Chincapin and His Pickaninny Revue. He came up with this name because I had made the movie *Hearts in Dixie*.

I was now an established child star. I had played the part of Chincapin in the movie. The revue worked, and we played to a full house every day and night. The engagement was for kids and parents at Oceanside Park at the beach on the pier. The show consisted of Mrs. Hightower playing the piano, Willie on drums, Red Mack on the trumpet, Jack Williams, Roy Presley, and Dorothy as a singer and dancer. Vivian Webster and Esther were dancers, and Amanda was a singer. (Dorothy and Vivian were my neighbors. We all lived on the same street, and I would ride to the beach with them to work the revue.) The children would pay ten cents and the adults twenty-five cents to see the show. They would walk up some stairs and walk around to stand in order to see the show. They would have to look down on us in the pit-like arena. To show that they enjoyed us, they would throw money at us for tips.

It was so much fun. All the rides would be free to us at the pier. We would ride the merry-go-round, roller coaster and go into the haunted house. As I look back, I'm sure the food of hot dogs and hamburgers were just ordinary, but back then as a kid they were scrumptious. It was a good thing that we enjoyed ourselves because General White ran off with all the money. Thank God Mama knew how to save for a rainy day.

After Nevin, I went to Ascot Elementary on Vernon and Compton. With the money I made from my first talking picture, *Hearts in Dixie*, I put a down payment on our first home. From fourth through sixth grades, I went to Ascot School. From Ascot, I went to McKinley Junior High.

Word was out that Lionel Hampton was looking for some dancers. He lived on Tenth Street, off of Central, in a little apartment. The band, which was a twelve piece ensemble, rehearsed in Lionel's one room along with Freddie and me tapping. We had to all work together in order to coordinate the show. We would go to his place and rehearse and rehearse until the show was perfect. No one could afford a studio room to rent — we had to use what we had. Things were not easy in those days, but when the curtain rose the show was sensational. Lionel's group was called Lionel Hampton's World Fastest Drummer and His Cotton Club Orchestra, with Miss Wilma Mae Lane as a singer. Freddie and I were known as his Rhythm Dancing Team. We worked with him at the Pavilion in Pismo, California, the Santa Barbara Convention Center, San Diego, Ventura, and up and down the southern coast.

I only attended McKinley for one year because we went on my personal vaudeville tour. After my vaudeville tour, I returned home to attend Polytechnic High School. Deep down inside I wanted to attend Jefferson, but my family felt that Poly had more prestige because of its reputation as an international school of all races and culture. All my relatives were present for our family discussion of my choices for high school. I sat there listening attentively. When the meeting was through, Mama looked at me and smiled, saying I would attend Polytechnic. I said that was fine. I knew not to disagree after the family had spent such a lengthy meeting concerning my future.

I was a friend to all the students. I made friends with a boy who was a cobbler. He's probably a millionaire by now because he had such a good trade. I became close to a Jewish boy named Leon Barowitz, and taught him a popular dance called the "truckin." He was so proud of himself "truckin" all over school and home. His dad had a dry goods store on Seventh and Ceres. I was invited to his house once at Fedora near Pico Boulevard. His mother made some pancakes. I tasted the pancakes and fell in love with them. From that morning on, when I picked up Leon for school his mom had to make pancakes for me.

I taught private dancing lessons on the side for extra money. I will never forget the 60-year-old white lady who came for dancing instructions. She had always wanted to dance when she was a little girl, but her family couldn't afford it. My method was teaching how to learn in four lessons. She learned to tap in that amount of time, learning both her time step and routine. Her body physique was thin and slender, and I would have to hold her arm and hand — they would be so cold — to help her. (I guess she had thin blood at that age.) She was grateful, and these lessons show how she held on to her dream: She didn't let her age stop her. She felt she could do anything and she mastered her goal and desire. Remember this woman as an example. Hold on to your dreams. Don't let anyone take them away from you. Work at them, though you may get tired. You can rest, but don't give up.

At Poly, I was in the Mask and Sandal Drama Club, the band and the Glee Club. Mrs. Feninsey was our drama teacher. I remember a play we did called *Babs*. In this hit play I played the part of a servant and created a dancing part in the play. Once the students found out that I was a professional actor, I became more popular than ever. *Cimarron*, a film in which I had a lead role, was still playing. The newspaper reviews from the well-known columnist Luella Parson made my face known throughout the school. During high school, I did many movies. In 1935 and 1936, I played "Eightball" in such Gene Autry movies as *Tumbling Tumbleweeds, Red River Valley* and *Guns and Guitars*. Other films were *Hearts in Bondage, The Lonely Trail* and *Wine, Women and Horses*. I did many musicals (*The Singing Kid, Born to Dance*) and comedy films. Sometimes the dancers and musicians would be given credits and sometimes not, which at times made documentation of my film appearances difficult.

I attended high school with some outstanding African Americans. Thomas Bradley was a track star who ran the 440. He was president of the student body, and later became mayor of Los Angeles. Homer Blair ran the 660. Melvin Nickerson ran the 880; his father was an executive at Golden State Insurance. Aubrey and Francis Warren were brothers who were football stars. Ruben Cordova was secretary of student body. Donald Butler was president of self-government. Mary Bishop was vice president. Hadda Brooks was an outstanding piano player who became a star known as the Boogie Woogie Queen; one of her hit songs was "My Desire." I met my elementary and junior high sweetheart, Martha E. Graham, at Poly. She later became an architect. I tried sports at Poly and went out for the track team. I wasn't able to practice like everyone else because I was making movies and performing in nightclubs and taverns. My show consisted of three or four girls, along with Freddie. I wouldn't get home until two in the morning. By fifth period I would be sleepy, which is why my grades were not as high as they could have been.

The Los Angeles School System was having a big track meet with all the high schools. Now mind you, I was an actor — not an athlete — but I went out for the 660 race against the best athletes from Manual and Jefferson. I had a lot of guts, faith and self-confidence. I gave it my all. I started off with speed. The entire school was rooting for me: "Go, Gene, Go." I was doing my best, but around halfway through the race I began to get tired. My legs and back began to cramp. I was running with all my might. With tears in my eyes, I was huffing and puffing to complete the race. I was the last one, and "I ain't ran in a race since." I decided to stick to show business, something that came natural. Try not to spread yourself so thin as I had done.

Mama met a man who was a musician, a serviceman from Fort Huachuca, Arizona. He had a shiny new horn, and came to our house and taught me to play. I was crazy about that horn, and I learned my scale in one week. I thought Mama was going to buy that new horn, but she shocked me by buying an old saxophone. That put a damper in my heart and spirit, so I put the horn under my bed for it to collect dust. I had no idea that years later I would be stationed in Fort Huachuca, playing sax and clarinet in the band. Economically times were hard, but I was always using my brain in an honest way to enjoy life's pleasures.

I knew Mama did not have any extra money to spare for extracurricular activities. I wanted to attend the football games, so I pulled that old dust-collecting sax from under my bed and joined the band so I could get in the games for free. I had a good ear, but I couldn't read music. This was my musical downfall. The band director was so nice. He tried his best to help me, but those students had been reading music for years. I was a good faker, but I stayed for only two semesters because I didn't want to hold back the band.

I took piano lessons in 1930 from a white fellow who had a technique called "Learn to Play the Piano in Twenty-One Lessons." I picked up on the piano quickly. On Forty-Seventh Place, I learned to play instruments in this order: ukulele, harmonica, piano and bass fiddle. The bass fiddle came from the choir room in my church, Wesley Methodist. A little old lady from my church had stopped playing it, and I asked if I could have it. I began to play around and because of my musical background, I was able to teach myself. I learned the tenor sax while recuperating from a stage performance accident. I was taught the clarinet while in the army in Fort Huachuca. The alto sax came naturally. This chapter has been a brief overview of my early days. The remaining chapters of this book will, in detail, tell the story of my life, beginning with how I became a child star.

2
Comedy Series

The situation seems to be worrying the powers that are at the Hal Roach Studio. They are trying to get along without Ernest Morrison, Sunshine Sammy, but the big question is will the exhibitors accept Our Gang Comedies without Sammy or a race star other than Farina. It is rumored that two of the Our Gang Series that were made without Ernest were returned from the Eastern exchange marked "no good." Word of mouth was out that Hal Roach Production was in need of a colored child to take Sunshine Sammy's place. It is a significant fact that they were in need of someone to carry the heavy acting.—*Quote from a studio gossip magazine in 1924 that kept abreast of what was going on in Hollywood.*

Hal Roach actually came up with the idea for *Our Gang* by unintentionally eavesdropping on some regular, ordinary neighborhood kids having good clean fun in a pile of lumber on a studio lot. Back then the studios weren't like they are today; early Hollywood was totally different from today. Some were actually like barns. In fact, Century Studio used to *be* a farm. We had what we called Poverty Row: the poor studios. That's right — back then Century Studio was not big time. Charlie Chaplin's studio was better than Century. His studio was about 20 blocks east of La Brea and Sunset. For a short while, L-KO (Lehrman's Knock-Out Comedies) used the same offices as Century Studio before Century moved in. Universal City was in the heart of San Fernando Valley. Hal Roach owned his own lot.

Some of the original *Our Gang* cast were contract workers within the Hal Roach studios. Johnny Downs was working in a Roach series with Charlie Chase. Ernest "Sunshine Sammy" Morrison was working on the lot. Mary Kornman was the still photographer's daughter. Mickey Daniels was Mary's neighbor. Jean Darling and Mary Ann Jackson lived in Glendale and Santa Monica. And so it all began...

OUR GANG (1924–1925)

The director of *Her Reputation* told my mother that Hal Roach was looking for a boy to replace Sunshine Sammy. Sammy's dad was taking him out of

the series because he felt
that Sammy deserved more
money. Ernest "Sunshine
Sammy" Morrison was a
seasoned, polished actor.
He was also the first black
child in *Our Gang*, while I
was the third. When he left
and did quite well for himself, the door was opened
for me. I met with Mr. Roach,
and he liked my natural acting ability. I did some impromptu acting, and he said
I had an open freshness with
a million dollar smile. He
conversed with me for a
short while, and I signed
immediately for a three-
year contract. He coined the

Historic reunion: Eugene "Pineapple" Jackson, the third
black child actor to appear in the *Our Gang* comedies, has
some fun with Ernest "Sunshine Sammy" Morrison
(right), the very *first* black child actor to star in the series.

name "Pineapple" for me in the series, which has been a permanent part of
my show business name.

When I appeared in the *Our Gang* series, the following directors, producers and cast members were involved: Hal Roach produced, while Robert
McGowan directed. The titles were by H.M. Walker, the stories were written
by Hal E. Roach, and the editor was Thomas J. Crizer. The photography people were Art Lloyd and Alvin V. Knetchel. The cast members that I worked
with over the years were Joe F. Cobb; Johnny Downs; Allen "Farina" Hoskins;
Mary Kornman; Mickey Daniels; Jackie Condon; Andy Samuels; Peggy Ahearn;
Wadell Carter; William Gillespie; Sam Lufkin; Dick Gilbert; Charles Bachman; Allen Cavan; Charley Young; Gus Leonard; Helen Gilmore; Lyle Tayo;
Jack Gavin; and Ernie Morrison, Sr. Mrs. Fern Carter was the school teacher
of the children for 23 years. I played "Pineapple," Farina's big brother, for the
next two years.

While in *Our Gang*, I never worked with Ernest "Sunshine Sammy" Morrison, but I did have the opportunity to work with his dad, Ernie Morrison,
Sr. It was a pleasure and honor to act with him because everyone knew how
famous his son was. Morrison, Sr., played the black doctor Royal Sorghum in
"Circus Fever." He was the father of Farina's girlfriend in "The Love Bug."
Both junior and senior Morrison were fine, established, respected actors who
did well in films and vaudeville.

I still have fond memories of the *Our Gang* comedies. My first day on the
set was gleeful. I had a dressing room, and we had a tutor on the set. We filmed

Our Gang in 1924: Eugene "Pineapple" Jackson, Jackie Condon, Mary Kornman, Mickey Daniels and Joe Cobb.

in different locations, such as Lincoln Park, Griffith Park, Catalina Island, the Los Angeles Zoo, a San Pedro ship, Union Southern Pacific train station, Venice Beach, Ocean Park and Santa Monica. Every two weeks Mr. Roach would have big name bands entertain us. Entertainers from Honolulu, the Philippines and Samoa were flown into the studio.

Every Christmas and Thanksgiving we would get new suits, toys and trains from the major department stores such as May Company and Broadway. I'd like to point out that these comedies marked the beginning of integration in the film industry. It has really been played down, but it shouldn't. All the children were treated the same. Whatever one child received the other children received.

About 40,000 children were interviewed for *Our Gang* parts. Only 41 were placed under contract, with salaries ranging from $37.50 to $75.00 a week. Roach had talent scouts that worked for him because he liked the gang to always appear as young children having fun. One of his scouts turned down Mickey Rooney and Shirley Temple as gang members. Jackie Cooper began in a 1929 *Our Gang* comedy, and George "Spanky" McFarland later replaced Joe Cobb. Mickey Blake and Peggy Eames were fortunate enough to be members at one time.

To be a member of the *Our Gang* cast held special privileges, like having our likenesses used around the United States as product endorsements. Faces of the gang members appeared on balloons, coloring books, lunch boxes, packs of gum, skates, shoes and clothes. Just as the parents and children of today are involved in the latest kids' craze, the parents and children were wild about *Our Gang*.

Top: Our Gang shoots a scene at a studio pond and (*BOTTOM*) with their guests from the islands.

TOP: Farina, Joe, Pineapple, Mickey, Jackie and Mary pose in their new caps. *BOTTOM:* Director Bob McGowan teases the gang.

For promotional purposes, the Roach Studio held *Our Gang* look-alike contests around the United States. Even our dog, Pete, was popular. (The public probably never realized that we had two Petes. Each one had a ring around a different eye.) Roach's idea of the creation of the gang worked. He expanded and gave unknown children a start in film. It paid off for him. Hal Roach loved children, and it showed in his work.

Since there is a rebirth of interest in the cast of *Our Gang*, I will explain my role as Pineapple in the series: From time to time Hal Roach used other supporting characters in the gang; the character of Pineapple was one of them. Pineapple was created to help carry the heavy acting load because Farina was so young. I was in a total of six *Our Gang* comedies:

"The Mysterious Mystery" (December 14, 1924). "The Mysterious Mystery" was about a rich kid named Adelbert Wallingford who wanted to play with the gang instead of being tutored by his teacher. Adelbert is later kidnapped. (The gang, of course, just has to get to the bottom of the mystery.) Mickey is Sherlock Hawkshaw, and Farina is Hawkeye. We capture someone that we think is the crook, but who turns out to be Detective Jinks from the police department. We unknowingly deliver a package to Mr. Wallingford that had a ransom note from the kidnapper. A pigeon was to return with $5,000 to the bad guys. The pigeon gets away and a fierce chase is on with the gang and Wallingford. Mickey, Joe and Farina hide aboard a plane to try to catch the bird. The pilot falls out by mistake, and Mickey must take the control. Joe goes on the wing and Farina on the tail to capture the bird. They follow the bird to a barn, crashing into the roof and exposing the kidnappers. Detective Jinks and Wallingford had been following in the car. When the crooks are discovered, Adelbert was rescued. The gang wins the reward for the capture of the kidnappers and the safe return of Adelbert.

"The Big Town" (January 11, 1925). The gang has been playing in an empty boxcar on the railroad tracks, and the door is closed by mistake. The next morning we find ourselves in New York. Earlier we had received a postcard from Skinny, who was visiting in New York, that made us want to visit New York. We had no idea that we would receive our desires so soon. Since we have disappeared, our hometown police chief in Elmira wires the police chief of New York to be on the lookout for six missing children. We have a ball in New York crossing the Brooklyn Bridge and taking a ferry past the Statue of Liberty to Manhattan. When Mickey drives the gang up Fifth Avenue on a double-decker bus, we are spotted by a New York policeman and sent back home on a train. While on the train, more trouble erupts for us. An entomologist is sleeping on board, and his large ants get loose. Farina helps in the mischief by placing the frightening specimens around the pullman car. When we arrive home, the gang is greeted by angry mothers who spank us on the spot.

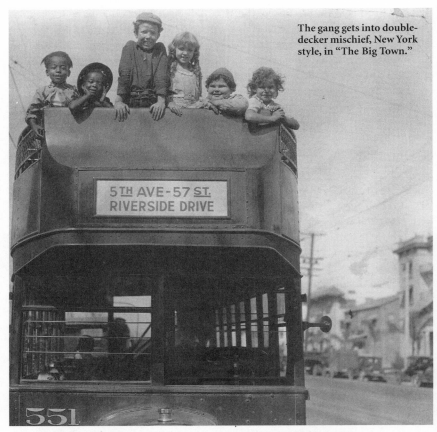

The gang gets into double-decker mischief, New York style, in "The Big Town."

Our Gang at the railroad

"Circus Fever" (February 8, 1925). The circus comes to town for one day only on June 2 at 2:00 P.M. Farina and I are in bed with "speckled fever" and unable to attend. Sammy's dad, Ernest Morrison, plays the black doctor who cares for us. Mickey, Jackie and Joe are angry because they must go to school. When they find out that Farina and Pineapple have "speckled fever," they come up with the idea of dotting their faces with red paint. They fool their mothers, but the family doctor isn't fooled. The doctor tells the parents that the boys have "circus symptoms." Mary drops by to tell them that school has been dismissed for the afternoon so the students can go to the circus. When the boys find this out, they are shocked. Their mothers will not release them to go to the circus. To make it worse, they are given a dose of castor oil and made to stay in bed.

"Dog Days" (March 8, 1925). Farina, Mickey, Jackie, Joe and I have trained pet dogs. We all think that our dogs are the best. We have a slogan throughout the film that we used: "Let's see your dog p'form that trick." Mary plays a high society girl. Mickey's dog stops her runaway pony, and she is so grateful that she invites the gang to her party. We enjoy ourselves at the party. During all the frolic and fun, it is discovered that one of the dogs is missing. When we find the dog, she has given birth to a litter of puppies. The proud gang member states, "Let's see your dog p'form that trick."

"The Love Bug" (April 5, 1925). This was a forerunner to some of the talkie shorts. We had a loveable old lady who was the grandma to the entire gang. When we needed advice, we would turn to grandma for comfort and strength. She was full of wisdom. Farina and Joe have love problems, so they turn to grandma. The gang decides to go off in the afternoon to visit Pineapple, who is working as a page in a beauty parlor. No people of authority are around, so the gang goes wild in the shop. Joe gets stuck in a steam cabinet, Mickey gives himself a mudpack, and Farina gives a permanent wave to his pigtails. Jackie plays around with the main control of different hoses until steam, air and water rush out of the control tubes. The owner appears just in time to save his shop from destruction. He is so angry that he calls the cops. The policeman is about to arrest the gang when grandma comes on the scene to save the day.

"Shootin' Injuns" (May 3, 1925). I want to give credit to Alvin V. Knetchel for the clever trick photography in this two-reeler. His camerawork exhibited the first use of superimposing more than one figure on the screen at the same time. This verifies the old saying that "there's nothing on film that hasn't been tried before." "Shootin' Injuns" opens with "Pancho Farina" not being able to find the gang's private underground hideout. He can't find it because it is camouflaged by hay. This particular Our Gang comedy is about the gang's fantasies of the wild wild west. We get our ideas from the nickel and dime novels that we read, and plan on running away from home to discover the West. We had been warned by our parents, but it was settled: the gang would meet that night to travel to a faraway country. Travel at night proves scary to us, so we run into a house because of the rain. This is not an ordinary home; it is a building full of surprises. Stairways, floors and walls turn into sliding chutes and panels, and skeletons, bodies and paintings come to life. Some fascinating scenes were those of the skeletons at the top of stairs. They all separate at the top, and slide down the rail individually. When they get to the bottom, they go back to being one skeleton. Alvin Knetchel knew how to use the proper timing in order to coordinate these scenes skillfully.

Another instance of Knetchel's successful camerawork is when Farina runs from the skeleton. Farina stops in midair; no movement is seen from Farina for a period of seconds, and it looks like he jumped out of his skin: Two Farinas are seen on the screen at the same time. When the parents arrive to help the gang, they become equally frightened by the house. No one knew that this house was purposely made as a haunted house to be sold to an amusement park. It was a nightmare for all.

As *Our Gang* (from left: Mary, Jackie, Mickey, Farina, Joe and Pineapple) was ringing in the new year of 1925, Pineapple was preparing to move on with a solo acting career.

During my time with *Our Gang*, my family and I rented a house at 1429 East Fifteenth Street. We lived off an alley. My grandfather also stayed with us. This was special to us, for this was our first house. In the past, we had lived in rooming houses. I was now making enough money for a house and car. We bought a 1924 Touraine. A Touraine is no longer being made, but it was like a convertible. It was built by the Touraine Model Company. It cost $950 from the Hal Roach dealership on Seventh and Central. Due to the fact that my mother could not drive, she hired young men to drive us around, but after spending $1,200 for rear-end repairs resulting from inadequate drivers, she learned to drive. Because I was in such demand, I left *Our Gang* when Farina turned five and before my three-year contract was up. I was as hot as a firecracker, popping from one studio to the next and working two or three studios a day. I would be picked up by a limousine at one studio and be dashed to the next. I was going solo as a child actor, and I ventured out into other comedies.

Top: Pineapple as a golf caddie in a 1926 Century comedy. *Bottom:* Swim plans are interrupted for Pineapple and the other Boy Scouts in this Century comedy short.

The Century kids (with two adults) on the alert in a scene from 1926.

CENTURY COMEDIES

Julius Stern was the producer of the Century comedies, while Alf Goulding and Fred Fishback were the directors. Fred had come to Century from Mack Sennett for higher wages. The Century comedies depicted Boy Scouts camping and hiking in the wilderness. I can still vividly recall some of those scenes. In one, the Boy Scouts are swimming in the creek in their underwear. A couple comes along looking for a lover's lane, and we are all surprised when we are spotted in our underwear. I run into a big hollow trunk to hide, which the script called for me to do. Not knowing that bees were in the hollow tree trunk, I sat on a bee and it tore my bottom up. My eyes got big, and I ran out as fast as a cheetah. The on-site physician had to be called to get the stinger out, a scene that was definitely not written in the script!

Another somewhat hazardous scene was to run into a spooky house where the room was pitch black and contained a live alligator. There were no black stunt men in those days, so we did all the acting — including stunts — ourselves. In an unlit room, I had to scurry up a drape above an alligator with his mouth open. I had to show fear with my eyes and facial expression. I could have been history but, as they say, God watches over fools and little children. In this particular scene, as I look back, I believe I was both! But this is what made acting fun back then. Impromptu moments sometimes made the scene work because they were natural and funny.

Top: The kids get ready for some fun in a scene from the *Buster Brown and Mary Jane* comedies. *Bottom:* Buster, Pineapple and Mary Jane are startled by burglars.

TOP AND BOTTOM: On the set of the Century comedies in 1926.

1926 Century comedies: Eugene "Pineapple" Jackson spies on a couple of crooks.

BUSTER BROWN AND
MARY JANE COMEDIES

I played an elite colored child in the *Buster Brown and Mary Jane* comedies. These children were older than the *Our Gang* bunch, and the clothes were quite different from the gang's. We wore pressed, buttoned clothes instead of rags. The field trips were situational comedies. Many scenes were in the home due to the fact we were middle-class children. Buster Brown and Mary Jane's family owned a big limousine, and we would play in it like the Prince of Bel Air.

MACK SENNETT COMEDIES

From *Buster Brown and Mary Jane* I moved to the Mack Sennett comedies. Mack Sennett produced major comedies, with Fred Fishback as director and actors Harry "Snub" Pollard and Buster Keaton receiving top billing. The Mack Sennett comedies were visual gags, but they were not as popular as *Our Gang* (To this day, I do not know why.) When I wasn't acting in front of the camera, I was making personal guest appearances at the theaters.

All of the comedies that I worked in were made in such a way that the atmosphere could never be recreated today, no matter how good the producers and directors. Everything that we did was raw, yet pure. It was just plain different from now. We were truly a family on set, easy to work with because we all had a goal of trying to please trying to do our level best. We didn't have the "big I and little you" mentality on the sets like some of today's sets. Show business was strictly show business back then.

When you see the old footage of us moving quickly in scenes, this was actually how we thought and worked. We thought and worked quickly — time was money. We didn't have a lot of money for anything back then. We didn't have the large budgets that the studios give out to producers and directors today. We had to think and make do with what we had. Everyone knew how to stretch a dollar. This philosophy spilled over into every crew member and every actor. We just didn't have time for a lot of nonsense on the sets.

Show business was show business. It was, and still is, a tough grueling business that one must do out of love for the art. It is that simple. If you don't love it, it is going to break you in every form and fashion. It's not kind at times, but that's show biz. The biz is like a maze at times. You have to be quick and always thinking in order to make it. An actor must be like a juggler. He must be able to balance, weigh and juggle everything to survive because nothing is promised in the biz. No sir, nothing was promised to us back then, not one thin dime.

We had to always be watching and looking for a break, a crack to squeeze into to make our way. But as I look back, that is what made the industry fun. If a bookie or agent asked if you could do something, that could mean an impromptu audition right on the spot. We were fast talkers. We were salesmen of our own craft and talent. We had to be; otherwise, we didn't eat. It was plain and clear that the actors back then had it all. We were definitely multitalented.

Will Hays was the censorship czar back then, and he ruled when it came to what was appropriate and what wasn't. Some of the mess we see with children on television and film today would not be tolerated by his department. He did not play around. He had rules that were going to be upheld and that was it. Some of the rules that he used to govern us need to be reinstated in television and films, especially when children are involved.

3

Silents in the Roaring Twenties

Before I made my debut in the silent films of the twenties, there was a very talented child star by the name of Ernest Morrison (better known as "Sunshine Sammy" from *Our Gang*), who paved the way for me. In life there will always be someone ahead of you. Remember this. Once you have made it, pull someone up with you. There is always room at the top. It is the bottom that is crowded.

The following promotional write-ups appeared in publicity publications before one of my films would run at local theaters:

> Introducing Gene Jackson, filmdom's brown bit of Sunshine! Ten year old Gene is the most famous juvenile in film today and his record as a performer merits the distinction. Probably his best liked appearance was with Ben Alexander in J. McDonald's film production, *Penrod and Sam*, based on Booth Tarkington's famous story and released by First National Studio. Gene is again with Ben. This time it is in the character role of Vestibule Johnson in *Boy of Mine*, another Booth Tarkington human interest drama which McDonald produced for First National with William Beaudine as director. The cast of *Boy of Mine* included Henry B. Walthall, Irene Rich, Bert Lytell, Ben Alexander, Dot Farley, Lawrence Licalzi, George Reed and Gene Jackson.

Another newspaper stated,

> The famous little colored star making big hit with movie fans, Gene Jackson, the celebrated little colored star who many consider the peer of all film youngsters regardless of race and who also seen in *Penrod and Sam* takes an active and more than interesting part in *Boy of Mine*. His work as Vestibule Johnson in this offering fall but little short of being a classic.

It was customary in those days for newspapers to use the word "colored" in reference to African Americans, but these press reviews made us feel so

Top: Eugene with costars Henry B. Walthall (left) and Ben Alexander in *Boy of Mine* (1923). *Bottom:* Ben Alexander and Eugene play cops and robbers in *Boy of Mine* (1923).

good. Press reviews can make or break a film, just as they can today. We were fortunate to always get rave reviews. I appeared in the following silent films during the 1920s:

Boy of Mine (1923). This was a J. McDonald film, with William Beaudine as director. The cast included Ben Alexander, Rockliffe Fellowes, Henry B. Walthall, Irene Rich, Dot Farley and Lawrence Licalzi. Ben played Bill Latimer, a fun-loving child. Irene played Ruth Latimer, and Henry played her husband, William. In this movie I played the son of a junk dealer, George Reed, and assist him in picking up junk from the rich white folks. I befriend Ben, the son of an aristocrat, and we play cops and robbers. Of course, I have to be the robber (what else?). William Latimer was a strict banker who doesn't want his son to have the life of a child. He wants to control every move. After his wife and son leave him for a short while, William realizes that a child must be allowed to be a child. He becomes a different person once they return. Many of the old films had good messages in the script. If parents today could model after some of the plots in those old movies, we would have better families. Better families contribute to a better world.

Penrod and Sam (1923). Ben Alexander and I had worked together in films before, and we were together again in this film. Bill Beaudine was a director from England who brought a different style and flair to the set. Ben played Penrod Schofield, Joe Butterworth was Sam Williams, Joe McCray (another black child star) played Herman and I played Verman. Madame Sul Te Wan, the first black film actress, was also in this film. Hollywood was crazy about her. Other stars were Buddy and Gertrude Messinger, and Newton Hall. Gertrude played Marjorie Jones, Penrod's sweetheart. Rockliffe Fellowes was Mr. Schofield, and Gladys Brockwell was Mrs. Schofield. We also had Mary Philbin as Margaret Schofield; Gareth Hughes as Robert Williams; William Mong as Deacon Bitts; Martha Mattox as Miss Spence, the school teacher; Vic Potel as the town drunkard; Bobby Gordon as Maurice Levy; and Cameo the dog.

Cameo was special to me because I had a dog myself named Jack. When we weren't shooting in the film, I would play with Cameo. This was a special treat for me to work on this film and be able to play around with a dog. Everyone knew where to find me if I wasn't nearby. I would be somewhere with Cameo, a smart dog who took directions very well. He was a playful, fun and loving animal. In the film he was Penrod's dog Duke.

This was another film produced by J. McDonald and based on a Booth Tarkington story. Distributed by Associated First National Pictures, this film was a combination of comedy and drama. Penrod and Sam are buddies who have a secret club that excludes Buddy and Newton's characters. The club is like a fraternity, and the boys play on a certain lot. The lot is sold by Penrod's

Eugene (far left) and the other children in *Penrod and Sam* (1923).

father to Deacon Bitts, and the table is turned: Buddy refuses to let Penrod play the lot. Penrod is heartbroken because his pet dog is buried on the lot. Penrod's father sees the grief in his son and decides to buy back the lot for Penrod.

Back then we had a lot of family movies. They were wholesome, with a small town atmosphere. This movie dealt with childhood rivalry, and it showed the love that a father has for his son. Rarely do we see these kinds of movies anymore. All of our movies are so full of violence. When I see films that are shown today, I am not surprised by the violence in the world. If we would spend more time making wholesome films, they would leave an image in a person's mind. When that individual walked away from a positive film, love would be in heart and mind. This would make that person want to go out and show love to all mankind. The film industry must begin to realize the power the media has on the world and begin to change in a positive manner to show all people fairly and perpetuate strong family values. This could help the world become a better place.

Thief of Baghdad (1924). Robert Dandridge was another colored kid star. He and I were picked to play page boys. Douglas Fairbanks, Sr., was the star

Little Annie Rooney (Mary Pickford) and her gang stand guard.

and title character. Sam Baker, another great black actor, was also in this film. He was a giant standing around seven feet tall. Sam and I were favorites of Mr. Fairbanks, and when his friends would come on the set he would call us to perform. We performed for such greats as Harold Lloyd, Rudolph Valentino, Charlie Chaplin, Ramon Novarro and others. I would do my shimmy dance with my fancy steps, and Sam would do his imitation of a roaring lion.

The cast included Snitz Edwards as an evil person, Charles Belcher as the holy man, and Julanne Johnston as the princess. The two princes were Noble Johnson and Mathilda Comont, and the slaves were Anna May Wong and Etta Lee. Jess Weldon, Scotty Mattraw and Charles Sylvester played eunuchs. Sam Baker played the Sworder. We also had a magician, Sadakichi Hartmann, and I would love to watch him perform magical tricks.

This movie was full of fantasy and adventure. The Thief of Baghdad starts out as corrupt until he falls in love with the princess. He is a liar, but decides to tell the holy man that he is not a prince. He is humbled and sent on a mission to find a magical chest in an effort to gain his happiness. He finally overcomes everything that has impeded his progress for a successful mission. He frees the princess from the Mongols.

Little Annie Rooney (1925). This film starred Mary Pickford, America's sweetheart. Her real name was Gladys Smith, and she worked her way up

Top: Little Annie Rooney (Mary Pickford) and friends. *Bottom:* Mary, Eugene and the other kids on the lookout.

through the ranks of theater and film with the guidance of her strong mother, Charlotte. Charlotte Smith ran the show for her child's career just as many mothers did. She knew how to hold on to a dollar, stretch it and invest it properly, which made Mary a very wealthy person. Mary was first married to Owen Moore, a black Irish actor. They had met at the Biograph Company. After they divorced, Mary later married Douglas Fairbanks. This marriage also ended in divorce.

Mary was attractive. Her most noticeable feature was the color of her hair. It was the color of honey, and her curls looked like gold. These were natural attributes, not dyed or false. Mary continued to have a youthfulness about her as she matured. When she was between the ages of 24 and 34, she was able to play the role of a 12-year-old. In *Little Annie Rooney*, she played the part of a tom girl. Children of several different nationalities were in the gang. I played the part of Humidor, and William Haines played Joe Kelly. Other cast members were Walter James, Gordon Griffin, Carlo Schipa, Spec O'Donnell, Hugh Fay, Vola Vale, Joe Butterworth and Oscar Rudolph. Spec played Abie, Vola was Mamie, and Joe portrayed Mickey.

This was a comedy type drama film. Annie's father is a policeman. Annie takes care of her dad and brother, Tim, but still finds time to get into mischief. Her father is killed in a gang fight, and Tim and Annie are determined to get even with the person that killed their father. Annie's sweetheart, Joe Kelly, is accused of the murder. Tim shoots Joe, but Annie continues her investigation of the real culprit until the actual killer is found. Annie then gives blood to save Joe's life.

This movie was full of action-packed suspense. The public didn't know who did what, which is so different from the films today. Nowadays they show who did it, along with a big chase, which doesn't make people think. When we made movies, they were full of everything. For instance, this movie dealt with a family relationship between a sister and brother, murder, revenge and life-saving sacrifice.

There was an electrical parade after we finished *Little Annie Rooney*. Mary Pickford had a float made from the actual set of her clubhouse on the east side of New York. The parade began around Fifth and Figueroa and went out to Coliseum. I recall that we played on the float and had fights, throwing plastic apples, oranges, tomatoes and false bricks at each other. The premiere of *Little Annie Rooney* was at the Million Dollar Theater, owned by Mary Pickford.

Uncle Tom's Cabin (1927). Harry Pollard was the director of this picture. James Lowe was Uncle Tom, with Gertrude Howard as his wife. (James Lowe was the first West Coast "heavy" Negro actor, and Gertrude Howard was an established star before Hattie McDaniel.) I was immediately chosen to play one of the sons at Universal Studios. I played a double roll because I had outgrown one and grown into another. My character names were Pete and Sam. The

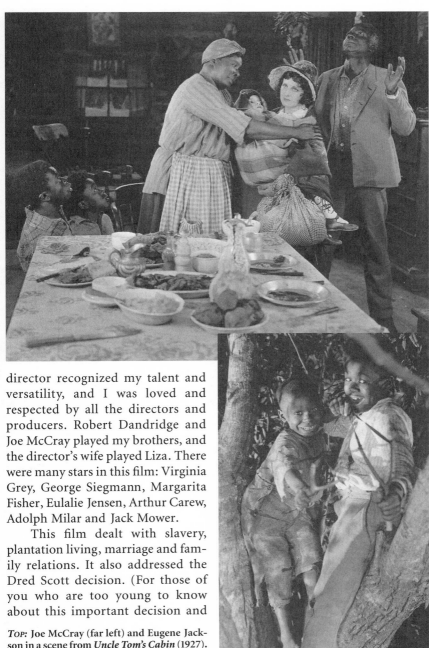

director recognized my talent and versatility, and I was loved and respected by all the directors and producers. Robert Dandridge and Joe McCray played my brothers, and the director's wife played Liza. There were many stars in this film: Virginia Grey, George Siegmann, Margarita Fisher, Eulalie Jensen, Arthur Carew, Adolph Milar and Jack Mower.

This film dealt with slavery, plantation living, marriage and family relations. It also addressed the Dred Scott decision. (For those of you who are too young to know about this important decision and

TOP: Joe McCray (far left) and Eugene Jackson in a scene from *Uncle Tom's Cabin* (1927). *RIGHT:* Robert Dandridge (left) and Eugene Jackson in *Uncle Tom's Cabin* (1927).

haven't read or been taught about it, the Dred Scott decision was a law passed by the United States Supreme Court. It stated if a person had one drop of black blood, then that person was declared black or African American, regardless of how light or white one looked.) Universal built an enormous white house called Shelby House, and hundreds of black extras were used. It took two years to make *Uncle Tom's Cabin*, which was my last silent film. I made the transition from silent films to talkies with *Hearts in Dixie* (1929).

4
Talkies,
1928-1937

Hearts in Dixie (1929). In my audition, there were 15 boys in Los Angeles auditioning for the role of Chincapin. Fox was searching for the best colored actor. William Fox went all over New York, Chicago and the South to cast my role. In those days, Hollywood liked dark-skinned blacks with kinky hair. I was actually too light, but was chosen anyway because I had the personality and the talent. Winning this role made me the first black child star in sound pictures, or "talkies." They would darken my skin, and the screen test was 30–45 minutes. One was given lines and then judged on timing, voice, facial expression and body language. In the early talkies, the voices of the colored actors came across better than white actors. The quality of the Negro's voice was richer in resonance, tone and quality, while the white actors came across sounding mousy and weak. Still, the screen tests were very competitive.

The following black actors were in *Hearts in Dixie*: Clarence Muse as Nappus, my father; Dorothy Morrison, sister of Sunshine Sammy, as my sweetheart, Amelia; Miss Billbrew and her chorus of 60 voices; Lincoln Perry, better known as Stepin Fetchit; Mildred Washington; Bernice Pilot; Vivian Smith; Robert Brooks; Richard Carlyle; Zach Williams; Clifford Ingram; the Fanchon and Marco Steppers; the Emperors of Harr, a singing group; the Four Covans Dancers; and the Evans and Weaver dancing team.

Fox wanted Charles Gilpin, a Broadway star, from New York because of his stage background to play my father. He had played Emperor Jones in New York. He had a great-sounding voice, but he drank himself out of this part. He was chosen over George Reed and Jim Lowe. He held up production for two weeks. They sent for Clarence Muse, a young new actor from Chicago's Lafayette Players. There were two sets of sweethearts in the film: Dorothy Morrison and myself, and an adult team consisting of Clifford Ingram and Mildred Washington. Bernice Pilot was Stepin Fetchit's wife.

The voodoo woman was supposed to be played by madame Sul Te Wan, but Mrs. A.C. Billbrew got the part of the voodoo woman. She had a singing

choir of about 60 singers, with her husband as the lead singer. She probably beat out Madame Sul Te Wan for the role because of her talent and the fact that her choir could be utilized. Madame Sul Te Wan was the first black actress in movies. She started out with producer/director D.W. Griffith, who directed *Birth of a Nation*. Madame Sul Te Wan had three sons, one of whom was still living at the age of 80 in 1990. My wife Sue and I took him to Oakland to receive an award for his mother's contribution to the arts. He lived

Top: Eugene Jackson stars as Chincapin in the 1929 film *Hearts in Dixie. Bottom:* Chincapin (Eugene Jackson) and mother Chloe (Bernice Pilot) in *Hearts in Dixie* (1929).

the life of a king for one week, as excited and thrilled as a child. The Black Film Festival at the Paramount Theater in Oakland held the affair to honor his mother.

Locations in Bakersfield, California, were used to depict the South. We started filming in Bakersfield and went back to Los Angeles to shoot a scene. Things had been going smoothly when all of a sudden Clarence heard someone say, "Bring that nigger over here." Now Clarence was an outspoken young actor from Chicago who respected himself and others. When Clarence heard that word "nigger," he went to the director and demanded an explanation. Clarence was very upset and had to be held by other actors. Words were exchanged between the two, and the director stated that they were referring to a "Go Bar" (a black device, about four feet by eight feet, that was used to dim lights). Clarence explained to director Paul Salon his dislike of the reference, and production had to be stopped. My mother and I heard that word before on sets. It had frightened us when we first heard it. We sat quietly and discovered that they were not referring to us.

Clarence, being a man of high principles and standards, would not back down. He wanted the name changed immediately because the word "nigger" was unpleasant to the ears and degrading to an entire race of people. I was so shocked and proud of Clarence at the same time. He was strong and so full of character. He was a man of high principle and worth. He stuck to his guns, his beliefs, until a change was made. I was merely a youth, but I was taught something that day that has stayed with me all of my life: If you know and believe in your heart that something must be changed, act on it. Do not let it ride, or it will eat at you the rest of your life. Take action as this man did. He didn't care if it cost him his part. He stood strong. He took the hump off our backs and gave us respect that day.

Clarence Muse is just one example of how the first pioneer black actors made a difference for black actors to follow. We were laughing and dancing on the scene and doing our job, but we were also making a road for other blacks to travel. This was why I must tell this story. Had we not acted in these roles written for us, the white minstrels would still be making money on our talent. Al Jolson and Eddie Cantor are perfect examples. They would blacken their faces and use black dialect to act and sing black songs.

Similar things are going on in show business today. They aren't blackening their faces, but our songs, styles and dances are being copied by nonblacks, which shows why we should be proud of our arts and talents: If they weren't good, then people wouldn't copy them. It is so important to think positive about oneself and culture. If a person doesn't think good of himself, his talents and his people, then how can he expect anyone else to think good of him? It is that simple. It is that clear.

In *Hearts of Dixie*, we had all the best adult dancers. We had the famous "Flying Covans," who had been around the world. They did a tap, flash and a wing act. The blacks who performed in early films had natural talent. Hollywood knew that and respected them all. Unlike today, there was no such thing as equipment to help enhance a person's voice. Acts had to be smooth and well-rehearsed. Jimmy Miller and George Jones of Los Angeles were our top tenor singers with A.C. Billbrew and their famous quartet. The female dancers were picked from Frank Sebastian's Cotton Club in Culver City, the Club Alabam and the Dunbar Hotel.

Many of the dancers would teach me some of their steps. I would master the routine quickly, which would amaze them and make them want to show me more. I caught on well and absorbed everything they demonstrated. (I would put this learning to use in my career.) It wasn't uncommon back then for established stars to share their knowledge and skills with someone else. I and other entertainers are recipients of this type of action and generosity from some of the great benefactors.

As a child actor, I had to contend with the jealousies of adults as well as children. While filming *Hearts of Dixie*, Clarence Muse had a radio show for publicity. Family and friends could not understand why I was not invited to appear on his show since I was the child star. One day I was told point blank that I was purposely being ignored because all of Hollywood loved me — Clarence did not like that. This is just one example of what I had to deal with growing up as a child star. It wasn't always peaches and cream. At times, it was very painful.

Fox Movietone Follies of 1929. After *Hearts in Dixie* in 1929, I played in *Fox Movietone Follies*, starring Sue Carol, wife of Alan Ladd. Stepin Fetchit played Swiftly. Other stars were John Breeden, Lola Lane, Jeanette Dancey, Sharon Lynn and Dixie Lee. It was a musical comedy about a southern guy who tries to dissuade his girl from going into show business. I have a dance partner, Jeanette Dancey, and we sing a song called "Break Away." Jeanette was a little colored girl who had a rich, mature voice like an adult. This early talkie musical was an all-star review: The studio tried to use a great deal of their contract stars in this film.

Cameo Kirby (1930). Irving Cummings was the director of this film at Fox Film Corporation. The cast members were J. Harold Murray, Norma Terris, Douglas Gilmore, Robert Edeson, Myrna Loy, Charles Morton, Stepin Fetchit, George MacFarlane, John Hyams, Madame Daumery and Beulah Hall Jones. This film is about riverboat gamblers on the Mississippi and is set in New Orleans. I play the part of a river boy who sells watermelons from his boat down the river. The river scene was filmed on location in Sacramento.

As a child actor, I was able to stay at the Senator Hotel in Sacramento with my mother and Mrs. Ducket, the first black school teacher of child actors and actresses. No adult Negro actors were allowed to stay there, but because I was a child star some doors were opened. At times, things were somewhat more relaxed for a Negro child actor.

Dixiana (1930). The stars of this RKO film were Bebe Daniels, Everett Marshall, Bert Wheeler, Robert Woolsey, Dorothy Lee, Joseph Cawthorn, Ralf Harolde, Jobyna Howland, Bill Robinson, Edward Chandler, George Herman, and myself. It was a southern film in which I played the part of a houseboy named Cupid — I was 13 years old. This film is about a singer who wants to hide her past in order to marry into an aristocratic family. Her background is discovered and her plans are foiled for a while. Later in the movie she is reconciled with her lover.

When I was told that my idol Bill Robinson was going to be on set, I became cheerful. Mama had always taken Freddie and me to see him at the RKO Theater whenever he would be performing in town. Since he was a dancer and I was a dancer, I felt we had something in common. It was special to be able to see him, and I was dancing pretty good at the time. One day I left the set for my dressing room and ran into Bill Robinson. I was about three feet from him. With excitement in my voice, I said, "Hello, Mr. Robinson!" He just said, "Hello, boy." He kept walking, acting as if I was invisible. I was so hurt. I ran upstairs and told my mother, and she told me to forget about it. I was feeling so down in the dumps. From that day on, until he changed in later years, I didn't like Bill Robinson for two cents — he was on my list. Some of the stars today treat people unkindly. This should not be, because the fans pay our salaries. Without loyal supportive fans, a star's popularity can fade, along with his salary. Everyone should be treated with kindness and respect, which is why I had so many fans. I treated everyone with the utmost reverence and consideration.

At the same time on the set, the original radio stars of *Amos 'n' Andy* were brought in from Chicago to make "Check and Double Check." (By the way, the original radio characters of *Amos 'n' Andy* were white.) I ran into Amos and Andy, and they were so cordial. They spotted me with my ukulele, but I didn't know who they were. They asked if I played, and I said yes. I played a song, then one of them took my ukulele and played chords that I had never heard. When they told me who they were, I was so surprised and elated. I asked if they would sign my ukulele. I didn't have a pen, so they waited patiently while I scampered upstairs to my dressing room to get one. I still have that ukulele.

Cimarron (1931). This movie won a 1931 Academy award and was directed by Wesley Ruggles. The screenplay was written by Walter Weems, based on the novel by Edna Ferber and set during the Oklahoma land rush. I costarred as Isaiah. The stars were Irene Dunne; Richard Dix as Yancey Cravat; George E. Stone; Edna Mae Oliver; William Collier, Jr; Nance O'Neil; Roscoe Ates; Robert McWade; Frank Darien; Delores Brown; Gloria Vonic; Otto Hoffman; William Orlamond; Frank Beal; Nancy Dover; Helen Parrish; Donald Dilloway; Junior Johnson; child actor Douglas Scott; Reginald Streeter; Lois Jane Campbell; Ann Lee; Tyrone Brereton; Lillian Lane; Henry Rocquemore; Neil Craig;

Robert McKenzie; Bob Kortman; Clara Hunt; William Janney; and Dennis O'Keefe. Estelle Taylor was also in this film. She was the wife of world champion fighter Jack Dempsey. Stanley Fields was the bad guy, and Deacon McDaniel (the brother of Hattie McDaniel), played the butler.

I will never forget the opening scene. Before shooting this scene, the director, Wesley Ruggles, came to me and said, "Gene, I have two cakes. They cost $125 apiece." If you fall correctly the first time, you can take the other cake home." Twelve people were sitting at

Top: Eugene starred as Isaiah in the 1931 Western *Cimarron*. Bottom: Eugene ("Isaiah"), Irene Dunn, and Richard Dix in *Cimarron* (1931).

A scene from *Cimarron*: Irene Dunn, Roscoe Ates, George E. Stone, and Eugene "Pineapple" Jackson.

the dinner table. I was placed above the table on a platform to fan the flies away. Richard Dix entered the room telling the family of the Oklahoma Land Rush. His voice was full of vigor and amusement, and I became so intense in his conversation that I fell down six feet into the cake. I made a bull's-eye. I made such an accurate fall because I *wanted* that second cake. (I was able to give all the neighbors a piece of cake.) When I land in the cake in that scene, I spring up with excitement in my face and voice, begging Massa Yancey to take me with them. My mama comes from the kitchen exclaiming that I won't be "goin' to no Oklahoma. I was goin' to take a bath." Yancey packs his family for Osage, Oklahoma, which was untamed country. I steal away in a rug because I want to be with them and have great feelings for the family; I felt that I am a member of his family. When they discover that I am in the rug they have traveled quite a distance, so they decide to let me stay.

When they get to Osage, Yancey Cravat establishes a printing press for business. Osage is open country, and outlaws pass through town regularly. My death scene received rave reviews by the famous syndicated columnist Walter Winchell. My highest accolade came from Louella Parsons. She had the dark, bold Gothic letters proclaiming, "THE DEATH OF ISAIAH WAS THE THE HIGH-LIGHT OF THE MOVIE." "With creditable performance on the screen this year when he was cast as the slave boy in *Cimarron* with Richard Dix."

A funny scene in the movie is when Richard Dix goes to church on Sunday. I play the part of a child who is totally devoted to him. I want to be around him no matter what. One day as he goes to church, I have dressed up in his clothes and hat that were too big for me. He is on the way to church when suddenly he hears something behind him. To his surprise, it is me. He uses psychology on me by saying that I could be more useful if I went back to guard the home front. He instructs me to do patrol duty and gives me his pistol. I run back home, slipping and sliding in his big boots, filled with excitement by my new job.

Sporting Blood (1931). *Sporting Blood,* produced by MGM, was filmed in Lexington, Kentucky, in ten days. The entire crew rode first class on the train to film. My mother and school teacher, Mrs. Ducket, were with me. The cast consisted of Clark Gable, Ernest Torrence, Madge Evans, Lew Cody, Marie Prevost, Harry Holman, Hallam Cooley, J. Farrell MacDonald, John Larkin, Gertrude Howard and Tommy Boy the horse. Gertrude played the character of an old mammy, Jolly John Larkin played the part of a stable man who had been around horses for over 30 years, and I played the part of a stable boy named Sammy. There were great write-ups in the newspaper about my past performances before I came to town.

The training for this film took place on the back lot of MGM. The director asked me if I could ride a horse. I said yes, but I had never ridden a race horse. He obtained a trainer to teach me to ride. The training took place on lot number two, which was like a forest full of green grass and trees. (It consisted of ten acres.) The trainer instructed me how to mount the horse and hold the rein. It was different from riding a stable horse. I rode around in a circle like a race track for about an hour. My mother and the trainer were watching me. The horse was walking slowly. I called out to the trainer, "What do I do to get him to trot a little bit?" He said, "Tell the horse to get up, and pull on the rein a little." When I did that, he shot out like he was in a race. I was holding on as tight as I could. He seemed to run faster and faster. Mother was on the ground screaming at the top of her voice, "Hold on Gene, hold on!" The trainer was hollering and yelling instructions. The horse then turned to run through the trees. I was afraid a limb would be hanging down from a tree and would knock me off the horse. I guess the horse got tired because to everyone's surprise and joy he suddenly stopped. My mother and the trainer had been running after us, and they were just as tired as the horse. I hit the ground fast — I was shaking like jelly. After the producer was told of this ordeal, he decided to get a double because he did not want anything to happen to his prize star.

When we arrived in Lexington, they hired a colored rider. My costume for the picture included a cap, a pair of torn pants, and a ragged shirt. When I arrived, I was filled with wonder at the farms. I recall telling the press that I wanted to buy my mother a farm even if it cost a million dollars. I had the opportunity to meet the owner of Dixiana Farms, Charles T. Fisher. Also, I saw Elmendorf Farm. I saw the great retired race horse, Man o' War, on the first day of location. Upon arrival, I was picked up in a limo and driven to the race tracks. I was amazed at the conditions of the living quarters for the horses. The stable had hardwood floors that shone like a dime. They had running water, and there wasn't a speck of dirt anywhere. I recalled thinking that some people didn't live as well as these animals. I was told the horses made millions of dollars. Because they were worth much, they had to be treated with love and care. We should value our children in this same manner. Children are invaluable — no monetary value can be placed on them.

I went to Kentucky weighing 115 pounds. I left twenty pounds lighter because the notorious flies nearly ate me alive. In between shootings, I would sit in the limo to save my flesh from the flies and the hot sun. One time I fell asleep, and when I woke up I was shocked to see the limo surrounded by white people. I was frightened. I thought I was going to be lynched, but to my surprise they were fans wanting my autograph.

We couldn't stay with the white cast at the hotel, so they found a respectable colored family who had a very nice home. They were the Smith family, with twin boys Marvin and Melvin, who were around my age. Every day when I would come home from work, the place would be crowded with kids looking for autographs. We would attend church with the Smiths on Sunday. We would be introduced to the congregation as celebrities from Hollywood. We were treated very well by the community: Different church people would invite us over for dinner every day. The pretty little girls would chase me but they had to get past my mother, which was a big task. But they did manage to get by for an autograph.

We left Kentucky to complete shooting at MGM, a studio that was known for rain shots in their movies. In one scene, a mare is giving birth to a colt in the rain, and I ride in the rain to get blankets for the colt. John Larkin, Ernest Torrence and I had to carry the colt inside for warmth. Immediately after this scene, my mother made me change into dry clothes. She tried to get John Larkin to change. He replied in a macho manner that he was fine and was not bothered by working in damp clothes. He continued to work in wet clothes all day and became very sick. He stayed ill for about a year until finally he died of pneumonia.

Another one of my favorite scenes is when I overhear two crooked gamblers discussing how they will sabotage the race. I told Madge Evans, and we decide to thin the rein so that when the jockey pulls the horse back, the rein will begin to ravel and eventually break. To the surprise of the jockey, he pulls on the rein trying to hold the horse back and the rein gets thinner and thinner. It finally breaks, and the jockey has to hold on to the horse's mane and neck. The horse goes on to win the race.

Sporting Chance (1931). This was another "horse" movie. The race track

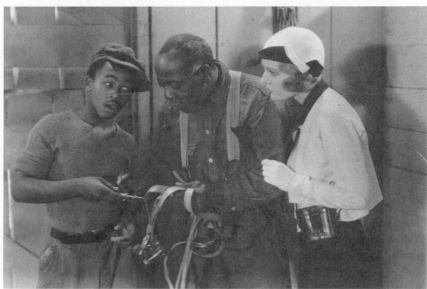

TOP: Sammy (Eugene Jackson) holds Tommy the colt in a scene from *Sporting Blood* (1931). *BOTTOM:* Eugene (Sammy) helps fix the reins in *Sporting Blood* (1931).

Eugene reteams with his *Cimarron* costar Richard Dix in *Secret Service* (1931).

scene was filmed on location in Oceanside, California, and the remaining portion was done on a set. The cast of this independent film consisted of William Collier, Jr., Claudia Dell, James Hall, Joseph Levering, Henry Rocquemore, Hedwiga Reicher, Mahlon Hamilton and myself as Horseshoe. I had a better part in this movie than in *Sporting Blood*. I did a tap dance routine, I did more acting, and I did a lot of riding on stable horses. I did a lot of comic scenes as a wide-eyed stable boy. This musical romance is historic because it was the first time that a steeplechase was ever staged for the screen.

Secret Service (1931). I did such a good job in *Cimarron* that I was requested to work with Richard Dix again in *Secret Service*. The following stars were in the film: William Post, Jr., Shirley Grey, Nance O'Neil, Harold Kinney, Gavin Gordon, Florence Lake, Frederick Burton, Clarence Muse, and Gertrude Howard. This movie was about impostors and impersonators. I was a house boy in a southern mansion who spies on the enemy to relay activities to Union soldier Richard Dix.

King of the Jungle (1933). This movie was based on a novel called *The Lion's Way: A Story of Men and Lions*; the working title of the film was *The Lion's Way*. The stars were Buster Crabbe, Frances Dee, Sidney Toler, Nydia Westman, Robert Barrat, Irving Pichel, Douglas Dumbrille, Sam Baker, Patricia Farley and Ronnie Cosbey. Buster Crabbe, the 1932 Olympic gold medalist swimmer, made his debut in this film. The film was shot on locations including a zoo, Mexico, Chatsworth, Santa Catalina Island, San Pedro, Laguna and San Francisco. Sam Baker plays the king of the safari, my father. As I remember one scene, a Caucasian family visits the jungle for a safari. I am giving the daughter a tour when suddenly a lion appears and I scare it away with my spear.

A lion trainer was on hand to direct us and help with the lion. Had the lion not obeyed, we would have been his supper. Later in the afternoon, one of the major white actors was killed by the lion. The star was wearing an animal skin jacket, and the heat from the sun mixed with the perspiration of his body made him smell like a real animal. The lion broke loose and attacked the star, breaking his collarbone and then killing him. This was a horrible disaster on the set for all. Buster was bitten on the leg by a tiger, though it was not a serious wound. This was a dangerous film to perform in.

Ladies Crave Excitement (1935). The stars of this film were Norman Foster; Evalyn Knapp; Esther Ralston; Eric Linden; Purnell Pratt; Gilbert Emery; Irene Franklin; Syd Saylor; Emma Dunn; Mary McLaren; Matt McHugh; Francis McDonald; George Hayes; Stanley Blystone; Russell Hicks; Max Wagner; Lynton Brent; Edward Peil; Robert Frazer; Herbert Heywood; Christian Rub; and Jason Robards, who was just beginning in films. In this film, a reporter and an heiress uncover a horseracing scam. I played the part of a stable boy.

Wine, Women and Horses (1937): The cast of this film included Barton MacLane, Ann Sheridan, Dick Purcell, Peggy Bates, Walter Cassell, Lottie Williams, Kenneth Harlan, Charles Foy, James Robbins and Lady Luck the race horse. This was another horse racing movie and with it Warner Bros. became the first to produce a film at the Santa Anita racetracks. I will never forget the tracks. In the middle, they had a bed of beautiful pansies of all colors.

Ann Sheridan was from Houston, Texas, and this was her first movie. She was a very pretty lady. I played Eightball, a barber shop shoe-shine boy and stable boy. The plot centered around Jim's character, a big time gambler. When I would shine his shoes, the gambler would tip big. Jim marries a self-righteous woman who is against gambling, but they divorce and he ends up with his old flame.

5
Singing Cowboys
and Dancing Crows

My second big break came when in 1935 Republic Pictures of North Hollywood produced the Gene Autry Westerns. They said they had an unknown singing cowboy actor from Oklahoma who was a heck of a marksman with the six shooter. They told me I would be one of Gene Autry's sidekicks. Things were tough in the movie business, and they couldn't pay much because Autry was not established. Westerns were new. Little did they know that Westerns would be a hit in the future or that Gene Autry would become a well-known star. They said it would be steady work, so I took it — I had to eat and pay the bills.

Our first picture was *Tumbling Tumbleweeds*. The plot was about a traveling medicine show. We would ride into town singing and playing, and I had to fake playing the violin while Gene sang. I would tap dance on the platform of our wagon, which was pulled by a mule. I incorporated some of the same tap steps I had used in a movie where I danced on a saloon bar. We were mostly on location in Victorville and Indio, California. Alan Ludwig wrote the story on which *Tumbling Tumbleweeds* was based, and Joseph Kane was the director.

Smiley Burnette played the accordion. We had the medicine man, George Hayes, who sold medicine strong enough to kill a snake. My costume consisted of a hat, khaki pants and shirt. When we put the medicine show on, I had a fancy black and white striped suit with a high white hat. The film was a hit, and I received complimentary newspaper reviews for my part as Eightball. However, even as a teen actor I couldn't escape jealousy from adult actors. Smiley Burnette was somewhat jealous of me.

The story has Gene Autry returning home after five years to find his father murdered. His best friend Brownie is accused of the crime. Gene doesn't believe this and gets to the bottom of the mystery by playing detective to bring the real murderers to justice.

Other actors in *Tumbling Tumbleweeds* were Lucille Brown, Norma Tay-

TOP: Eugene Jackson ("Eightball") and a young Gene Autry. *BOTTOM:* Gene, Doc and Eightball (Eugene Jackson) ride into town in *Tumbling Tumbleweeds* (1935).

Eugene Jackson ("Eightball"), Gene Autry and Smiley Burnette provide saloon entertainment for the locals.

lor, Edward Hearn, Jack Rockwell, Frankie Marvin, George Chesebro, Tom London, Cornelius Keefe, Cliff Lyons, Tracy Layne and Champion the Horse.

This picture was filmed at Republic studios on a small budget. Because Gene was unknown, studios were reluctant to issue a large budget. Studios didn't take big risks on unestablished artists back then. Directors and producers had to make do with what they were given and had, which brought about a great deal of creativity in the film industry.

We made *Red River Valley* and *Guns and Guitars* in 1936. Some of the cast of *Red River Valley* were Gene Autry, Smiley Burnette, Frances Grant, Boothe Howard, Jack Kennedy, Sam Flint, George Chesebro, Charles King and Champion the Horse. My character's name was Iodine. The title of the movie is based on a Western song that is referred to throughout the movie. A new dam is being built, and some people are unhappy about it. Mishaps began to occur, so Gene and Smiley pretend to be ditch-diggers in order to solve the accidents at the construction site. Laughter was continuous in the film because of Gene, Smiley and myself. Our roles kept the spirits high in this film.

In *Guns and Guitars* I returned as Eightball, along with Champion the Horse. Frankie Marvin played Shorty. Other cast members were Gene, Smiley, Tom London, Charles King and Denver Dixon. Autry is accused of murdering the sheriff, so in order to clear his name and jail the bad guy he becomes the sheriff. The song "Ridin' All Day" is sung throughout the movie.

I did the Civil War movie *Hearts in Bondage* in 1936. James Dunn, Mae Clark and Henry B. Walthall also starred. Frank McGlynn, Sr., played President Lincoln. The theme had a soap opera–type plot with two naval heroes and the conflict of the Civil War. The battleships *Monitor* and *Merrimack* are a big part of the story. Lew Ayres directed this film.

Hattie McDaniel and myself worked with the Duke, John Wayne; Ann Rutherford; Cy Kendall; Bob Kortman; and Sam Flint in *The Lonely Trail* (1936). I played a dancer. John Wayne was just starting out in film — no one knew that he would someday become an icon in the movies. The Duke returned to his hometown in Texas and is shocked to find that it is full of corruption. The governor hires Wayne to clean up the place from carpetbaggers. The town folks don't take to the Duke at first because he is a Union soldier. Over time, though, he is able to win over the people with his actions.

Musical shorts were shown in theaters after feature films and newsreels. They were short musical stories that would sometimes last around 35 minutes. Musical shorts would also be in clubs and taverns, where people would put a quarter in a machine to see a show.

Herbert Jeffrey was the first black singing cowboy. In 1938, he starred in a musical short called *Rhythm Rodeo*. Freddie and I, rhythm tap dancers, did an eccentric cowboy comedy dance in the dirt. The musical shorts also starred Troy Brown, who was about 300 pounds. He was an actor and entertainer who could sing and dance. It was truly something to see a 300-pounder do a full split to the floor, then rise and continue to dance. He was real funny. Jim Davis was an actor who was creative with horseriding tricks, roping, swimming and diving in the movie. He also did a lot of *Tarzan* features.

In 1943, the musical short *Moo Cow Boogie* was released. It was a West Coast Colored Production that featured Rosa Lee Lincoln as the star cow-dancer. Other cowgirl dancers were Mildred Boyd, Juanita Moore, Louise Ritchie and Etta Jones. The Four Tones sang the western songs. Many of the same actors and dancers used in *Rhythm Rodeo* were used in *Moo Cow Boogie*. Dudley Dickerson, a black cowboy comedian, was the star comedian at Frank Sebastian's Cotton Club for years. The dancers in *Moo Cow Boogie* were the Mosette Dancers. In this short, Dorothy Dandridge sings "Cow-Cow Boogie" in a nightclub, and I am her piano player. (Dorothy was an unknown actress at that time, having been discovered in a 1938 Columbia film called *You Can't Take It with You*.) My brother Freddie and I did the street dancing in this movie. The Dandridge sisters were in this movie, but of the Dandridge Trio, Dorothy was the one who became a well-known star.

DANCING CROWS: *DUMBO* (1941)

Our unknown big break came when I was around 17 or 18, between 1935 and 1937. The reason I call this our unknown break was because we never received any big money for our contribution to *Dumbo*, which was released in 1941. No one knew it was going to become a classic in the animation industry. In fact, animation was new back then in the movie business. During that time Walt Disney was just beginning, and he had acquired a loan for this film. Freddie and I did some dancing for Disney artists to go by in animating the crows for the film. The making of *Dumbo* wasn't easy for us as dancers. We didn't have all the modern technology of today. When it wasn't right, we had to dance over and over again. Sometimes even if it was right, we still had to do it more than once because we didn't have the equipment of today.

I had forgotten about this work until some old footage was found in a Disney vault. One of the elder workers just happened to recognize me in the footage. He knew that I was still alive, and I was contacted. The Disney executive had a limo sent to my home to pick me up for an interview on November 21, 1995. The Disney executive told me that they would be coming out with a series of books giving credit to African American dancers for their part in helping create the foundation for the Disney film animation. No mention of sharing this film's royalties with me was ever discussed, but that's show biz. What I would like to see would be a Disney film showing how animation was done back then, superimposing Freddie and me dancing with the crows. Ah, that would be a movie that children would love.

One can never foresee the future. This was true especially back then. The movie industry was truly in its infancy. This is why the artists of today have smart lawyers who know contracts. Back then the lawyers — and people in general — were innocent and honest. We were trudging in a field that was new. No one knew what would take off in the future, what would be a hit or turn into a classic. We didn't have people that were able to sit back and observe or predict what we were doing in the motion picture industry and what would sell or be a blockbuster. What we did have were hardworking artists like myself and so many others, like Walt Disney and Hal Roach, who did things all because we loved it. We did not know we were making history.

6
Vaudeville Tour, 1932–1933

What was vaudeville? Ah, vaudeville. Vaude was a part of history that can never be recreated no matter how hard modern technology tries today. We had our own flavor and style. Yes sir, we vaudevillians had style that could be noticed by anyone. We moved our bodies differently. We had expression. We had flair. We were exciting to talk to. A vaudevillian always had a story full of adventure because we had been all over. We never had a lot of time to sit still. We had places to go, people to meet. We had to be about the business of finding that next gig, hopping the next train. Vaudevillians were quick. Here today and gone tomorrow. We had to be fast or we could be left out. No vaudevillian wanted to be left out of any show that was jumpin'. A circuit with good acts could only enhance your act. It wasn't easy, but I wouldn't trade those memories for anything in this world.

Vaudeville was raw and fresh. It was real, and it was hard work. It was theater at its best and sometimes at its worst. Nothing today can compare to vaude. Vaudeville was love, a love of the art and craft of being able to make someone laugh who may be hurting within. The driving force of the vaudevillian actor was to see that facial expression of merriment or even tears, or to view the movement of the body from enjoyment, or to hear a chuckle, cry or sign. We thrived and strove for applause. It was live family entertainment, which meant no cursing or swearing. Saying the wrong word could put you off the circuit.

Vaude could make you cry. Yes, it could make you cry from the long hours and low pay, the carrying of luggage, the driving of cars, the riding of buses and trains. Yes, it could make you cry from the practice, the practice that was a must. There were no retakes. The audience would make or break your act — you were aware immediately if your act was entertaining to the crowd. There was a rapport between the audience and entertainer, and we reacted from each other's responses. It was like playing ball, playing catch. The entertainer would throw a line or skit to the people. They would react either favorably or unfavorably. If you threw a curve that they didn't like, you struck out on the spot at that very moment. That was it. No one's feelings were spared — that's just the way it was. It was demanding and grueling, yet fun. The audience had no mercy. They had spent their hard-earned money, money that very well could or should have been spent on a bill. But people wanted a lift in their life. They wanted some sunshine, a ray of hope that promised things would be all right or could get better. The vaudevillian provided that type of hope. But vaude could also give you the blues, the blues of having low funds and needing to stretch that buck a little farther. However, it provided laughter and joy for us and the public.

The goal of every entertainer was to strive for a good vaudeville circuit. To have your personal vaudeville tour was special. You were top dog. Vaudevillians were different: We had our own style, class, talk and mannerisms. It was a way of life, our life. We were a family. We had camaraderie. Vaudeville will always be special to the entertainment world because it was an art that was truly international. It crossed all waters and barriers to bring delight. No period of history in the entertainment business can ever match vaude. Simply put by Abel Green and Joe Laurie, Jr., vaudeville was "show biz."

In November of 1931, Freddie and I now had a great act. We had worked ourselves up to the "big time" playing the Orpheum, Million Dollar, Warner Bros., and RKO theaters. Playing on these circuits meant you had made it to the big time. The theaters would show a feature film, then the newsreel, a cartoon, and then the vaudeville act. We had been dancing for many years before we went on my personal vaudeville tour throughout the United States.

We had been working vaudeville locally. I had learned to do many imitations of celebrities. I learned to do Amos 'n' Andy and later would have a part on the television series as the bellboy. We were well-seasoned, and I had done a number of films. While performing in Los Angeles and surrounding areas, we were known as the Jackson Brothers. Our act consisted of ten minutes, and the entire stage show lasted about an hour. We would open up as a team, singing and dancing. I would come back to do my imitation of Amos 'n' Andy, Rochester, Jimmy Stewart, Rose Murphy, and the Chee Chee Girls, and Freddie would come back and sing.

We would close with a double tap stair dance. We danced to the tune of "Melody in F." We did nine-and-a-half courses, medium stop time beat, on the cue of "let's go." The tempo would be picked up fast, two-and-a-half courses. We would do a fast time step on the floor, make a fast break up the stairs, turn around and tap, make a fast break down the stairs, then pull the trenches twelve bars into a split. The crowd would go mad. They would jump to their feet.

We were known as the fastest double-stairs tappers. I created this routine from watching my idol, Bill "Bojangles" Robinson, do a stair dance routine.

He would start on the floor, then he would go up and down the stairs. It was sensational. (He was famous for tapping up the stairs.) Freddie and I changed it to two people and added three more steps, making it a total of six steps that we would tap up and down on. What made our stair dance so different is that the last two-and-a-half courses would be picked up with a real fast tempo.

In preparing for our big act, we practiced long and hard. We practiced this routine for months on our front porch steps. In fact, we did all our dancing in the living room and on the porch. We always had a street audience. People would pass by. They would stop to look and applaud, and would make constructive comments that we would listen to. There is nothing like rehearsing in front of a live audience. It's the everyday people who add the flavor and knowledge of what is good and what isn't.

I believe our first team song and dance was "Keep Your Sunny Side Up." I would come out and do a song and dance called "I Fall Down and Go Boom." We would follow that with jokes. Freddie would come back and sing a song called "Romance." Then we would do a double tap drill to the tune of "Sweethearts on Parade." We would close with a fast tap dance and a song called "Running Wild." We rehearsed and rehearsed until it was a smooth act. We were ready for vaudeville. We made our costumes by scrounging around and putting this and that together. We went to Kress Five and Dime Stores on Forty-Fifth and Central for our costumes. We had some pictures made, then we checked the phone book for booking agents.

VAUDEVILLE, HERE WE COME!

Jean Michael, John, Bob, another Bob and Bernard were agents for the Bert Levy Agency, located in the RKO building which was on Hill Street. The Bert Levy Agency would do all of our northern bookings. The Fanchon and Marco Agency on Sunset booked us on the Fox Circuit, which went all over the country. (Roy Wolff, a famous band leader, was the brother of Fanchon and Marco.) The Johnny Beck Agency was in the Warner Bros. building on Hill Street. A Mr. Krammer was also my agent. These were our Jewish agents who gave us our start.

Al Wager, on Seventh and Broadway, had cheap jobs but they kept us working. Sometimes, he would come up with a big-paying one. He booked us at a little theater in San Pedro, California, called the Beacon. This audition was a matinee in which we received a small amount of pay. His right-hand man, Nelson, caught the matinee and reported back to him that we were ready for vaudeville, for the "big time." From then on we would get jobs on Saturday and Sunday for $25 or $35 an act. We played at the Hippodrome on Main Street about 30 times a year. We also played at the Arrow on Fourth and Main for two days.

Vaudeville, here we come! Eugene (right) and brother Freddie.

Things were rough. We received $15 for two days, and our car wasn't running. My mother, Freddie and I walked from Fourth and Main to Forty-Seventh Place in order to save money. Our mother was a stalwart, vigorous in spirit, mind and body. She is the reason I'm successful today because she taught us how to save and survive. After we played all the little theaters, we were able to get the bigger agents. We played two theaters named the Strand: one in Whittier and the other in Long Beach. I will never forget a hard rain when we were playing in Long Beach. It rained so heavy that we had to spend the night in the theater. The streets were flooded, and the bridge was washed out.

After hard work, we finally got to work in the State and Lake Theater in Long Beach. We were on the same bill with Burns and Allen, Arthur Lake and Charlie McCarthy. Al would book us all around. He would book shows for us at the CCC Camps for wayward boys in Victorville and Lancaster in the mountains. We would be taken up in army trucks. We would make six or seven dollars and be given donuts. President Roosevelt founded the CCC Camps. They were founded on love to get youth back on the right track and help them become citizens in the world. I believe these types of camps are needed today to help today's youth.

Working our way through vaudeville introduced us to people who would later go on to become stars, like the Garland sisters, who were on the show with us at the Garfield Theater in Alabama. We had worked together at different theaters. While at the Garfield, Judy's mom told my mom that MGM's talent scout was coming out to catch the show that Judy Garland (whose real name was Frances Gumm) was in. They liked her and signed her, and we never saw Judy again. The rest is history.

When we would play at the Orange, a small neighborhood theater, we would work the matinee and appear with regular acts. Johnny Beck would book us on stag shows, where the girls would do a song and dance routine. Nothing but men would be in the audience, and they would boisterously clap, yell and whistle. We made more money on stag shows because they were illegal and because they were only one-night jobs.

A funny thing happened while performing one stag show. One day Johnny Beck called me to get some pretty colored girls to strip in Burbank. The girls really didn't want to do it because they knew we would be on the same show and would see them. I finally talked them into it and said that we wouldn't look. While the girls were performing someone yelled "Raid!" and the cops were there. Everyone began to run, first for their clothing and then for the door. Freddie and I had already performed, and we all made it out safely.

We continued to break in our act for vaudeville on Friday, Saturday and Sunday at the Tivoli Theater, which was located on Forty-Third and Central Avenue in the heart of the colored section. We played up and down the coast of California, appearing in such cities as Huntington Park, Santa Barbara, Ventura, San Diego and Orange County. The April 21, 1931, edition of the *South Gate Daily Tribune* carried a story stating that we were performing with the Warner Bros. Theater Circuit and Everett Hoggland. From there to San Diego we went on the Bert Levy Circuit, which covered the Northwestern cities such as Seattle, Vancouver, Portland, San Diego, San Jose and San Francisco.

We were appearing with Horace Heidt and his band at the Golden Gate Theater in San Francisco. Horace would feature successful stunts and gimmicks in his performances. The Bell Ringers from Europe were on the same show. There were so many of them that I wondered how they all got paid, because pay was low in the thirties. We were dressed in bellboy outfits, and the band was on stage. Freddie was sitting on one side, and I was on the other. Our job was to take the microphones out to the performers to sing. We would tap dance out with the microphones. We would be featured next, and we would do our dance routine. We were there for six weeks.

We went to Seattle to play at the Beacon Theater for one week, then returned to San Diego to play at the California Theater. We were playing and doing well. While other acts were on stage performing, Freddie just happened to look up and see the curtains burning. We were downstairs in the dressing room, and Freddie ran down yelling that the stage was on fire. The sprinkler system was on and water was everywhere, but we all got out safely. We held a benefit show for the actors and called it the Burnout Revue. In our act, I added more imitations of famous radio and movie stars. I was now able to do Lionel Barrymore, Uncle Sam's P.38 and the Air Bombers, Peter Lorre, Alfred Hitchcock, and race cars at the Indianapolis Speedway.

While we were playing at RKO Theater on Eighth and Hill, a Jewish booking agent by the name of D.P. Robinson saw our act. He came backstage to talk to my mother. He was a typical New Yorker. He was dressed in an expensive silk suit, he wore a mustache, and he smoked a cigar. He told her how impressed he was with our performance and said we were great enough for a vaudeville tour. Mama invited him to dinner, and he enjoyed Mama's cooking. He started telling us how great I was in *Cimarron*. He told us how many stars were making tours and personal appearances. He made the big money seem so beautiful. He was polished and slick. He said he would get one, two, and four-sheet billings: billboards like the ones in the circus. We would have electrical lobby displays. We agreed to make the tour.

We did not know D.P. had a drinking problem. He liked his scotch and whiskey along with blonde female companions. He was a smooth operator in all forms. He was precise. He was a negotiator. He knew the ropes. We did not know that later down the road, he would hold out on our money. (Back then it was hard to check a person's background. People took a person's word as being his bond. We didn't have computers to verify anything.) This made the trip harder. He took advantage of us. We knew nothing of the weather in northern California or any other parts of the United States. If we had known what we know now, we would have never agreed on a tour in the dead of winter.

We were on tour during the Depression. We didn't realize how bad things were until we went on tour. People would spend their last dime for laughter. Since I am older, I can now see how laughter can be the best medicine in hard times. While traveling, I saw the devastation of the Depression on families. This is why traveling is so important: It broadens one's outlook. One sees everything from a different perspective. Traveling makes people more receptive to various cultures. I discovered that people are more alike than different. Our family was fortunate. We used our money wisely. I was 16 years old when the Depression plagued our nation. From the time I started in the movies in 1924 through the Depression, I worked with my vaudeville tour.

We started preparing ourselves for the tour. First thing we did was to have our 1930 Graham Sedan overhauled with tires, battery and brakes. While we were preparing, D.P. Robinson was preparing the billboards and electrical lobby signs with my picture on them. Thousands of window cards and four-by-eight sheets were posted on sign boards. My brother was 13 years old, so we could not leave the state of California without a school teacher. We had to find a school teacher with good credentials who could travel. The board was strict back then. They kept a close watch on the education of children. It was not as lax as it is today. Parents weren't able to disappear with children from schools without someone knocking on your door and checking.

We searched until we found a teacher: a professor who majored in mathematics. He could also sing. His name was R.C. Jackson from St. Louis. (He was not related to us, not even close.) He was able to travel and was approved by the Board of Education. The next real big thing was to find a versatile piano player who could travel. We found Jessie Gipson. He came from a musical background family and was an excellent player. (He had a younger brother by the name of J.T. who at the age of 12 was playing the trumpet like Louie Armstrong.) Everything began to fall in place. Our next task was to get our wardrobe together. Mama made sure she got us heavy winter underwear, wool shirts and pants. She got the clothes together for our act that consisted of tuxedos, derbies and black patent leather shoes. Our outfits were made by Glover and Son, the best colored tailors in town.

We bought a new trunk to carry our clothes and wardrobe. We had portable steps made for our act. The stairs were six feet long and four feet wide. Our steps were not made by skilled vaudeville craftsmen who knew exactly what was needed. They were made from oak and pine and were thick, bulky and cumbersome. They worked out, but they were just awkward. Our stairs were heavy, whereas the stairs made by the skilled craftsmen were light. The sides of the stairs were used on the side of the trailer to make it higher. The steps were placed on the inside with our other gear. The trailer was seven feet by four-and-a-half feet. We had a special iron bar tongue made to be attached to the back of the car.

Time was winding down to leave. The countdown began on February 1, 1932. One, two, three, four ... we were panicking. The last minute things were making us nervous. We were all in an uproar trying to make sure we had everything. "Do you have this? Don't forget that. Where did you put that? Got the maps?" We had been living and performing in sunny, southern California all our lives. We had no idea what was ahead for us in terms of weather and lifestyles. My personal vaudeville tour consisted of 89 cities and 16 states. It was a pleasurable, educational experience that I will treasure all my life.

On February 5, 1932, we left 1161 East Forty-Seventh Place. All the family, close friends and neighbors were present to bid us farewell. We left behind Aunt Hazel, Aunt Joe, Uncle Leon and my grandfather Joe Foster, who was ill. Mama had made a big lunch for us. We pulled off and drove down Central Avenue over to San Fernando Road and then 99 Highway. The 99 is now the 5 Freeway. We had to travel the grapevine and ridge route, which had a high elevation. It was scary coming down the curves from the grapevine. This was my first time driving on the highway. I was pulling a 1,000-pound trailer that was attached to the back of the car. My palms were sweating, and my heart was beating fast. It was total silence in the car. You could have heard a pin drop when we drove down the grapevine. We were so happy and rejoiced to see a straight road leading into Bakersfield. It was a straight shot of 33 miles. I had traveled this road before in a bus with Fox Studios when we made *Hearts in Dixie*, but I had never driven. It was all flatland highway to Oakland.

D.P. Robinson was in Oakland getting us bookings. The title of my group was now "Eugene Jackson and His Family of Five." It consisted of my brother Freddie; Mr. R.C. Jackson, my teacher; Jessie Gipson, the piano player; and Mama Lil. My 16 vaudeville states were California, Nevada, Wyoming, Utah, Colorado, Nebraska, Iowa, Missouri, Kansas, Illinois, Wisconsin, Michigan, Indiana, Oklahoma, Texas and Louisiana, with stops in major and small cities totaling 89. I have fond memories of all those cities, even if I'm not able to recall them by names. For the most part, we were received warmly and treated like kings and queens during our tour.

My cross-country vaudeville act was different from the vaudeville act that Freddie and I did in Los Angeles and the surrounding areas. While we had only two performers in Los Angeles, we now had five. Our total act was 35 minutes of nonstop, electrifying toe and fast tap dancing. I would open up in my *Cimarron* attire and recite some of my dialogue from *Cimarron* to make the audience remember whom I was portraying. Next, I would sing and dance. Then I would introduce my brother Freddie, who would sing a song called "Romance." While he was singing, I was changing into my *Sporting Blood* costume. We would then act the selling scene of Tommy Boy, the horse I raised in *Sporting Blood*. (Freddie had made a wooden camera to pretend he was the director and cameraman. It looked like a real one, but it was a prop to make the people think we were actually filming. Freddie was outstanding in building items from wood. Had the doors been open for blacks in the skilled craft area of Hollywood, he could have gotten a job in the industry. He was very gifted.)

I would open with a monologue to Tommy Boy. I would tell him how they were getting ready to take him away and that I would miss him. I would do this monologue with tears in my eyes, saying, "Goodbye, Tommy Boy." The background music playing was the song "My Old Kentucky Home," played by our piano player, Jessie Gipson. I would announce my school teacher, Mr. R.C. Jackson, who would come out and sing "Old Black Joe." Next, I would introduce my mother: "Now, ladies and gentlemen, I would like to introduce to you someone who has stuck with me through thick and thin, no one other than my dear sweet pal, my mother, Mrs. Lillie Baker. She would come out and sing "River Stay Away from My Door" with Freddie and me. Our second song would be to the tune of "Dixiana," also the title of a movie I starred in as Cupid with BeBe Daniels.

Freddie and I would close the show with our double tap stair dance. We did this same routine over and over in every city and town. There weren't tapes or television for instant replay — we had to act fresh, alive and excited about our part in order to keep the audience interested. They had paid their hard earned cash for entertainment. It had to be right the first time, or the audience let you know on the spot. They were an active part of the show.

My first stop in California was in Oakland at the Lincoln Theater on Seventh Street. Driving into the city of Oakland, we began to see our publicity. Billboards were placed everywhere. One billboard read:

> In person, Hollywood's most famous piccaninny! The unforgettable Isaiah "Cimarron," remember him? Eugene Jackson, the Cimarron kid, with his family of five in a sensational singing dancing and comedy hit! A WOW! The talk of screen land! Remember him in the original "Our Gang"? He tickled you in "Hearts of Dixie," won your hearts in "Sportin' Blood," grieved with you in "Cimarron," scored again in "Secret Service," and rollicked his way to greater fame in "Sporting Chances." You cannot afford to miss this treat! ONE DAY ONLY!

When we saw this, we became excited. I couldn't wait to get to Oakland. With my head bopping from side to side, I began to whistle, hum and sing some of the tunes to our acts. Everyone in the car gleefully joined in.

In Oakland, we met D.P. Robinson at the Lincoln Theater on Seventh Street, which was the heart of the colored community. We opened on Monday, February 9, 1932. This was the Golden State Theater Circuit. The billing said, "See him in person, Eugene Jackson, star of Our Gang Comedies and one of the most clever screen comedians. Adults 25 cents, children 10 cents, loges 35 cents." ("Loges" were the big seats, the booths.) We were a big hit on our opening date. I signed autographs for an hour. The weather was cold. We stayed with a lady named Miss Jefferson. She was the cousin of Mary Tolbert, a good friend of my mother's from Houston, Texas. Mary told us to contact Miss Jefferson for lodging. She had a big two-story house that was very neat and clean. (Miss Jefferson was a seamstress for the whites in Oakland.) We performed at the State Theater in Napa, California, on February 18 and 19, 1932.

D.P. Robinson had made arrangements for us to broadcast from the famous Claremont Hotel in Berkeley. We did 30 minutes. The object was to let people know that the little kid star, Eugene Jackson, and His Family of Five were appearing in their local theaters. My past film credits, *Cimarron* and others, were mentioned. We played in Martinez, California, on February 21 and 22, 1932, at the Avalon Theater. The billboards read:

> See Eugene Jackson who starred with Richard Dix in Secret Service. He's the year's highlight in person, Hollywood's most famous and beloved piccaninny, screen land's newest idol and future great star and his family of Five. Highly talented performers in the season's most sensational, whirlwind of singing and dancing comedy. Enjoy him now in the season's greatest stage show.

Notice how I was referred to as a "piccaninny" in white newspapers. I had no control of this. When write-ups appeared about me in Negro newspapers, however, I was given the utmost respect.

On February 24 and 25 we performed in Colusa, California, at the Colusa Theater. Their local newspaper wrote:

> Movie director says Colusa is an unusual city. Mr. and Mrs. D.P. Robinson of Hollywood are here with the Eugene Jackson Company now appearing at the Colusa Theatre. Robinson is a well known Hollywood director. He has directed such stars as Mary Pickford, Marion Davis, The Mack Sennett Comedies and Eugene Jackson, Hollywood's favorite piccaninny actor. Incidentally, Robinson was a boy of 13 who played in a picture with Mary Pickford. That was 22 years ago. Henry Walthall was in the picture. It was directed by the old master D.W. Griffith. Robinson said that in an interview that 22 years ago the silent movie industry was in its infancy. Robinson has been in every town in the states of 500 people or less. He was impressed with the 2 newspapers, the fine schools, streets, homes and theatres. In his view, it was an ideal town.

D.P. also told the reporter:

> This will be Eugene's last appearance at the Colusa Theatre tonight. The boy gets a salary of $45.00 a week for fifty-two weeks in the year whether he works or not. Jackson is under contract with radio stations and movie picture studios. This is the first town in Northern California in which he has played. He came to Colusa because he had heard so much about this city, the fine Theater of which N.C. Steele is the manager.

D.P. told all of this to the *Colusa Daily Sun* newspaper; D.P. Robinson was quite a promoter. That was not my actual salary, but he knew how to build for a show. He was a natural promoter from his heart. He knew all the tricks and gimmicks of the trade to build excitement and fill a theater. He knew and did his job well.

Next we went to Petaluma, California, where we played two days at the California Theater. On March 2, 1932, we played in Fairfield, California, at the Solamore. I recall that the people in these little towns had never seen movie stars, white or black. Our next stop was Dixon, California. We played at the Dixon Theater March 3 and 4, and from there we went to Modesto, California, at the Lyric Theater which was a packed house. We moved on to the Empire Theater in Santa Rosa on March 6 and 7. We played at the Broadway Theater on March 11 and 12 in Burlingame, California. On March 14 and 15, we performed in San Bruno, California. It was getting colder and colder the farther north we went.

Everything was going pretty smooth until we played in Chico, California, at the Senator Theater. We played there for two big days on Saturday and Sunday. On Sunday night after the show, we were packing our dancing stairs and putting our wardrobe trunk in the trailer. There were fans at the back stage door, talking to us and begging for our autographs. We didn't know we were being set up for a big steal: They stole our wardrobe trunk with all our clothes in it. We called the police, but they couldn't find anything. We were sick and cold. The local newspaper wrote, "Thieves loot on trailer auto home. A trunk containing the clothes of the Eugene Jackson Troupe valued at $500.00 was reported stolen from the show at the Senator Theatre Sunday night. The trunk was found in an orchard on Guill Avenue a day later with the clothes missing." That put a damper on our spirits for a while, but the show had to go on.

We replaced our items quickly because we had to move on to Yuba City, and then to Elko, Nevada, for our next engagement. Time was of the utmost importance. In leaving, we chose to look at the bright side of life. We reminisced on the fact we had started out as a smash hit in our own state with valuable experience from working with the Golden State Theater Circuit, the Fruitville Circuit Theater that covered 12 cities in California. We may have lost some material items, but had gained wisdom and pleasurable memories.

We were booked in Nevada for the Hunter Theater in Elko. Their local newspaper was called the *Daily Free Press*. The hit movie at the time was a thriller called *The Deceiver*. The *Daily Free Press* wrote, "The highlight of the year in person Eugene Jackson, Cimarron kid, and his family of five are highly talented performers Tuesday only March 15, 1932." We appeared at the Grande Theater in Reno. The *Reno Evening Gazette* newspaper wrote, "On Wednesday March 16, 1932, Hollywood's famed piccaninny will be here tomorrow at the Granada Theatre one day only."

It was so cold in Reno that we had to buy new clothing which put a heartbreak on our pocketbook. We had only been on the tour for a little over a month when we noticed D.P. was drinking a great deal. He claimed he was drinking to keep warm. Our next date was Fallon, Nevada. The Fallon Theater manager, Mr. Evans, said he felt extremely fortunate in being able to get the attraction of Eugene Jackson and His Family of Five. We left for Medicine Bolt, Wyoming. It was cold and snowing. The town was very small and had the look and feel of a European coal mining town. We played one day there and stayed with a light-complected colored family that was very nice.

The next day we left for Cheyenne. They said they would *lend* us a shovel because they said it was bad luck to *give* a shovel. They knew what type of weather we were going into. We had no idea. We thanked them for the shovel. We started toward Cheyenne on the gravel roads. We drove for about 100 miles until we got to a road where the bridge was out for about 50 feet. I said, "Lord, how are we going to get across?" I said that we would have to go off the road to get to the other side. I went out there with a stick poking in the water to see how deep it was. Mama hollered, "Gene, be careful, watch it." The piano player and the school teacher were sitting in the car while I, a mere child, did all the work.

They did nothing but sit. I put it in fourth gear and turned the car to the right, down into the river banks to the other side. We made it. I was so happy to get out of that mess. I didn't know what other messes lay ahead. We started on down the road, no cars, no nothing. Wyoming had red mud that was as thick as glue. It began to get dark while we were driving. We could see the trains for miles ahead, but no cars. I was driving on the gravel road, but our Graham Page was built low to the ground. Large trucks with deep wheels had made an impression in the mud before me. I drove directly in their tracks, and the Graham Page came to a dead stop. The whole car just sat down and the wheels would only spin around and around. I got out and looked, and so did everyone else. I got the shovel and started digging the red mud from under the car and wheels. It got dark and the grown adult men in the car had not done one thing. Mama had a candle in the car to keep us warm. That was all we had. We could hear the coyotes while I dug all night getting the mud from around the car.

Finally, I got the mud from under the car. In the morning, we could see the sun coming up. The mud was now away from the car, and we could finally get traction. I started the car. It began to move. I had been driving for about 15 minutes when all of a sudden we looked behind us and saw many cars. It looked like nine thousand cars were traveling behind us with no problem. We had smooth sailing after that.

We were too late for the engagement in Cheyenne, so we cut over and headed to Denver, Colorado. But before Colorado we went to Salt Lake City, Utah, and got rave reviews from major newspapers. Then it was on to Colorado. We gassed up and hit the Rockies to Colorado. The mountains were so high and full with snow. It was difficult pulling that trailer up those steep mountains. The highway was slippery — I had to be careful. We were climbing higher and higher. It was deep, and looking down on the trees was scary. We eventually reached the top of the summit, but we then had to go down the icy curves, around and around. I put the car in low gear. I was scared, but we finally got down on the level. What a breather!

The sign said Denver, but we had to turn for Pueblo, Colorado, and Colorado Springs. Now on our way there, Mama was sitting in the back with the school teacher. All of a sudden Mama looked in the back window and yelled that the trailer was loose. All of our things were on the highway. Luckily for us, no cars were behind us. The trailer was zigzagging, and clothes were flying in the air all down the highway. We stopped. We all got out and picked up our clothes from the highway. We drove about a mile and found a fellow who was a welder. We got the trailer to his shop, he built us another strong bar to pull the trailer, and we continued on to Colorado Springs and then to Pueblo, Colorado.

We stayed at the Prothos. It was a nice hotel. I met a girl there. I fell in love. I forget her name. This shows how much love *that* was. (Later, she came to see me in California. I was too dumb to know what was happening. She was very much interested in me.) We performed well in Pueblo and moved on to Denver, where we played at the Empress Theater. We played one week there and lived in the colored section called Five Points. We played at the Brown Palace, which was an exclusive hotel where millionaires lived; we also played in the colored clubs.

We had to leave our piano player in Denver because he had an abscess in his jaw. He was in great pain. From that point on, we used piano players in each town as we traveled. When we would arrive in a town, we would quickly put out a call by word of mouth in the black community that we were in need of the best piano player in town. We would audition them until we found the best. We never had trouble finding the top piano players in an area. Every musician was always interested in taking part in a jam session.

We left Denver for Nebraska. We had some cousins who lived in Omaha, so we stayed with them. We played at the small, colored Lincoln Theater. We also played in Scottsbluff. At that time a strike was going on across the country for the stagehands and electricians. We honored the strike and only played three or four days. Then we headed for Illinois. We went through Iowa from Nebraska. Iowa had the worst highways in the world. They were skinny and full of curves. The highways were so narrow. When the trucks would come by, you would have to get off the road to let them pass. That was hard driving. While in Iowa, we stopped for gas in a little town that was full of gnats. I couldn't imagine how residents lived there.

Before going to Illinois, we had bookings in Iowa, Missouri and Kansas. In Missouri we played in Joplin, Hannibal, Springfield, Salem, Kirksville, St. Louis, Canton, Edina, Rolla, Sullivan, St. James, Lebanon, Leclede, Kansas City and Knox County. When we got to Kansas City, we picked up a piano player by the name of Dozier Williams. He played with us in Kansas City and St. Louis on through to Chicago. We played for the whites at the Paseo Park in Kansas City. A big band by the name of Benny Moden played behind us. We were very successful.

After each show, I would autograph in the lobby. Many nationalities were there, especially Italians. In Kansas, we played in Kansas City, Lawrence and Topeka. From there we were booked at an Indian reservation in Lawrence,

Kansas. Lawrence had a free college for Indians. We were able to go on campus. I was walking around campus looking for Indians until someone explained to us that as long as anyone had a percentage of Indian blood, however small, that qualified them to go to college free. I was glad someone explained that to me because I kept saying to myself, "I only see white people. Where are the Indians?"

We headed for St. Louis. My reviews in the newspapers were great. The *St. Louis Globe Democrat* wrote that I was appearing at the Club Plantation at 911 N. Vandeventer. I was presenting my new revue "Rhapsody in Rhythm," starring Eugene Jackson, the kid star of *Cimarron*. Admission was $1.00 per person weekdays, and $2.20 per person Saturday and Sunday to cover amusement tax. The show was staged by S.H. Dudley, Jr. Other stars on the program were Ruth Harris Boatner and Houang Yuen, Lillian Goodner, Mistress of Ceremonies and Eight Plantation Girls, and Walter Stanley and His Plantation Stompers. Houang Yuen was really a Caucasian who was an imitator of Ching Ling Foo, an Oriental who was the master of magicians during vaudeville days.

The newspapers went on to list the other places we were performing. They had an all-colored revue. We had a band to play behind us. They had a donkey act and a comedian. We were there for two weeks, and it was very exciting working there. There was a 16-year-old chorus girl who liked me. She ran away from home and lived next door to the club in a hotel. A popular song back then was "Willow Weep for Me." She played that song when I met her. She tried her best to get me to her room, but my sweet guardian angel, Lillie Baker, was always there to protect her son from temptation. She was better than any hired bodyguard. Mama was on the case to make sure that nothing materialized.

The theater strike was still on in St. Louis. We played for the Negroes in a small colored theater named The Star. For whites we played at the Garrett Theater, which was a high-class burlesque house. Vaudeville acts and burlesque queens performed there, and Evelyn Meyers was the star burlesque stripper. There was always a singer. Performers were Wally Veron, a comedian; a sixteen-member chorus line; strippers; plus two extra white comedians; and a star colored banjo player named Pat Patterson, who could play the banjo and make it sound like a band. He had a muffler between his knees which would make the banjo cry "wow-wow." He also played a small harmonica. We did our regular vaudeville act, and the crowd went mad. Since we were working in burlesque, Mama tried to keep us from watching the ladies. We would sneak upstairs and watch, but the girls didn't care. They continued to do their thing.

We stayed there on Enright Street with a real nice colored doctor. (The street was named after him.) Just before we were getting ready to leave, I walked to the store. It was very cold. While walking down the street, I ran into another entertainer from out west. He was walking towards me. I saw a big, big figure of a man with a khaki coat, boots and a McCarthy hat. He was about

6'2" and 225 pounds. I looked up, and there was someone I knew. I said, "Cliff."
He was amazed to see me. He screamed, Gene!" and squeezed me real tight.
He asked me what I was doing in St. Louis. I told him I was doing my personal vaudeville tour. He wanted to know when I left Los Angeles. I told him
February 5 and asked him what he was doing in St. Louis. He said he was on
his way to New York to audition for the part of the Lord in *Green Pastures* when
his car broke down. He asked where Mrs. Baker was, and I took him to Mama.
He asked my mother to loan him $25 to get his car fixed. When he borrowed
$25 from us, it was like $1,000. Money was tight, but Mama always had a heart
of gold. She always had a helping spirit about her. I guess that's where my
goodwill nature came from.

Cliff made it to New York and got the part. We read in the paper that he
was a big success. I never saw him again until I came home from tour in 1933.
When Mama made the loan, he had promised to send us our money. That
never happened. When we arrived home, I found out that he was staying at
the Dunbar, a famous colored hotel. I went to see him to remind him of the
$25 loan. It wasn't given back as freely as it was given. I had to chase him
down — he acted like he didn't want to pay me back. I had to remind him that
had it not been for my mother having a kind heart, he would never be the star
that he was. We had helped him to the top. He wanted to forget that, but I
wouldn't let him.

We played in a college town called Kirksville, Missouri, at the Fox Theater. It was an all white town, but they were crazy about me. They gave us a
tour of the campus and took us to their campus osteopathic facilities. When
they opened the door, there were 40 dead bodies. It was quiet as a mouse. Oh
what a weird feeling. They said most of their patients were hobos from the railroad tracks. We were told that from the human skin the students could make
purses and belts. One of the student guides jokingly told us if we had a knife
they could cut us a piece of skin as a souvenir. Mr. Jackson, our school teacher,
always carried around with him a pocket knife for his eating apples. I asked
Mr. Jackson to let us use his knife. Mr. Jackson said no way. He said that he
used his knife to cut apples, not human skin. We all laughed.

As we were leaving St. Louis, the *St. Louis Argus* newspaper wrote that I
had completed a show at the Roosevelt at 810 North Leffingwell, leaving audi-
ences spellbound. Reading positive write-ups would give us energy to jump
another hurdle. Next, we went to St. James and played at the small Lyric Theater.

When the show was over in Edina, Missouri, the crowd was so elated. They
didn't want us to go home. When they asked where we were staying, we told
them right behind the stage would be our room since we couldn't find lodging
because of our color. They felt so bad that we couldn't find a place. They stayed,
and we talked for many hours. The owner had to ask them to go because we had

to get up early in the morning to leave. The next day we were getting ready to continue our tour. When I started the car, it caught on fire. All the wires in the car burned, so we took it to the garage to have it repaired and rewired.

The owner of the garage had seen our show. I guess everybody in town saw it. He rewired our whole car. We asked him what we owed him. He said, "You don't owe me anything. I enjoyed your show. You all are such fine people." This goes to show you how God brings a ray of light in one's life. Even though we couldn't find lodging there, the generosity of this fine white man showed the love of God in people. It showed the spirit of true kindness and giving. The only problem is that sometimes blacks are not given the opportunity to prove themselves merely because of the color of their skin. We are not judged as individuals but as a group, which is not fair. If one black person messed up, that could ruin it for other blacks.

We had to stay on the move. We went to Charleston, Illinois. The *Charleston Daily Courier* wrote on June 16, 1932: "The public should see Eugene Jackson and his family of Five. Come see the Cimarron Kid." Charleston was a nice small town. The only colored people were a couple of shoe-shine boys and porters. From there it was on to Pana, Illinois, to open June 20, 1932, at the Palace. They had a newspaper that was called the *Daily Palladium*. The masthead for this newspaper was "the paper with a soul." I want you to know that there wasn't a soul around there.

The next place was Nokomis, Montgomery County, Illinois. On June 23, 1932, the *Free Press Progress Community Newspaper* of Montgomery County wrote that I was an upcoming attraction. We had played in many small towns and theaters. As we got closer to Chicago, the atmosphere in the car was full of an energized spirit. The automobile was full of stories passing from one person to the next about the windy city.

The opening night at the famous Regal Theater in Chicago was electrifying for us. The Regal had a fabulous stage and was black-owned. Our billing read, "Come see Eugene Jackson, Chincapin of Hearts in Dixie, the Our Gang Kid and Company of Five in person for four days and three big hits, adults twenty cents, Friday, July 8." This was one of the first and biggest colored theaters we played. The organist performed and would set the mood before we came on stage. We went over real big. The audience could feel our energy, and they reciprocated.

Our act was great, but while we were on stage performing someone was upstairs stealing everything we had. We went to the police and they took fingerprints, but basically there was nothing they could do. We were staying with my mother's brother, Cuney Foster, who was a businessman, a plumber. One day we were playing with some children and Mama spotted one of our shirts on one of the kids. We followed them home, then called the police. We recovered everything. We were better detectives than the police!

We were booked in Cicero and Mama told Uncle Cuney where we were playing. We were told that Cicero was Al Capone's territory. I didn't even know who Al Capone was at that time. Uncle Cuney refused to go, and we couldn't get any colored people to go with us. We weren't aware of the racial boundaries in the cities — we were just entertainers trying to do our job of bringing joy and laughter to the hearts of all. We went and played at a big theater with no problems. We came home and weren't touched.

In Milwaukee, we played at the Cool Garden Theater. The *Milwaukee Sentinel* wrote, "A triple star stage program, Eugene Jackson, kid star of *Cimarron* and 'Our Gang' will be on program with the Hallelujah Quartet at 6:30 P.M. Friday." We were also appearing at another location. We had completed a full day's work at the Granada Theater. Mama had received a wire earlier in the day which Freddie and I knew nothing about. The old cliche "the show must go on" was definitely true back then. There was no such thing as cancellations. Once the curtain went up, that was it. We had to perform, rain or shine. If we were ill, we still gave a top-notch performance. All the benefits the stars have today with unions were not strong and available in the early days of show business. It was plain and simple: If you didn't work, you didn't eat. It was very important to leave a good track record because if you didn't, it could result in you not working in the next circuit.

Show business was strictly business in the olden days. Stars didn't cancel shows like they do today. Mama knew this, and she was not going to jeopardize our bread and butter. She was a businesswoman, a professional from her heart. She didn't tell Freddie and me until that evening about the telegram. When we had finished performing, she told us that Papa had died. I remember Mama performing without tears in her eyes. That took courage. She was strong. I know she had to be hurting inside, but she was an entertainer. An entertainer performs even when hurting because it's a job. I can imagine how she felt not being able to go to her father's funeral.

We moved on to Kenosha, Wisconsin. The *Kenosha Evening Newspaper* wrote that we had a "sister" starring with us. She was none other than Dorothy Lee, who had joined us for the local shows. She was from the area and could dance like Bill Robinson. Shirley Temple had nothing on her. She was a great tap dancer. The reporter asked who my favorite stars were. I said actress Jean Harlow; next to her were Constance Bennett and Irene Dunne. My favorite male actor was Richard Dix. The article ended by saying that I was Hollywood's most famous juvenile. In Wisconsin, we played Milwaukee, Kenosha, Racine, Green Bay and Sheboygan.

We decided to leave D.P., our manager and agent, because he was holding out on our money. He began to drink heavily. Once we left D.P., we played a lot of small theaters in Chicago and surrounding states to survive. We began to do our own promoting. D.P. wired us from New York, saying he wanted us to come to New York from Chicago. He said he was booking us in Europe. My mother's brother, Cuney, however, claimed to be psychic. People would come from all over to hear his predictions. He convinced Mama not to go to New York. He said he had a vision of us getting stranded. Mama listened to him, and that was the end of our relationship with D.P.

As I think back now, I wonder how my career would have been if I had gone to Europe. The Nicholas brothers made it big after they came from Europe. In fact, most colored entertainers who went to Europe made it grand after coming back to the States. Black actors had more freedom to perform in Europe. When they returned to the States, their track record was built. Doors that were once closed would be opened because of the European exposure.

We decided to stay in Chicago to work to get money to return to Los Angeles. We played at the theaters owned by Ballin and Katz. We played at such theaters as the Franklin on Thirty-First and Calumet, the Imperial Theater at 2329 West Madison Street, the Willard Theater, the Avenue Theater on Thirty-First and Indiana, and the Prairie Theater. We would play one or two days. Admission would be 15 cents for adults and 10 cents for children. We lived all around in Chicago on the south side. I remember South Parkway where the Reds would have their communist meetings. They would pass out flyers.

While we were in Chicago, there was a new Walgreens that was opening on Forty-Seventh and South Parkway. Mr. Brown, the manager, had me there signing autographs for a promotional grand opening. On the same side of the street was the Regal Theater. The Metropolitan Theater, featuring the famous Whitman Sisters Revue, was across the street. The Whitmans were a weekly attraction which consisted of one of the sisters' sons, Pop Whitman and his partner, Eddie. They were great dancers. They were born into show business like Sammy Davis, Jr. It makes a difference when one is born into show business because the parents know the ropes, but as I look back Mama did pretty good. She was respected by all. I had to pick up steps and steal jokes from listening to others. I had no coach, only natural talent from God. It was the pure, raw endowment that made me famous.

The Mills Brothers were coming into their own at the Tivoli Theater. They were the hottest thing going at that time. "Fatha" Hines played at the Grand Terrace Night Club. We also had an opportunity to perform at the Grand Terrace for a social engagement. Chicago was our headquarters; we stayed there for five months. We would go into the little towns then come back to the windy city. A favorite dish of mine in the windy city in the thirties was a dish called "State Street Chicken Special," which in reality was neck bones. You could order this title anywhere in the city at a black restaurant and they knew what you meant.

The *Chicago Defender* newspaper kept me in the news. They wrote, "Eugene Jackson, the boy star, is still playing in the Chicago territory making personal appearances. He has been doing his show in the district for several months." While in Chicago I met Mr. Fuller, the creator of Fuller Products.

He was one of the black pioneer million-dollar businessmen. I was taken to his business headquarters. This was a high point in my life. He was strong in character, and this showed in his posture. I met another giant, Mr. Murray of Murray Products. He supplied me with the Murray hair grease. I remember slicking my hair down with that grease before my shows.

We performed in surrounding states like Michigan and Indiana. In Indiana, we played in Michigan City on Wednesday, July 31, 1932. This was a nice town, but it smelled from the slaughtering of animals. We were well received in a town called Marion, Indiana, where just a year before we arrived some people hanged a black youth. We also played in South Bend, Indiana, in small theaters and clubs.

In Chicago we attracted a young man of 18 who volunteered to help us drive back to California. He was about 5'5", of medium build with dark brown skin and a close hair cut. He was a smooth talker who knew how to act in a way that made us think he was a nice, well-mannered young man. (In those days everyone was helpful, and one could get all the help needed.) We were all very appreciative of his gesture. However, once we got on the road, his true personality appeared. He began to sass us. In reality, he was a jerk. His family was probably glad to get rid of him, because of his ways, and sad to see him return. We tried to leave him in Edina, Missouri, but he went to the police on us. We had to pay his way back to Chicago. Stars were always approached by townspeople who were like hustlers, especially in large cities. They always felt that we had more money than they, but sometimes they unknowingly would have more money than we did. This is why the stars of today have bodyguards to fend off groupies.

Even though we had played Edina, Missouri, before with D.P. booking us, we still had difficulty obtaining lodging. The theater manager fixed us a room at the back of the theater again, which showed just how tough it was back then. The entertainers today don't know how blessed they are to be able to walk up to any hotel or motel and stay. Our itinerary continued in Canton for Thursday, February 2, 1933, at the New Gem Theater, with admission being 20 cents for adults and ten cents for children. On February 3, we played in Kirksville at the Fox Kennedy Theater. We performed in St. Louis at the Longwood Theater at 9409 South Broadway.

On the way home, we took the famous Route 66. We had decided to stop and play at some of the same places we had performed while with D.P. We incorporated the song "California Here I Come." The crowd loved it. We played at high schools, marathons, anything that would pay an honest wage. We performed two shows in one day in Springfield, Missouri. We performed at Lincoln High School for the whites, and a show for the black residents was held from 7:00 P.M. to 9:00 P.M. It was a task, but we did it. We also performed at the Marathon Palace stage in Springfield.

After leaving Missouri, we stopped in Tulsa, Oklahoma. While we were in Oklahoma, news came over the radio about the big earthquake in Long Beach and Los Angeles. We were all nervous about our family and home, wondering if our place was leveled. The 1933 earthquake literally destroyed Long Beach and other towns. We wired home, and my aunt told us our home was fine. Relieved to hear this news, we continued our journey westbound. We met some very influential colored people in Oklahoma. I had the opportunity to visit the area of the Negro millionaires. (Back then the colored people owned oil wells.) I saw wealthy Negro people wheeling and dealing in business. Even the *Oklahoma Eagle* newspaper was black-owned. On March 4, 1933, a nice article was printed about me in this newspaper. While there, we performed at the Booker T. Washington High School. The people in Tulsa were very nice to us.

After leaving Tulsa, we headed for Guthier, Oklahoma. We were traveling on a Saturday night about 9:30 or 10:00 P.M. on Route 66. I was driving 35 or 40 miles an hour when all of a sudden this car hit my fender and front bumper. A car swayed off to the left into the field. I pulled to the side of the road and stopped. We all got out to look at the damage. A young white woman was staggering and crying. She was dressed in a white party gown. I told her that she came across the line. She was drunk and scared. Cars were coming up the highway, and then a patrolman drove up. I told him what had happened. He saw that she was drunk and put her in his car. I asked him about getting her name and license — I wanted her to fix our car. He just told us to get in our car and keep going. The fender was rubbing the tire, so I had to drive slow.

We got to Ada, Oklahoma, late that night. It was so cold we had to stay in the car all night. When daylight came, we found a garage for repairs. We found the colored section of town and got settled; we were appearing at a walk-a-thon that night. We had been traveling for months and hadn't seen many colored people since Chicago and St. Louis, but in the state of Oklahoma we began to see Negroes. We were lucky to run into a big-time promoter by the name of Jimmy Allard. He had a big white show called the Southern Brevities. We joined his show and were featured as "Eugene Jackson, the Cimarron Kid and his brother, Freddie."

The Jimmy Allard show was unique because he was the owner and manager. We were very impressed, and it felt good to work with him. He was a southerner around the age of 25, around 5'8" and thinly built. He was a fair, professional businessman. His show consisted of 16 gorgeous girls; the Dixie Four, a singing group; the Louisiana Buddies Star Band; Rosetta Langdon Dancing à la Carte; and Pauline Thomas, a stage girl. While with Jimmy, we played in Oklahoma City, Stillwater, Ada and Chickasha.

In Oklahoma City, there was a lovely colored lady by the name of Mrs. Alridge. She was a very distinguished lady, and everyone respected her. She had both Indian and Negro blood. She taught school and was the principal. She owned her own theater, mortuary and the *Black Dispatch* newspaper. She was one great lady. She wrote the following in 1933 in her newspaper:

The Our Gang star at the Alridge Theater Wednesday, Thursday and Friday in a big time singing and dancing act, March 15, 16, 17, 1933. The talented brothers Eugene and Freddie will be in company with their mother, Mrs. Lillie Baker, who manages the act and a special tutor, Mr. R.C. Jackson.

On March 22, 1933, the *Daily Oklahoma* newspaper wrote that we were performing for whites only at the Reno Theater. The newspaper also stated that we were performing at the Club Boga with a big white orchestra leader, Coon Sanders. He was very well known and highly regarded. The newspaper went on to say that "Tonight, Thursday there will be a double tap floor show featuring Eugene Jackson Hollywood's most famous piccaninny from the picture Cimarron." We had write-ups in all of the town's local newspapers. We were featured in the following newspapers: the *Stillwater Daily Press* on April 7, 1933; the *Daily Express* on April 12, 1933, in Chickasha; and April 16, 1933, in the *Seminole Producer* newspaper and the *Daily Ardmore*. We had worked those towns thoroughly and made good money. We told Jimmy we had to get home.

We proceeded to Oklahoma City continuing on Route 66. We left Oklahoma for Texas. In Dallas, we couldn't get one booking at any white theater. We were able to get a booking at the colored State Theater. We were received there warmly because my mother was born in Houston. The Foster family had a lot of cousins throughout the state of Texas. Word of mouth that the Foster family had people in show business made it easy for us to play to a full house wherever we went. My mother's cousin was a school teacher in Dallas.

While in Dallas, we met some fans. I remember a particular young lady around the age of 12 or 13. Her name was Lillian Cumber, and she was so excited about meeting us. She expressed an interest in coming to Hollywood. Years later her family moved to Los Angeles, she looked us up and we became good friends. I introduced her to her second husband. Her dreams and desires came true. One could tell she was a very determined individual, which resulted in her becoming the first black talent agent in Los Angeles. She is still Hollywood's top and most recognized talent agent. In my later years, she became my agent. She is well seasoned and knows the ropes of the business inside and out.

Having so many fans on the road made us feel good. They gave us the ability to face the next show, town or situation with strength. God and our guardian angels were always with us wherever we went. We carried Him in our hearts and in our shows. This is why we were so well received by all. While I was on the road, a young guy told me how he loved me in *Cimarron*. He told me of his desires to come to Hollywood. He, too, was a determined person, for one day, after we had been home for some time, he appeared on our door step. He told us he had hoboed out. Mama fixed him a big meal. He left with joy in his heart and a bag of goodies to hold him over to his next destination. This was not uncommon for fans to show up on my door step unannounced. I do not know how they found my home, but they did. They would appear on our door step on Fifteenth Street and on Thirty-Second Street. Mama always made them welcome.

After Dallas, we moved on to Houston to work and visit for three weeks. We stayed with our cousin in the Fifth ward and got engagements at Phyllis Wheatley School and Jack Yates School. It made us feel good to know that so many remembered us. I was surprised and delighted to discover so many great musicians coming from these high schools. The band director at Jack Yates was Mack Day. Some of his students went on to stardom. This just goes to show you the importance of a good teacher. They are the foundation for our youth. Outstanding sax players were Arnette Cobbs, Gus Evans and a kid called "Illinois Jacket." Russell Jacket played the trumpet, and Illinois was his kid brother. Illinois went on to New York to record with Freddie Simon.

We went on to Beaumont, Texas. My mother had relatives there also. Their names were Irene and Alfred Foster, and they had two children, a daughter and a son. Their son was a big-time doctor. (He and I later met in the army in 1945 because of our induction into the military at Fort Huachuca, Arizona.) We appeared in the *Beaumont Journal*, which stated that on Monday, May 29, and Tuesday, May 30, 1933, at the Joyland Theater, the public could see "the Wonder Kid Actor and his Gang in a hot one hour stage show attraction, extraordinary in person, Eugene Jackson, admission fifteen cents." The *Beaumont* [Texas] *Enterprise Journal* wrote on May 31, 1933: "Tonite Midnight Ramble for whites only at the Joyland Theater, Eugene Jackson, the Cimarron Kid. The most sensational singing, dancing and comedy whirlwind of the year in a hot hour, stage show admission twenty-five cents."

We refused to play at the white theaters in Fort Worth, Texas, because of the Jim Crow law. Our people would have had to sit upstairs to see us. We said we weren't going to go for that, proving that the colored entertainers in those days did take a stand on issues that affected blacks. We may have grinned, danced and smiled as if we were happy-go-lucky, but we took a stand on issues of color, no matter how small they may seem today. We made a difference. We had standards and morals. When we performed, it was a job, a job that may have looked easy and carefree, but wasn't. People are instrumental in making changes on the job. The entertainment industry *was* our job, and we made changes. We paved the road. We made it easier for the young by taking a lot of insults and ridicule. We made people laugh, but we also made changes. We had relatives at Fort Worth, where we did small performances at the Elks Club. We also did shows in Galveston.

We continued on our way to the state of Louisiana, where we stopped off in Lake Charles to perform in a road house (another name for a nightclub) located on the outskirts of town. We were making our way to California inch by inch, state by state. "Let's hit Route 66 for home. California, here we come."

When we saw the sign saying welcome to California, we were elated. On the highway we saw signs saying "San Bernardino, El Monte," then we drove to downtown Los Angeles onto Central Avenue. We were happy to reminisce. We turned on Forty-Seventh Place to see our two-bedroom home that looked like a palace to us. Everyone in the neighborhood greeted us with open arms.

7
Roles for African Americans

The parts for Negroes between the time of 1920 through 1940 in those days were mainly plantation and slavery movies. After that the roles were butlers, maids, shoe-shine boys, and porters and waiters on trains. When talkies came in, my first talkie was *Hearts in Dixie*. With the money from that film, I bought our first home at the age of 12. The average American kid was not able to make that kind of money and investment.

We moved up the financial ladder by my work in movies. Had I not been working in movies, even though I got paid less than the white actors, I would not have been able to help and improve the conditions of my family. I would have had menial jobs that didn't pay what I was making in the movies. I might have shined shoes or sold papers for a great deal of my childhood, but because I was in the movies I had available to me more funds and a more stable opportunity. Back then many jobs for African American people were maids, butlers and chauffeurs. My mother was doing day work in Hollywood in homes and apartments — these were honest employments. We should not be ashamed of our past. These were the only opportunities made available to us. We were not robbing or stealing. We worked long and hard hours and got paid little wages.

The Negroes contributed a great deal to this nation: One finds many inventions by blacks because we were in the service business. We cared for this nation and invented things to make our work easier for us. We were cooks, so A.P. Ashbourne invented the biscuit cutter. W. Johnson invented an egg beater. Augustus Jackson invented ice cream, while A.L. Cralle invented the ice cream mold. Figuring out a way to preserve the delicious meals we had prepared, J. Standard invented a refrigerator. Frederick M. Jones invented an air conditioning system for trucks and train cars. Since we were always opening doors for people, Osbourn Dorsey invented varieties of door knobs and door stops.

We cleaned streets, so Charles Brooks invented the street sweeper, while

Eugene Jackson (far left) in a scene from *Secret Service* (1931).

Sarah Boone invented the ironing board. We were always cleaning, so L.P. Ray invented the dust pan and Thomas W. Stewart invented a type of mop. W.A. Deitz devised a new type of shoe, Jan Matzeliger invented the shoe-lasting machine, and John A. Johnson invented a new wrench. We cut and manicured the lawns, so John A. Burr invented a lawn mower.

It didn't surprise me that young Tiger Woods won the Masters because George F. Grant invented the golf tee. We were there on the golf course before Tiger, making the road easier for him and other blacks to follow. They really didn't want us to learn to read and write but we did, and W.B. Purvis invented a fountain pen. Paper and the alphabet were invented by Africans. John L. Love invented a type of pencil sharpener. F.W. Leslie invented the envelope seal. While we privately learned to read and write we had to have a way to see, so Michael Harney invented an improved lantern.

Burridge and Marshman invented a typewriter, Alexander Miles an elevator, and Tom J. Marshal a fire extinguisher. Because we were up all hours of the night laboring, Latimer and Nichols invented an electric lamp to help us see. We've always raised and cared for children, but when we got tired from carrying them W.H. Richardson invented the baby buggy. Lyda Newman created a type of hair brush, and George Washington Carver invented peanut-based lotion and soap so we could have smooth, soft, clean bodies.

Eugene poses on the 20th Century–Fox lot.

So that the children could enjoy themselves while playing, David Gittens invented the skooterboard. A ride which we all love so much is the roller coaster, invented by Granville T. Woods. The mind game of chess was invented by Africans. We were chauffeurs, so Garrett Morgan invented the traffic signal to help keep us safe while driving. Paul E. Williams invented the helicopter. To keep everyone safe, Washington A. Martin invented a new kind of lock. While times were hard, we had to find a way to release our pain and turn it into joy and pleasure, so Joseph Dickinson invented the player piano. Giving us something to play the low-down, dirty blues on, Robert Flemming, Jr., strung together some strings and made a new variety of guitar.

We knew how to save; we knew how to depend on God and others in our churches and community. Back then, all neighbors knew each other. We could look out our window or door and see black men and women going to work neat and clean. Because of segregation, we saw the different professionals in our community: Black doctors, lawyers, and business men and women lived next door to us all. Everyone was respected in our community. We saw people working, not standing on street corners selling drugs. As actors we played maids, butlers, servants, shoe-shine boys and porters, but we were contributing to society. Our bent backs helped the world.

Yes, the white media didn't show an abundance of black professionals and should have. Both sides of our lifestyle should have been depicted with balance. The black actor worked and lived in two worlds. We knew our culture back then, and we lived it. We were taught it by our elders, by our community. As Negro actors in those times, we were able to separate our culture and lifestyle from the screen very easily because of the times. We were grounded in our roots in a positive way because of our communities. I knew what we had in our community, and each area was unique.

One of the main ingredients that helped me along the way was the love shown by all, which helped build my character. Because I was a kid acting, I never thought about stereotypes. I was so glad and happy to go on auditions and beat out both black and white children actors. All I knew was that I was going to give acting all I had. I've done this all my life.

I believe that the old-time black actors are sometimes ridiculed for the roles we played, but I must say that we did not control Hollywood; just as the black actors today do not control Hollywood. They have more power and control now than black actors did when I was performing. If we had refused a part, they would have given it to a white actor, who might blacken his face to portray the role. This would have taken money from black actors who desperately needed work. Similar things happen today, but we do have more African American directors, producers and independent film companies that make a variety of opportunities available to black entertainers. When I started out, we did not have the abundance of African American writers like we do today. We need more quality African American filmmakers.

We trailblazers are sometimes beaten down for the parts we played. In our day, most black actors were very seasoned and talented. Our talent may have been taught, or it may have been a gift from our creator. I know my abilities were a natural endowment. We had to be able to do more than one thing, or a more versatile person was chosen. We worked long and hard hours for less pay than white actors. We took a lot back then. We had the black organizations like the National Association for the Advancement of Colored People

Eugene in a scene from the 1948 film *Scudda Hoo! Scudda Hay!*

(NAACP) on our backs. At the same time, while trying to act and perform on locations, we would not be able to eat, sleep or walk freely down certain streets. All of this added pressure on the Negro actor. To top this off, we would still be expected to perform royally, which we did because of the love of show biz.

We were entertainers: top quality, first rate and first class. The stars and people of today have not walked down our path, so it is difficult for one to understand why and how we did what we did. We took a lot from both sides. It was hard to please both sides when you had to eat. We had families to support and maintain. It wasn't easy to hold a family together in show business. Being black and trying to hold a family together was even harder. We were always looking for work. We had to be thrifty and still play up the Hollywood image. No wonder so many stars of both races became alcoholics, resorted to drugs, or just plain lost their minds and ended their lives. It's a business that can break you in all forms.

We were doing a job — just as someone else may have been a plumber, we chose acting. A plumber would do his best to fix the problem, while an actor would do his best to please the producers and directors. That's what it was about — and still is. It is that plain and simple. It was our job, our employment.

Eugene, with dancing partner Miss Lucey, at 20th Century–Fox.

Please be proud of our roles and hard work. We did contribute. We did make a difference. We used our brains to make the world a better place. We have all contributed to this nation to make it great.

I want the world to know that I and other black actors always did our job with pride. We were pioneers, people who took our job seriously and did our best. Look at our skills and our craft. Judge us by what we endured to stay on top and keep the door open for the young African American actors. Don't blame us, for our hearts are heavy from carrying such a full load. We've seen and experienced it all, believe me. We've held on to the art for the young. Try to understand what it was like. Accept us, for we are a part of you. We are a part of the world. No matter how you critique us, the bottom line is that our roles made our mark in history.

8
Directors, Producers, Residuals and Agents

FAMOUS DIRECTORS AND PRODUCERS

When I was a kid actor, people were just people to me. I wasn't knowledgeable of who was considered to be tops in the fields of directing and producing. I've been directed by so many over the years that I may have forgotten who directed me in a particular film and who produced the film. I've thumbed through my albums to read the newspaper clippings to help refresh my memory. Some of the big names were Hal Roach, Bob McGowan, Mack Sennett, J. McDonald, Bill Beaudine, Harry Pollard, Irving Cumming, Wesley Ruggles, Paul Salon and Cecil B. De Mille.

I worked so much as a child because back then word of mouth from one director to the next kept me busy. You didn't have agents to pick up the phone and get you work. Your trail followed from your determinism, your style, and what you put in from your heart. The director only had to tell or describe to me once what he needed or wanted. I was known by all directors as a kid who was easy to work with, a kid with a pleasing personality, a kid who listened, watched and gave the directors more than what they asked for, which kept me hopping from studio to studio. I would work for this particular production company, then be swept in the limo to another studio, all in the same day. In order to be able to do this, I had to be prepared. I had to have the lines, scenes and settings memorized in my head in order to deliver a smooth performance for the director.

Back then we didn't have time for retakes. We had to be quick and good. That old adage of "time is money" was practiced by everyone. We didn't horse around on sets like they do today. Time wouldn't allow that because it took so long to shoot and make a movie. Everyone did his best to be precise and exact.

My reputation preceded me before I even knew that I was considered for a part. By the time I was approached for a part, it was already settled in the minds of the producers and directors that Eugene Jackson was their child star to be cast for the role. I was able to change my expressions and moods to fit the moment, which kept me working and would add to increases in my contract from one film to the next. Because I worked so hard, the directors and producers would approach my mother with bigger and better deals. Even though I didn't make as much as the white child stars, I did pretty good.

Mama was a smart business lady; she learned from Papa's businesses. Mama knew she had a son with talent. She did the best she could for me in handling my career. She was honest, respected by all directors and producers, and never went to the casting couch for a deal.

I'd like to say to up-and-coming stars that you should believe in yourself and practice hard. Don't resort to anything that will belittle you or bring you disrespect. Stay away from anything that is negative. It is easy to go wrong. Before you know it, you have slipped down the wrong path. It is harder to follow a straight and narrow road for success because you must practice, practice, practice, and practice to be good. It takes a lot of time to be skillful, but once your skills have been fine tuned you will be sought after. Nothing comes overnight. Even at my age, from time to time, I get calls from directors and producers asking if I can do this or that.

Yes, the times have changed on me and it seems that all has faded. But when I get that call from someone that remembers me for my skills and craft, I become energized: One day my wife, Sue, answered the phone. The person on the other end said his name was George Peppard. My wife didn't hear him clearly, so he repeated himself. She said, "Oh, yes," and handed me the phone. When I got the phone, he introduced himself again. His tone was full of reverence and respect. He told me that I had worked with him some time back and he was doing a movie. He wanted to know if I had time in my schedule to work with him again, and I told him that I would be honored. After I hung up the phone, I almost fainted. It made me feel so good and special that this man did not let his secretary or agent call me. He wanted to ask me himself, out of respect. No matter how small the part is today, when I walk on that set, and whatever the director and producer request, I'm able to deliver — because I'm a showman.

RESIDUALS

In order to make it back then as an entertainer, one had to work constantly. Residuals were unheard of. There were no such things as insurances or funds available for actors. The actor had to save and be thrifty at all times, because in the business of yesteryear an actor could end up not getting paid for work or a show could close without notice or reason to anyone. This could leave an actor in a bad way because of daily living expenses. When the curtain

1606 East 103 Rd Place
Los Angeles, California
May 9, 1931

IN AGREEMENT:

THE JACKSON BROTHERS, MANAGED BY MRS.   BAKER, MOTHER,

AGREE, TO APPEAR IN PERFORMANCE FOR ONE HOUR OR PORTION

THEREOF IN A SONG-DANCE AND NOVELTY ACT AT THE GERMAN

TURVINE GYMNASIUM   (BLUE ROOM) AT 938 WEST WASHINGTON

ON WEDNESDAY EVENING, MAY THIRTEENTH (13th) AT 8:30 P. M.

ON THE GOODYEAR RUBBER COMPANY PROGRAM FOR THE TOTAL

CONSIDERATION OF TWENTY DOLLARS INCLUDING AN ACCOMPANIST.

IN AGREEMENT WITH FLOYD C. COVINGTON, ENTERTAINMENT MANAGER.

SIGNED _Floyd C. Covington_

Floyd C. Covington, Entertainment Mgr.

Mrs. Lillie Baker

Mrs.   Baker, Manager

A 1931 contract for Eugene and brother Freddie, signed by their mother.

fell, the actor had to survive. Many times it meant the actor had "to rob Peter to pay Paul." This was how and why entertainers at times had bad names and reputations while performing in towns. The townspeople sometimes wouldn't do business with us unless we had cash up front — we weren't allowed to pay later. And needless to say, cash up front would be hard to obtain and keep.

So, an entertainer was considered by some as being someone to watch very carefully in doing business with because his lifestyle was not stable. We were stars in the public's eye but business was business, which meant we had to have hard, cold cash to make it. The lifestyle of the entertainer appeared flamboyant to people, but at the same time people sometimes thought of us as fast-talkers and swindlers. This was why Mama was so strong and honest at all times. She used to say, "If the Jackson family had nothing else, the Jackson family has a name to uphold." To Mama this meant integrity, standing by what one knew was right. A good, solid deal was a deal to uphold.

Residuals are good; however, they still don't cover dancers, musicians and nonspeaking roles. I have never gotten residuals for my musical and dancing contributions in film. This is why it is very important for dancers and musicians in film to have a good lucrative contract. The more unions you are involved in, the more protection and pay you will receive. I'm a member of Local 47 (a musician's union), Screen Actors Guild (SAG), Screen Extras Guild (SEG), Equity (the theater guild), and American Federation of Television and Radio Artists (AFTRA).

A smart, sharp entertainer had to budget and continue to be number-conscious of everything at all times, meaning that no matter how much one wanted something extra, one had to think of the necessities first. We always had to keep in the back of our heads that nothing from nothing left nothing. So the entertainer always had to be thinking about how to obtain that next gig in order to put some money in the cookie jar (or your mama's bra or stocking). It was clear-cut. The entertainer had to be a quick thinker and talker in order to beat out another potential act, since there may have been room for only one more act on the payroll. The entertainer had to survive. The creation of residuals is wonderful because it helps the actor continue to be able to maintain and function in a less stressful manner.

In our heyday we were riding high as kid actors. No one thought about how we were going to live in the future. Unless you had a smart family member, or someone who had made solid investments while acting and would be willing to share his knowledge with you, you could end up penniless like so many stars of my era. The July 1996 article in the *Classic Images* newspaper concerning my good friend Joe Cobb of *Our Gang* did not surprise me. None of us got residuals for our participation in the film industry when it was in its infancy. The article called Hollywood "heartless." I don't blame Hollywood for this because we were all innocent rookies back then. When Hollywood realized that no provisions were set aside for child actors, all kinds of protection laws were created. There are all types of relief funds and organizations set up now for actors.

Remember to always save for that rainy day because rain comes unexpectedly; and sometimes when it rains, it seems it is never going to stop. If you have prepared for that day, then you can sit back and watch it rain with enjoyment. When the sun shines again, begin to save for the next downpour. Don't let time pass you by without that nest egg, that security blanket. Love yourself enough to take care of yourself in the future. Be aware of the fact that everything revolves around time. Look at the four seasons and pattern your life around them: Blossom and bloom in the spring and summer. In the autumn and fall, gather your nest egg to save and invest. Don't sleep and hibernate in the winter months. Use that time wisely for planning and setting goals. When spring and summer roll around again, you'll be able to skip and jump rope with joy and pleasure because you thought ahead. This plan will secure you your own residuals of a lifetime.

Agents

Agents? Oh my goodness, who needs them? We do in this time period. The way Hollywood is set up today, one now must have an agent. You have to have an introduction. Your agent is that introduction, your bridge, your foot in the door. Once in the audition, you must sell yourself. You must perform in order to get that job, that gig. But sometimes agents will not work in your best interest, which is why actors and agents sever relationships from time to time.

One agent messed me around not once, but twice. I had won an audition as a musician. We were to go on location to San Francisco. I hadn't heard anything, so I called my agent to get the particulars. This was when she told me that the production company had chosen someone else. In reality, I found out that the production company really wanted me. My agent had someone else she wanted to push and sell. So you see how agents can sometimes be a double agent by not working in your best interest.

It's hard to trust people today in the business because times have changed. In the past, a handshake and a verbal response were a person's bond. They stuck to it. But in the industry of today, even if it is in writing, you may still not get the job. Agents are out to make as much money as possible. This is their job. If they believe they can make more on a particular individual, that is the one who will be pushed. Since they work on commission, agents think in terms of high returns. It is important to be capable of many things because an agent can make or break you. He will be able to plug you here and there for some quick money.

9
Beer Joints, Nightclubs and My Dancing Girls

Freddie and I worked all over, so I thought it was time to change our act. After seeing an acrobatic group in 1938, I tried to copy a flying trapeze act of jumping in the air, coming down, and going into the splits. It looked so easy to me, but I didn't realize that gymnastics came with a lot of hard work and practice, just like my tapping and acting skills. I thought I could do it without much practice. I was a kid who would try anything at least once.

Freddie and I were performing onstage. I jumped up in the air and landed on the floor in a split position. I was in so much pain that I couldn't get up, and Freddie came out to do his part. He didn't know I couldn't move. The audience showed shock and concern. The manager, who was smaller than I, had to be called. He helped Freddie pick me up and carry me off the stage, then he drove us home. This happened during a matinee at the Japanese Theater on Jefferson and Vermont. I went to the doctor, who informed my mother that I would be in bed for at least six weeks so the torn ligaments could heal.

While lying in bed, I began to think about my future and not being able to dance again. I recalled that horn under my bed that Mama had purchased years ago. I didn't like that horn because it wasn't shiny. However, I discovered that it didn't have to shine in order to produce — it released the same sweet sound as a shiny one. I was now grateful for that horn. I was always thinking ahead. I thought that if I couldn't dance anymore, then I should learn to play an instrument to make money.

I had been listening to the radio while in bed and began to play around with the sax to the music on the radio. I have always had a good ear for tunes. I began to play by ear, and in six weeks I had mastered the instrument. I bought some drums for Freddie for $25 and came up with the idea of forming a musical group. Had I not had the accident, I would have never picked up the skill of playing the sax or formed my group. From then on, my group would be my bread and butter for the rest of my life.

When Freddie was ready to graduate in 1938, they needed a band. The administration in charge of the prom asked Freddie if he could get a band. I immediately jumped at this opportunity and told Freddie we could make this money ourselves since we weren't working. I would play sax, Prince Beaver would play the guitar, Jessie Purdue played the trumpet, Lady Will Car was on the piano, and Freddie on the drums. This was the beginning of the Eugene Jackson Band. The dance went terrific. Everyone loved it. It went so well that we began to play in beer joints making two, three, and four dollars a night.

Mama had an RCA Victrola and lots of old opera and classical music. We would listen to them and practice. I knew to get a good piano player who could carry the band, one who knew more than I did and was seasoned in playing nightclubs and different settings.

Around 1938, I incorporated our dancing music into floor shows and hired beautiful, brown, fine-framed dancing girls. I would use various girls for different events at such clubs as the Dixie Castle, the Cricket Club on Washington and Vermont (which was owned by the champion fighter Bud Taylor) and the Boulevard Stop. The Mosette Dancers — Juanita Moore, Myrtle Fortune, and Lucille Battle — were my dancers.

My girls that danced for me at the taverns were Nettie and Helen Mitchell; Geneva Nickerson, the daughter of famous Frisco Nick, a dancer from San Francisco; Marian Anderson; Bell Tavern; and Fannie and Precilla Bufford. The Rosa Lee Dancers consisted of Flora and Mildred Washington. The Peters Sisters, who weighed around 200 pounds apiece, were a singing trio who worked for me. They eventually went to Europe and became very successful. I used a lot of girls from the area.

Sometimes I would get a call for stag shows. I had certain girls that I used for stag. A lot of the girls didn't do stag, but things got so tough that the ones who never participated began to do stag. They would say, "Gene, I'll do stag on the side." They would want to know where the location was. When I told them it was way out in Hollywood, they'd say, "I'll take it because ain't nobody gonna see me."

The manager of the Rosebud Theater had moved to the Lincoln Theater on Twenty-Third and Central Avenue. His name was Mr. Wolf. He knew me and gave me an opportunity to showcase my talent. When my pictures were showing, he would let me in free. My Harlem Revue consisted of the band and the girls, and we were showcased at the Lincoln. Mrs. Geneva Williams was the lady who told me about the Dandridge Sisters.

I was told that Mrs. Dandridge had two daughters, and they had a friend named Etta Jones who performed with them. They were known together as the Dandridge Sisters. Mrs. Williams knew my mother, so I went over to see

Eugene gets his dancing girls into the act.

Mrs. Dandridge at their home on Fifty-Fifth Street and met the girls. Etta happened to be there rehearsing. I told them I'd like to use them in my shows, and Mrs. Dandridge said she was very particular about who her girls worked with. They knew I was active in the movies and had been teaching tap since high school.

I had to be a mature guardian or they would not be able to work with me again. The girls were around 12 to 14 years of age; Dorothy was 12 years old. The Dandridge Sisters along with Etta Jones were my theater stage girls. I started arranging gigs with the girls, and we would play one-day engagements. (Though I was young, I was already acting as my own business manager and promoter. The organizational skills came naturally from my mother and from watching D.P. on my vaudeville tour.) This was in the thirties, and money was tight.

I remember we had a job in San Pedro at the Midway Club. It was a white sailor joint, but it was a job. I used Dorothy and Vivian Dandridge, and Etta Jones. We were called the Five Rhythmatics, with Freddie, myself and the girls. It was a one- or two-night gig. The girls were so pretty, and they went over big. The guys would try to get dates with them, but I would make them go upstairs to their dressing room and stay there until the next show. When we finished working, we would leave straight for home in my black, 16-cylinder 1931 Cadillac. Freddie and I would always deliver the girls home safe and sound. From there, we got jobs in Victorville at different clubs. There were special clubs that enjoyed seeing us, and we were asked back time and time again.

Coming back from Victorville one evening, we almost had a terrible accident. We had done an outstanding job performing and were exhausted. Freddie was driving, while Etta and I were in the front seat nodding off and on. Dorothy and Vivian were in the back seat. We were up 3,000 feet, and the highway was full of curves. All of a sudden, Etta opened her eyes and saw Freddie going to sleep. He was going off the road. She screamed, "Gene, wake up! Freddie is going off the highway!" I immediately had him to stop so I could take over the wheel. I was fussing and hollering, "You big dummy!" These were my favorite words. I then said, "Why didn't you tell me you were sleepy?" I drove the rest of the way home. That could have been a very tragic accident like the one in which Sammy Davis, Jr., lost an eye.

We worked the following places to rave reviews: the Paramount, the Strand in Long Beach at the Pike, the Million Dollar Theater, the Orpheum and the Hippodrome. The Hippodrome was where we broke in our act as the Five Rhythmatics with the Dandridge Sisters. These places were a showcase for acts, and booking agents would come to see performances.

We would all open up together. Freddie and I would come back and do a single act with fast double-tapping. The girls would come out and do their trio number in harmony, then I would come back and do my imitations of Amos 'n' Andy, Rochester, Peter Lorre and Lionel Barrymore. Next, all of us would come out and close with a fast-moving, 15-minute routine. An agent saw us perform this act and booked us in a movie called *You Can't Take It with You*. We did the streetdancing in the movie along with Dorothy in the film. We worked together for quite a while until the girls went to Europe. Dorothy came back from Europe a big star.

From there we were booked at the Million Dollar Theater with the Jay Brener Band, and then at the Paramount Theater. We were booked all over. We received gigs at the big clubs in Santa Barbara. We would play for our mother's social club. (She was an active member of the Eastern Star, an old group that is still functioning today. It was started to help improve the conditions for Negroes in the community.) After we finished working in Santa Barbara, we headed for the theater work. We worked up and down the coast, performing wherever there was an opening.

Established bands were in demand. Some of the well-known groups were the Les Hite Band, the Leon Heffert Band, the Louie Armstrong Band, and Fess White. They all played at respectable clubs like the Cotton Club. The top dancers during this period were Rosa Lee Lincoln, Flora and Mildred Washington, and Mildred Boyd. I had my big band at the Lincoln Theater, and the show was called "Rhapsody in Black Rhythm." The marquee read, "Eugene Jackson presents his Rhapsody in Black Rhythm with Freddie, his brother, Alma Travis, the Dandridge Sisters, Fess White, the Rhythm Gentlemen and Pat Patterson." Pat was the man who played the banjo in St. Louis in September of 1933. I had met him on my vaudeville tour. On the screen at that time were Bill "Bojangles" Robinson, Fats Waller, and Jeni LeGon, a black tap dancer from New York. They were starring in *Hooray for Love*.

There was a club around Fifth and Main by the name of the Waldorf Cellar. Emma Walton was the producer of the Black and Tan Show, which performed at the Waldorf Cellar. We were included in the act, though we were only around 15 or 16 years old. We shouldn't have been dancing in nightclubs, but we did. It helped the family out, and we loved it. We worked at Stillwell on Seventh and Main with the Sonny Clay Band and chorus girls. We performed at Pappy's on Ninth Street, with the Charlie Echols band, to a mixed crowd. Charlie's style was similar to Cab Calloway. Charlie was a swing-band entertainer. He had a light complexion and wore a white suit with tails. At intermission, white chicks would give him diamond rings. They loved him. He had a daughter named Nita, who I used in my group around the time I had the Five Rhythmatics.

In those days, girls made money by going to tables singing "risqué songs." They would make a lot in tips, so Freddie and I decided to do one during our intermission. Our risqué song was called " In Room 200 and 2 Where the Walls Keep Talking to You," a skit that added to our bankroll.

In 1938 there was a colored club in Pasadena that was closed. When Freddie and I went to see about buying it, there was a janitor cleaning up. We got closer and found it was Charlie Echols pushing a broom. We were shocked and thought our eyes were playing tricks on us — we never saw the former star again. This just goes to show you how one must save money in show business because it can get away from you so fast. Every penny I made, I invested. I bought real estate and purchased my dance studio.

There was a local colored union, the 767, on Central. Elmer Fain, a businessman, was the walking union delegate. The president was Mr. Bailey. Paul Howard was the secretary, and Florence Covez was the office secretary. Elmer Fain, who always wore a suit and hat, was hot on our trail. We would be playing and having a good time onstage, looking out at the audience, and to our surprise in would walk Elmer Fain.

The police could have used him to crack mystery cases: We never told him where we were performing, but somehow he found out. He would stand in a certain way and area to make sure we knew of his presence. During intermission he would always come to us and say, "You know you boys need to be in the union." We would respond respectfully, "Yes sir, we will." He wasn't the kind of man you could shake off.

One time I was playing by myself on the piano in San Pedro when I turned to a knock on a nearby window. When I looked out the window, there was Elmer Fain. He was a doggone good detective. He would have made a great FBI or CIA G-man. He was slicker than they were. To this day, we still don't know how he found out about all of our jobs. He was pursuing us because we were "hot as firecrackers." We had jobs to the ceiling and hadn't joined the union, and there wasn't anything he could do about it. We had been booking and arranging our own gigs.

We finally joined the union in 1939. By the time we joined, we were seasoned. We were playing and doing great. The value of the union was that we had insurance. If we didn't get paid, the union acted as negotiator. However, we always got paid because people would want us to return. On Thirty-Third Street there was a friend of mine named Monroe Tucker, who had paralysis and couldn't walk. He was a brown-skinned man with large lips and a flat face. He had a wonderful personality. He was a happy-go-lucky guy and was very jovial.

Monroe had a friend named Garland Finney, and they did a piano duo. Monroe and Garland played a lot of house parties. (In those days, people had house parties to pay rent. They were called "Chicken and Chitlins" parties.) I met Monroe at one of those functions and was impressed with his style. I used Monroe in about a dozen engagements and I would have to carry him to the car and restroom. His paralysis did not slow him down with the ladies. He had a good talk and rap with the girls. I would have to take him upstairs to the girls' room and wait for him in the car. He was getting all the girls. The chicks loved him. But he was messing up my action, and I let him go.

My Graham-Paige wore out so I bought another big car, a Pierce Arrow. I'd pick up the girls to go to work at the clubs.

10
Honolulu Tour, 1941

There weren't a great number of films being made in 1941; Hollywood was dead. Mrs. Butler, who had been to Honolulu before, received a call asking her to return. She called to ask me if I wanted to join her troupe of five girls in Honolulu. She owned a dancing school, and her troupe consisted of Doris Randolph, Wilma Mack, Dorothy Moon, Sylvia Perry and Melba Young. Eddie Davis played drums, Dave Henrix played the tenor sax, and Mrs. Butler was on piano. I would be an emcee, singer, dancer, and barker. (A barker is someone who beckons and ballyhoos the crowd by hollering and drawing attention to the platform, saying, "Hurry, hurry, step right up!") Even though I was going to be a barker, I took my sax with me.

When I stepped off the ship, I felt that I was on a different planet. Honolulu is an experience that I will never forget. When you get to be the age of 21, you are considered a man. I had been home with my dear mother all my life, but now I had an opportunity to travel on my own by going to Honolulu. This would be a good experience for me. That *Matson* ship left from San Pedro, California, on October 25, 1941. I was so excited. We walked up the plank to the ship, while Mama Lil (with tears in her eyes) and Freddie were on the ground waving. We were in third class but it was nice, and the food was great.

We sailed from San Pedro to San Francisco to Honolulu. It took five days on the *Matson* ocean liner. As we were getting off the ship, we were met by a big Hawaiian band with singers. The beautiful Hawaiian girls put a lei of fresh, pleasant-smelling flowers around our necks as we walked down the plank. We were given a welcome by these young ladies and escorted down the plank. I felt like I was in heaven. The lovely blue sky and water were so peaceful. I had nothing but a smile on my face. We immediately went to the circus headquarters, where tents were pitched on the vast grounds of the Mormon facility. (E.K. Fernandies was a Mormon who owned a large circus on the island of Oahu. He was a soft-spoken, polite and honest businessman who wore silk sport clothes.)

Our first booking was Hilo, on the island of Hawaii. We got off the big boat and onto a tugboat to Hilo. The water was so rough, and the waves were huge. We were bouncing and tossing up and down so much, we thought we would turn over. The trip was about an hour to Hilo. We stayed at a hotel for lodging, and the circus tents were set up on the fairgrounds. The variety show consisted of three acts: white entertainers, black entertainers, and the animal acts. Three separate tents were pitched for each act, with the main tent being the largest. Our tent was called the Black and Tan Harlem Strutters. We stayed ten days on this island.

On the day of the opening of the show, they built a stage and the drums and piano were put on it. The girls' and boys' dressing rooms were put on the side of the tent. This was all new to us, but I had done a lot of performing in vaudeville so I knew how to ballyhoo. The people would come in and fill the tent, and the show would last 35 minutes. When the tent would empty, I would begin ballyhooing to bring the people in. The girls had worked with Mrs. Butler, but this was our first show together. When the curtain rose, we were performing and rehearsing at the same time. The audience was unaware of this. The crowd loved the act — we did 12 shows.

We were taken on sightseeing tours of the big volcano and the man-eating plant. At 21, I was very adventurous and I met a Haitian girl at one of our shows. She and I enjoyed each other's company, but she failed to tell me she was married. The word all over the grounds was that her husband was looking for me. I said, "Feet, do your stuff." I was sure I'd rather tug with the waves than tug it out with him.

We went back to Honolulu to obtain our lodging. We were there two days and did not perform. Instead, we were taken on more tours. Mrs. Butler and the girls stayed at Mr. Fernandies' house. I stayed with a Hawaiian boy named Sam, one of the workers at the circus, who was strong as an ox and lived with his dad in the Kankakee District on the slope of a mountain. You could see down on the island of Pearl Harbor and the ocean.

When we weren't performing, I had free time to go downtown. I ran into some colored musicians from Los Angeles, and we had a ball talking and laughing. One guy's name was Buck Clayton. He had been around the world and told me they were staying with Marie Dickerson. I was surprised — I told them I knew her from Los Angeles as a dancer. They took me to see her, and we hugged and kissed. Previously married to comedian Dudley Dickerson, she was an entertainer in Honolulu. She liked it so much that she bought a house and stayed, renting rooms to entertainers and musicians who came to work in Honolulu. She was very financially established.

The next day I met the troupe at the docks for Maui. This ride was much better, and the waves were smoother and calmer. I stayed at an immaculate Japanese rooming house. I can remember looking under their houses and noticing how neat and clean they were, unlike Forty-Seventh Place back in the

Honolulu tour, 1941: Eugene in the middle of a song-and-dance hula.

States. The tents were pitched when we arrived. I began with the same routine as I did in Hilo. I barked, and the tents would fill. I was used to performing four shows a day. We did 23 shows a day for $35 a week, and we performed for three days. The girls were beat, and were crying about their aching feet, legs and backs. Because I was both emcee and barker, I felt I would lose my voice.

I met five Japanese guys who took me out on the town. Our first stop was an armory dance. When we walked in, all I could see was wall-to-wall gorgeous girls. They had layers of pleasant-smelling flowers around their necks, and the atmosphere was like paradise. I had a ball dancing with those sweet, innocent girls. We moved on to a tavern. We started drinking sake, which was like a wine. I had never experienced sake, but it went down real smooth. I got drunk and had a headache the next day. I do not understand how people can drink it; I guess the Japanese must be accustomed to it.

We went back to Honolulu, which was our headquarters. E.K. had booked a show for the Japanese people on River Street. On Sunday I had some free time to do a jam session at a restaurant called the Pearl Tavern, near Pearl Harbor. The owner and crowd had never had anyone play a saxophone, dance and sing like I did that day. My style and personality were different from previous entertainers. The owner wanted to sign me, but I was under contract to the circus. I told him that as soon as my contract was up I would work for him.

The tents for shows were pitched on Mormon grounds in front of the big temple. On December 4–6, we performed at Schofield Army Base for about

1,000 southern soldiers. (I remember that when we were passing through checkpoint, the MPs came on the bus asking if we had liquor. We could see at the guardpost the confiscation of liquor from the soldiers.) We performed to a full house on Friday, Saturday and Sunday. Since these were southerners, I changed my routine a little. I sang "You Are My Sunshine," "Deep in the Heart of Texas," "San Antonio Rose" and "Home on the Range." These were their favorites, and it made them feel at home. This was my goal. I knew they were far from home and that some may have been homesick. They loved the show.

It started to rain and became very cold. The soldiers gave me a little liquor to drink, and Mrs. Butler asked me to get some whiskey so she could make a toddy to warm the girls. (Now that I look back, I wonder if it was for the girls or if it was really for Mrs. Butler.) The soldiers were able to accommodate me. We had been performing to packed houses in the auditorium. The feeling of harmony was in the air, and everything was so peaceful and serene. We boarded the bus for home, with soldiers following, waving and throwing kisses. No one had an inkling that we would be bombed the next day. We dropped off the girls and Mrs. Butler, and I was taken to Sam's home. I said my prayers for bed.

The next morning, December 7, 1941, Sam woke me around 7:00 A.M. screaming and hollering, "Wake up, Gene!" I asked him what was wrong, and he said that Pearl Harbor was being bombed. I was shocked. I remember looking down from the house seeing and smelling the smoke. I tried to see San Francisco. My eyes filled with tears. I immediately told the family we should get food. I spent $35 for groceries, which was a lot in those days. I wired Mama some money. It was a good thing that I did go to the market because a curfew was soon enforced. All grocery stores, nightclubs, bars and liquor stores were closed — we were under martial law.

There were curfews and blackouts imposed instantly. Lights had to have blue cellophane over them for blackout. Citizens were being shot for ignoring the law and trying to loot. The island was in chaos. Fear and confusion were everywhere. My heart and soul were filled with grief, but I tried to remain calm and sensible. I was getting low on cash, so I went to Mr. Fernandies because he owned me a week's pay. He said he was unable to pay me because he needed his money to care for Mrs. Butler and the girls, who were staying with him. I had to get a job.

It came over the radio that they needed men to work in Pearl Harbor. I went downtown, took the bus to Pearl Harbor, and signed up to do manual labor. The director of personnel recognized me. He knew I was an entertainer and wanted to know what I was doing there. I told him there were no ships leaving and that I needed work. After I finished at personnel, I was taken by truck to the docks where the *Arizona* was sunk. The docks were totally destroyed. I cannot express the fear I had in my heart. My eyes shall never forget that sight. From that moment on, I realized that we could all be blown up in a matter of seconds. To comfort myself, I had to rely on my religious teaching from my mother and Sunday School teacher. I prayed constantly.

I was paid 60 cents an hour. The foreman gave me a 75-pound jackhammer to break boulders. It shook my entire body. Tears came to my eyes because I had never done manual work before. It was very painful mentally and physically. This went on for about three or four days when one day I saw Coco, one of the musicians. He said, "Gene, what are you doing?" I replied, "Man, can't you see what I'm doing?" "I'm breaking these rocks that the bomb destroyed." I noticed how well dressed he was and asked him what he was doing. He stated that he was a pipe fitter and his rate of pay was 75 cents an hour. I learned something that day: The one who does less work gets paid more. When I applied for work, I was unaware of the different positions available. All I wanted was work for pay. I had to laugh and chuckle to myself about my rate of pay versus Coco's.

All the laborers would meet downtown to be transported by an army truck to work at Pearl Harbor for eight hours. We would return downtown to wait for a bus to take us home. This routine went on for a number of days. One day while I was washing my clothes, I received a call from E.K. Fernandies. I had been calling him daily to see about transportation home. He said there was a cargo ship leaving for the States in two hours. They were taking passengers who wanted to get out of Honolulu. That was music to my ears. I threw wet clothes and all into my bag. I was so happy. I called a taxi and told the driver I was in a hurry to catch the ship that was leaving the docks for San Francisco. I told him the name of the ship and the dock. He asked me where it was. I said, "You've got to be kidding." He was a Hawaiian driver. I said, "Don't you know?" He answered "No," so I said, "Start driving." When we found the right docks, the ship had already left. I was sick to my stomach. I was so angry at the dumb cab driver. To top it off, it cost me $10 for missing the ship. I thought that I had better quit my job at the docks so I could be at home just in case E.K. called. It was a good thing that I missed that particular ship because it was full of cattle.

The next day I went to the personnel office, where they knew I was a movie star. I told the director of personnel that I wanted to quit. "What?" he said. "You can't quit. We need manpower here." I informed him that I lived in Los Angeles with my mother and that I was needed there. He said, "We need you here." I felt I was a prisoner on a beautiful island. Tears came to my eyes. I pleaded and begged, telling him I would do defense work in Los Angeles when I returned home. He said it was against his good judgment, but he would release me. He told me not to tell a soul. I told him my lips were sealed.

The next day, I was sitting around home listening to the radio about the war news in Honolulu. It was a good thing that we had stocked our cabinets. I had plenty to eat, but no job. I began to think about when I first got to Honolulu. I had met an opera singer who sang with the Hawaiian symphony orchestra. She had a car and owned a pineapple plantation. I thought she was the girl for me, and we fell in love. But when Pearl Harbor was bombed, I didn't see her anymore because of the blackout. I couldn't get around. Everybody was in a panic.

The blackout and curfew were still effective. Some people were still ignoring the rules and were being shot at night while trying to steal. All nightclubs, bars and liquor stores were still closed. While I was listening to the radio, an announcement came across asking for musicians and entertainers to put on a Christmas show for the underprivileged children. They said there would be no pay, but plenty of food. This was right up my alley. The next day, December 14, 1941, I got up and took a bus to the orphanage. The Christmas decorations throughout the building were beautiful. I was received with open arms. There were a lot of island entertainers. They fed us first, and the food was great. All kinds of acts were present. I did my singing and dancing act. After I finished, I watched the other acts. Two Chinese brothers, Inny and Gunny Young, were a singing team. They were about seven or eight years old, and they sang popular songs and had good harmony.

While I was watching them, they reminded me of Freddie and myself. I got a little homesick and wanted to cry. One never knows who you're sitting next to. I just happened to mention to a lady sitting next to me that they reminded me of my brother and myself. She told me that they were her nephews. I told her that all they needed was a good tap routine. She said that I would have to talk to their mother and father. I asked how I could meet them, and she said they were at their place of business, which was a café.

After the program, I rode with them to Young's Café. Young's Café was a big, fine place. Mrs. Young asked if I wanted to eat and I said I did. They had about 12 cute little waitresses. Mrs. Young asked me what it would cost to teach the boys how to dance. I needed the money badly, but didn't want to say too much and mess the deal up. I told her $35 a week, and she agreed.

The next day, I started teaching them tap dancing at their home. Their front room was like a small ballroom. The whole family would come and sit around the room to watch me teach them. When I went into the café to eat, the girls would all run to serve me. They treated me like I was a king. A person feels very good on the inside when people of different nationalities learn to love each other. I was welcomed into the homes of these people. We treated each other with the utmost respect. This is what life is all about. I was so happy being with nice people, especially during a time when the environment was so tense. Every day I would call to see if any ships were leaving. Inny and Gunny picked up tapping fast. I was glad because I did not know when I would get a call to leave. On December 24, 1941, E.K. called and said a ship called the *Lurline* was leaving the next day. It was such a nice gift to be able to leave for home on my birthday.

I told the Young family I had a chance to leave. They didn't want me to leave, and they all had tears in their eyes. I left the café in a hurry to go to E.K.'s to get my ticket. I put my ticket in my sock so that I wouldn't lose it. I was determined and desperate to leave. At the same time, I didn't really want to leave the Young family, but I had to see my mama. I was concerned about the condition of my entire family. I told myself that I wasn't going to miss the ship.

I was on the dock at 6:00 A.M., sitting on my bag with my saxophone to my side. Nobody was there but me and the ship. I was elated to see it. At 8:00 A.M. the gangplank was lowered. I was the first to board the ship. I received my bed in A deck, and I did not put my sax in storage. The ship was crowded. We were escorted with three torpedo warships, one in the front and the other two on the sides.

Three ships left that day as a convoy. The *Matson* carried all the military personnel with their wives and children. The *Mariposa* carried all the sick or injured sailors and soldiers, and the *Lurline* carried civilians. This was an experience I will never forget. There was always a feeling of suspense and fear. While walking on the *Lurline*, I met a lovely white girl named Irene from Pasadena, California. She was a college student on the island. I told her that I was an entertainer.

Another white girl named Dorothy joined our conversation. She said that she was traveling by herself because her husband was afraid to leave. He was scared the ships would be bombed. She said she was willing to take a chance. I asked her what kind of work she did. She said she played the piano. I said, "You're kidding," but she said she wasn't. I told her that I played the sax. Immediately the idea of a jam session popped into my head. I asked her if she would like to participate in playing some music. She said, "Why not?" I don't have a dime to my name." I'm so glad I had my horn with me on deck instead of in the storage compartment.

I went to talk to the captain and he thought it was a good morale booster since we had been in blackout for three weeks. The captain advertised the event in the ship's newsletter. We started the jam session in the Crystal Ballroom. We pulled the drapes together so no lights could be seen. The people danced until dawn. We met the next night and performed again.

Our tips totaled over $100, giving us around $52 apiece. Irene came up with the idea of a variety show. She felt there was a lot of unknown talent on the ship. I went to the captain and told him of our plan. I told him we would donate half of the money to the Red Cross. He said that was fine, so the next day we searched the ship for talent. Some people said they hadn't performed in years. All agreed that they were low in funds and could use some extra money.

The word was out about the dance and entertainment in the Crystal Ballroom. The people were wall-to-wall; there wasn't elbow room available. Both performances were packed. I took the proceeds to the captain's cabin. He would not accept the money, and took only ten dollars for the Red Cross. He said we had brought so much joy to the hearts of all and that this had been the most enjoyable trip of the *Lurline*.

There were about 10 or 12 acts, each one receiving $35 apiece. Irene and I split the rest, which gave us $135 each over three nights. She said she was so happy she met me. For three nights we played to a packed audience. The jar on top of the piano was full with tips. When the show was over, I had difficulty finding a place to count my money. Everywhere I turned, people were congratulating me for an outstanding job. I finally went to my room and jumped in my bunk with a flashlight. I pulled the cover over my head to count the money. I was surprised how much money I had made. I thanked God and asked him not to let the Japanese bomb the ships. The next day all the performers came to thank me. They told me that God had sent me to them.

The last night at sea brought a lot of people on deck to see the lights of San Francisco. Boy, that was a beautiful sight. Those lights meant something special to us all: They meant home soil. We arrived in San Francisco on December 29, 1941, around 9:00 A.M. Because I'm such a ham, when we docked the first thing I did was to kiss the ground and say "Allah, Allah, Allah, Allah." I grabbed a handful of dirt and an arm of that train for Los Angeles. Mama, Freddie, Aunt Joe, Aunt Hazel and friends met me at the train station. Away we went down Central Avenue to Forty-Seventh Place. Man, Central Avenue looked good to me. "There is no place like home" might be a cliché, but it was exactly how I felt. My home on 1161 East Forty-Seventh Place, my mama Lil, my brother Freddie and my Aunt Hazel meant so much to me. I did not realize this until the war broke out.

11
Army Days and Defense Work, 1942–1943

When I got back from Honolulu, I informed the studios that I had returned. I started working at Warner Bros. in *The Singing Kid* with Al Jolson. I danced with a group of dancers in this film. Before I left Honolulu, I had promised to do defense work, which was why I was released to return home. I am a man of my word, so I signed up at Douglas Aircraft in El Segundo. I was active with my trio. We were working in Long Beach at the Four O Club at the Pike. I explained to the owner of the club, Mr. Pappy Gerrot, that I could work from seven to eleven in the evening. I had to be at Douglas Aircraft in El Segundo at twelve midnight until six in the morning. I would leave Douglas Aircraft at six in the morning and go to Warner Bros. Studio for a full day of work. After that I would go home, eat, take a bath, lie down for a few hours, then go to the club. I worked three jobs around the clock, plus playing the field with the ladies. I had a girlfriend at the club and one in El Segundo at work. This went on for one year from 1942 to 1943, until I got my call from the army.

At that time, everybody was trying to avoid the army. Guys were getting 4-F deferrals. A guy on the avenue was selling a powder to increase your blood pressure so your system would be messed up for the physical. When I got my papers, I went on the avenue in search of the guy who sold the powder. I gave him fifty dollars, and he told me what to do. I told Mama. She was very concerned and asked if I knew what I was doing. She felt I could be taking something that was harmful, but I took the stuff. He said not to drive, so I decided to take the streetcar. I was waiting for something to happen, but nothing did.

At the center, I became nervous watching all the fellows line up. I sat there feeling normal. They called me from the long line to go in. They examined me and said, "All right, 1-A." I said, "Ain't this a drag. Doggone it, oh shoot! I'm gonna go out tonight to have a ball. I'll call a girl up." I got on the streetcar going home when all of a sudden that stuff started to work. I began to shake and sweat on the streetcar and could hardly get home.

When I got home, I fell on the bed. Mama said, "What's wrong?" I said, "Well, it's working now. When I wanted it to work, it wouldn't." She said, "I told you about spending that money on that stuff." My last night was spent at home in bed, sick. I had to leave the next day to join the army in Fort Huachuca, Arizona. This just goes to show you that if something is for you, then nothing is going to stop it from happening. I was inducted for service in World War II on April 23, 1943.

I informed the local musicians' union 767 that I had been inducted into the army, and they wrote a letter recommending me for the army band at Fort Huachuca. I was sent to San Pedro for three days to the reception station. I received my clothes and army ID. From San Pedro, I went to the Union train station for Fort Huachuca. Mama and Freddie saw me off from the train station. The train was full of young men going off to war. Looking around the train, I couldn't help but think to myself that some of us might not be returning home.

The train stopped at a depot station in the small town of Fry, Arizona. We were picked up in an army truck. While riding to the camp I noticed the prairie. In front of the camp was a small town called "The Hook" (because they had female hookers). As we drove into the camp, some of the men were dropped off. I was dropped off at the old post, which was the band quarters. My barracks were pointed out to me, and I put up my stuff.

I met Sergeant Andrew and he introduced me to Colonel Nelson, who was white, and Captain Joe Jordan, who was black. I had my saxophone with me. I told the colonel that I was an entertainer from Los Angeles. I stated that I could dance and play the saxophone, and he said he had a piano player for me. To my surprise it was Harold Brown from Los Angeles, one of the great piano players from the city. I didn't know he had been drafted. We hugged each other, and the colonel was elated to see that we knew each other. I suggested we play "I Got Rhythm" and did my whole routine of singing and dancing. The colonel said, "Okay, we can use him in the band."

It made me very happy to be with some friends. Harold told me that when I went to the band room I would meet more guys I knew from Los Angeles. I saw Wesley Prince, who had played bass for Nat King Cole; Pete Collins, a trombone player; Allie Grant, who played trumpet; and Chuck Thomas, a buddy of mine from Los Angeles who played the sax.

I got settled in my room of about 50 men and noticed a man in the corner with a net over his bed. They called him net man. He was a dark, short, thin guy who stayed to himself and didn't associate with any of the guys. He was a career soldier and a saxophone player who had been in for over 20 years.

Sergeant Andrew was from the Tenth Cavalry. All of the older men — Sergeant Andrew, Sergeant Hoskins, Sergeant Hall, Sergeant Gillard and Sergeant Slewy — were from the Tenth Cavalry.

A lot of recruits couldn't eat the army food because they said it wasn't any good. They claimed it messed up their system, and would go to the PX and spend money for food. I said, "Shoot, I ain't going to spend any money." I ate what they gave me and liked it. I ate so much that they named me "Chow Hound." I was always first in line. I would run like mad to be first.

On the second day, we had band rehearsal. I got up early that morning for reveille and roll call. After we cleaned up around the camp, I left for rehearsal. There were rumors going around camp about me being a hot saxophone player. As I sat down, I could hear the whispers of "Who is this guy coming in?" I could feel the envy. I was very tense. I didn't read music, but they didn't know it. There were about 40 men in the band. Sergeant Andrew, the band director, instructed me to sit in the front row. He put a sheet of music in front of me, and the tension began to build as I looked at the music. I was scared to death. I put my horn in my mouth. He said, "All right, we're gonna play this." He hit the music stand — one, two, three, four — and the band started playing. This went on three times, and my horn was silent.

I could feel all eyes on me. I said, "Sergeant Andrew, sir, I can play the horn. I can see the music, but I can't read music." There was complete silence in the room. I was perspiring from shame. The palms of my hands were wet. The men began to whisper again. They looked at each other in surprise and shock. I even heard a few chuckles of amazement. He ordered the group to settle down by tapping on the side of his stand.

Sergeant Andrew said, "Well, what we'll do is to put you on clarinet. I'm going to put you with Sergeant Hoskins." He had a lot of saxophone players, but he needed a clarinet player. Sergeant Hoskins was a career man who played the clarinet like Benny Goodman. He played it with so much expression, and he read extremely well. Sergeant Andrew said, "He will teach you to play the clarinet. It's up to you to learn to play or be shipped overseas." I didn't want to go overseas, so I agreed and began practicing the next day with Sergeant Hoskins. He taught me the musical scales, and I practiced for three or four hours a day in the latrine and at band rehearsal.

They had a four-chair clarinet section, and I was the fourth chair. I got better and better and moved up to third clarinet. I continued practicing daily. I stayed in the third chair for a while, but whenever the second clarinet had to go someplace, I would get the opportunity to play second clarinet. I felt good to finally be accepted. I had made an accomplishment. I'd like for young folks to get this message of working hard to succeed. What drove me was that I did not want to go overseas. Use whatever you can to motivate yourself. You will be a happier individual as a result of your accomplishment.

I got into the special service group for entertainers. This was a group of selected entertainers from the band who performed for the army at various functions. There were many people from New York in special services. The New Yorkers were Maceo Anderson, one of the Four Step Brothers; Lawrence Wiznoff, an opera singer; and Orlando Roberson, a singer. Later, Fayard Nicholas of the Famous Nicholas Brothers joined once he was inducted. Special services kept me busy, along with playing in the army band for the soldiers.

Taps would be played at the end of the day at 5:00 P.M. Walter Williams would have to get up at 6:00 A.M. to play the trumpet for reveille. He would be juiced the night before, but somehow he always made it. He would stagger out there with a hangover, cussing and fussing to himself. It would be cold out there, and one would think he'd mess up. But when he put that horn to his mouth, nothing but sweet music would come out. He would hit those high notes so crisp and clear. You would not be able to tell that he was drunk when he was playing.

I learned all the music of the band. Maceo Anderson and I got together and formed a team. He had been on the Ed Sullivan Show with his group. Then I got word that Freddie was being drafted, so I went to the colonel and asked him to get my brother stationed at Fort Huachuca. I pulled strings to get him there because he could have been sent to Europe or some other place. Freddie came up with his family. Since he had three kids, he was able to get a three-bedroom house; he did very well. Freddie immediately joined us on drums in the army band and special services.

After Freddie arrived, we started working together. One of our big shows was "G.I. Rhapsody." The Wacs (Womens Army Corps), and they had a lot of girls who were singers and dancers. We trained them as a part of our "G.I. Rhapsody" show. We put Fayard Nicholas in the show, and traveled all over the state of Arizona with the show to promote war bonds. We raised millions.

Within the military band, Austin McCoy had a great swing band that went down to Los Angeles to the Hollywood Canteen for a week. It was great because I had an opportunity to see Mama. Also, we were on the radio. We put on a floor show at the Canteen with the band. The Hollywood Canteen was located on Hollywood and Vine; it was a place where soldiers would go to meet girls and have a few beers. Civilians also visited the Canteen, but it was mainly a place for soldiers to enjoy. It was great to get away from the post.

I adjusted to army life quite well. I fell right into the flow of things, but a lot of fellows didn't and tried to get out. I gave myself a pep talk by saying that I should make the best of my situation and use everything to my advantage. Children today must adopt this philosophy in order to succeed.

One guy was so dissatisfied with the military that he almost starved himself to death. He ate only sardines and crackers, and got very thin. He had been transferred there from the South. He was a famous dancing entertainer who

Maceo Anderson, Freddie and Eugene dress up as Wacs for their "G.I. Rhapsody" show.

had made a movie with a white lady. She came to the base where he was stationed in the South to perform for the soldiers. When she saw him, she ran
up to him and hugged him. The white soldiers were furious about this. They
didn't like her showing affection toward him and they were unaware that show
business life was totally different from civilian life. A riot almost broke out,
and he was shipped to Fort Huachuca immediately. This broke his spirit. After

he had made up his mind that the army was not for him, his plan of not eating worked: After six or nine months, he was discharged.

It was rough for us back then. It wasn't all roses and happy-go-lucky. The West wasn't that much better than the South in regard to race relations. There was also prejudice on the West Coast.

When we would be assembled on the grounds for parades, General Armon would come on base and show disrespect for our black colonels and captains by calling them niggers. He would try to degrade them in front of us, but that just made us respect the officers even more. The colored colonels were all big-time doctors from civilian life; many came from Chicago. These men were immediately made colonels because of their fine educational background. However, some of the white officers didn't care where you came from or what credentials you had behind your name. All they saw was black skin — to some of them black skin meant inferiority, so they would try to belittle them in front of their men.

The old soldiers who were there before us had been through all of the disrespect; that was a way of life. Many of the Negro soldiers felt civilian life wasn't much better, so they tried to make the best of the situation. The view of the career man was that at least he had a job making $21 a month and a place for his family. The hearts, eyes and souls of those old colored soldiers have seen and experienced a lot of hurt and pain. The world didn't know that black soldiers prided themselves on being in the army. Though never treated properly with respect and dignity, the Negro soldiers fought proudly for their country. They worked at being the best, whatever the position or task entailed. We had some of the top men. We had the 92nd, the 93rd and the 337th medical and special services.

On camp we had a large hospital with Negro doctors and nurses. We had black lieutenants, captains, colonels and majors. The 92nd was a top company coming mostly from the South; they were known as Buffalo Soldiers, and they were sharp in everything. The troops would do drills on motorcades and would go on bivouac for three or four days at Fort Huachuca. In the back of our camp were miles and miles of empty space perfect for army maneuvers.

A lot of wives would come to visit their husbands, but would arrive after the men had left for bivouac. The soldiers left on base would sometimes take advantage of the wives and take them to clubs, which brought about some divorces and a couple of fights that led to a killing over a woman in the 92nd and the 93rd. The 92nd and 93rd had some nice little musical combos, but we were never able to get together and play because of our busy schedule. Fort Huachuca was mostly all black when I was there; now it is mostly all white.

The 93rd was at Fort Huachuca before the 92nd, and they didn't take any mess. They were a top group that trained hard and were highly physically fit. Nevertheless, I recall one sad incident very vividly. I knew exactly how they felt, for it happened to me while I was in the service. They went to Phoenix on a parade and were refused service of ice cream and a Coke at the Walgreens drugstore. This was quite a surprise to me because I had been treated royally in Chicago on my vaudeville tour at the opening of the Walgreens on Forty-Seventh and South Parkway (managed by Mr. Brown, who was colored). The 93rd were highly offended and tore up the town. The army immediately sent them to the South Pacific, where many of them were killed.

I'd like to say to the young people that sometimes things can be handled differently. This particular incident could have been handled in a more diplomatic manner, which would have saved the 93rd from going to war. It sometimes isn't good to let your emotions take over your entire body. There is always going to be someone in control who will quickly show his authority. One must realize that our lives are not valued as highly as whites. This is why it is so important for us to value and respect each other. We must treat each other as if we were precious jewels. The officials of the army should have researched what caused the incident.

In those days the army gave the black man little respect. The army did not face the core of the problem. The army took the view that if the soldiers wanted to destroy, then the army had the power to send the soldiers somewhere to be destroyed with the blessing of the government. We had a big show for the 92nd Buffalo Division since they were leaving. We put on about two or three shows because so many were being shipped out. The train came on base to pick up the soldiers for Europe. They made the musicians feel so good when they said we lifted their spirits. We made them feel like no war was going on. They left in laughter. Our work was not in vain.

Special services would play at the hospital for the sick soldiers. I ran into my uncle Alfred Foster from Texas. In civilian life he was an established, respectable physician. He was inducted with the rank of lieutenant. We were happy to see each other. He asked me where I was living, and I told him I was living in the older part of the camp. He lived in the newer section, which had just been built. He promised to visit.

When Alfred did come, I noticed he had developed a drinking habit. He didn't have a problem in civilian life, but he was not able to deal with the situations at hand. Many men were not able to cope. Some men were destroyed, and others were built — it all depended on the character of the individual. I knew how it felt to be well-respected in civilian life. To be in the army and be disrespected by white men was very humiliating. One had more freedom in civilian life than in the army. A person had to recondition his brain to survive mentally and physically. Alfred asked if he could borrow some money. I said, "You're a lieutenant. You have no business being broke." At that time, the men were gambling and drinking. I loaned it to him, but it took a while for me to get my money back.

"Adjustment" and "flexibility" are words that I want to leave with the young. Learn to adapt, learn to move with the flow of things. Don't be rigid.

Use your mind, your talents, to the fullest to make things for the betterment of yourself. The more education a person has, the better he will live. Education ranks highly; it puts one on a higher level. This was true in both the army and civilian life. In the army, the more education a person had, the more rank and better living conditions were made available to that person. In civilian life, a better education puts a person in a higher paying job and a better neighborhood. It is to the advantage of the young to get as much education as possible. It is about education and economics.

We had a theater on the old post, and Freddie loved the movie projector. The guy who ran the theater knew and liked him. In his spare time, Freddie would go there to operate and watch the movies. What I loved about the army base was that it had everything a person could want. It was a small version of a city. A person did not have to go off base for anything, not even entertainment. I finally got my trio together. I found a piano player by the name of Herb Gordy, and we would play at the NCO club on Saturday evenings. I began teaching tap dancing in a recreational room on the base to people of all races. I had military personnel and civilians from the laundry, machine shop, garages, and about three or four church congregations and civilian business owners.

I was always looking and searching for ways to make more money. Freddie and I went to the historic bandit town of Tombstone. I checked out a saloon about having some dancing and told the owner that Freddie and I would come on our day off on Saturday to play dancing music. We played one Saturday night to make some extra money. A doggone soldier in our company reported us, and they put us in the stockade. Soldiers would come by laughing and cracking jokes at us. We were in the jail for one day. They took the money that we made and bought belts for the band. This shows how jealousy interfered. We did not know that we had to seek permission from our head officer.

On camp was a dark-skinned lady with nice features who ran the NCO club. Her husband was Sergeant Black, a career staff sergeant. She would get us to perform there on our days off. She was crazy about me and had a lot of civilians who visited the club. We had an established name on base and in residential life. The closest town was Tucson, which was 90 miles from the fort. Since there was no place to go, the NCO was the hottest place around to go for a good time. Freddie, Maceo Anderson and I would perform at the USO officer club. The next town was Phoenix, where we would perform in small clubs called the Dug Out and the Elks.

I had a friend by the name of Allie Grant who had been in the service for some time. He had a car and was using it to his advantage. He was "hustlin' and bootleggin'." He would take the soldiers to Nogallis, Naco, Alcapreata, Mexico and Douglas, Arizona. He would have a roll of money. I said, "Gee, man, you're loaded." He said, "Man, you fool. You have your Oldsmobile. You could be doing the same thing." He said that he collected the money at the end of each month. I had been busy practicing my clarinet because I didn't want to go overseas. That was my main objective, which I had accomplished. I now had free time. I was getting $21 a month. I would send part of my money to Mama and keep just enough for me to live on. I thought that was a good idea.

So man, I started hauling soldiers to Naco and Alcapreata. I went mainly to Naco because it was only an hour away. Nogallis was farther and in the opposite direction. I began hauling soldiers to Naco and Douglas and buying whiskey. I sold the whiskey for $10 a bottle. During the night the guys would want something to drink. I would let them put the whiskey on their tab, and I really began to make money. Because I was making more money, I was able to pay off my house on Forty-Seventh Place.

I was getting into the groove of bootleggin'. I was hustling like mad, getting accounts and hauling soldiers up and down the road. I would take them to see girls in Naco. These were "sporting girls" for the soldiers; they would go to have fun. I would go so much until I was given the nickname of "Papacita," meaning "old man." We were allowed a gallon of liquor a month to take from Mexico. It was cheaper than in Arizona. I would buy Water Fill Frazier, which was a cheap Mexican whiskey.

I was doing pretty good. I was making money taking soldiers here and there. I would never allow the soldiers to bring any tea from across the border. (In my day, marijuana was called tea.) I didn't want to take any chances getting my car impounded. I would let them bring the whiskey, but that was it. One day my bass and piano player was getting a furlough to go home to New York. He wanted to take some tea to New York, and he wanted me to take him across the border to get the tea. He offered me ten dollars. I told him I would take him over, but that he had to get the tea back some other way.

By transporting tea, I could lose my car and be put in the stockade. I drove him over and parked at a bar full of girls. We agreed to meet each other in two hours at the club. He was to stash the tea on the American side. He met me at the club. I asked if everything was under control, and he said, "Yes, I got it across the line." I drove to the gate. At the border the MPs asked me if I had anything, and I said no. It was dark as hell driving back to camp. All of a sudden while driving, I heard my passenger fumbling. I asked him what he was doing, and he said everything was all right. He brought out a five pound sack of tea he had hidden under my dashboard.

I was shocked and upset. I said, "What the hell is going on?" He said, "What do you mean?" I began to steam when he said, "Man, be cool." I said, "How can you tell someone to be cool in their own car?" I went on to say that if they'd found that stuff in my car, I would have gone to jail. I was very angry at him and wouldn't let him ride into camp with me. I put him outside the gate. He paid me and went on his way. The guard on camp asked if I had anything. I said, "No. I'm clean." The next morning the bass/piano player got the train to New York City. I was glad he made it, but not at my expense. He sold all of the tea. This just goes to show you how people will use you to their advantage. Had we gotten caught, I could have lost my car. Another guy was making a lot of money bringing tea across the border. I did not get involved in that.

They began to send a lot of men overseas, and I thought I might be sent one day. The men would come back from Italy saying that I would love the French and Italian chicks, but I had a lot of sense. I said the Mexican chicks look just like the Italian and French chicks. I was safe from fighting the war; I was doing fine at Fort Huachuca. The colonel said they were keeping me on base because I made them happy. I kept the camp lively. With so many soldiers gone, I had a field day going back and forth across the border.

Maceo was always talking about New York. When he invited Freddie and me, we decided to save our money to go in June. We caught the train to New York's Grand Central Station, and I was thrilled. There were so many people in the station, I couldn't believe my eyes. I was looking all around, turning my head from left to right. We took a cab to Harlem for One Hundred and Twenty-Fifth Street. Next we went to my Aunt Lula's on Lenox Avenue. We hadn't seen my aunt since she came to California while performing in *Porgy and Bess*. She had been to Europe and was renting a room from Mr. and Mrs. Bob Lowe. She told us about meeting two sharp, cute girls by the name of Jan and Sue. I said that we were going to go to Harlem on One Hundred and Twenty-Fifth to see what was going on.

We met Maceo, and we all walked around together. I couldn't believe the wide streets and all the people. The girls were beautiful; I was so excited that I could hardly get over them. The conversation came up that soldiers were getting mugged going up to apartments to see girls. That scared us, and we said, "Oh, Lord, no way." We only had a three-day furlough. We went back to the house, and our Aunt Lula took us to meet the girls, who had their own place on One Hundred and Forty-Eighth Street between Convent and Amsterdam. It was nice and clean. After being introduced, we talked for a while. When guys in the army met girls with their own place, it was like utopia.

We went out that night to Luckey's Rendezvous and then on to stomp at the Savoy, where they had a band that played many Billie Holiday songs like "Lover Man." We danced and had a good time. We moved on to Small's Paradise. They had a floor show. We were holding hands a lot, and I was beginning to like the girl I was with. I kind of felt she liked me, too. We stayed out late, painting the town and seeing everything we could. Sue didn't have to be at work until 3:00 in the afternoon, so the night was all ours. We stayed out until 5:00 A.M. We all said good night and went on our way. The next night, I went by her house after she got off at eleven. Things didn't start jumpin' until late, around eleven or twelve. We got kind of chummy this night. I told her that I had a ring on my hand that I had gotten in Arizona. It was turquoise, like a birthstone. She saw and admired it, and asked if she could see it. She wanted to wear it, so I put it on her finger.

The second day we went sightseeing and went to the top deck of the Fifth Avenue bus. We saw Greenwich Village, the Empire State Building and the Statue of Liberty. We took the subway back to her apartment. I said to myself, "Man, we can make out at their place." She gave me a peck on the cheek, and I was sent on my way. That was it. I was leaving the next day, so she came down to the train station. I always carried so much junk and was loaded down with suitcases. I thought we might catch a gig to make some extra money, but the girls took up all of our fun time. We were all in Grand Central Station. It was crowded. I said, "Oh, give me my ring." She asked if she could keep it. (I had never given a girl a ring — dresses and stockings maybe, but no ring. This was serious and special. That's probably why no girls were ever able to catch me around Los Angeles.) I said, "My ring? Does that mean that you like me? Do you want to be engaged?" She said, "Yes." That scared the hell out of me. I said, "Dang, wow!" I tried to get romantic by walking between two pillars. I said, "With this ring we will become engaged." I told her to write me every day for six months and I would return to marry her. That is exactly what happened.

On the way home on the train, I began to think to myself what I was going to tell the three or four girls I had been dating. There was a particular lady, a civilian who had her own house and car. She was a very successful woman; she had sponsored my way to New York. The other girls took it all right, but my main girl, Dimples, was very upset. She was a pistol packin' mama — I was glad she didn't shoot me. Sue's family had the same number of family members as Dimples: three sisters and one brother. However, Sue and Dimples had different personalities.

I had cleared the way for Sue, so now I had to make some extra money to bring her to Fort Huachuca. Since I was only making $21 a month, I began to rack my brain for money-making ideas. I got the idea of a shoe-shine stand. I went to Colonel Nelson and told him I'd like to put up a shoe stand next to the PX because I had gotten engaged. His concern was whether or not I would have time for my assigned duties. When I told him I would operate it between band rehearsals and all my other activities, he gave me the green light to proceed.

I found a carpenter to build a two-seater shoe-shine stand right next to the PX. It had a little awning over it. It was nice. I had Mama to go to the shoe-shine supply store and mail me the brushes, rags and polish. I had my sign made that read, "Daddy-O's Shoe-Shine Stand." I went to the members in the band asking who wanted to help shine shoes. I knew Freddie would help me, but I still needed more help. They said, "Man, I don't shine shoes. I'm a musician." They were above this type of work. I told them they should want to make some extra money since we only made $21 a month, but they weren't interested.

Eugene Jackson (front), proprietor of "Daddy-O's Shoe-Shine Stand" at Fort Huachuca, Arizona, during World War II.

    I opened with Freddie and myself. We had shoes from the soldiers, the Wacs, civilians on post, nurses and doctors. I shined shoes diligently. When the soldiers in the special service band would come up and want to borrow money, I would give them some polish and a rag. They had to make their money shining shoes just as I did. After that, I had plenty of help.

I would shine shoes in the latrine until all hours of the night. I would pick up shoes at the hospital and from the newer part of the camp. The civilians claimed their shoes hadn't looked that good since they first purchased them. There was a great deal of dirt and sand on post, so I worked at my stand every chance I got. I made enough money to pay Freddie and the guys and was able to put money in the bank. It was getting close to the time to pick up Sue.

I was making $20 to $30 a trip for hauling five or six people in the car to the Mexican border. The only problem was flat tires. Tires were hard to get; therefore, I kept three in the trunk. They weren't making an abundance of them. I also had to ration my gas stamps. Stamps were a dollar apiece. You were allowed so many stamps a month per car. Some guys had black market gas stamps and several guys had cars, which allowed us to haul and bootleg to make extra money.

Bill White, Allie Grant and myself were doing quite well financially. Bill was a trumpet player who enjoyed doing comic drawings on different band members. We called him "the vulture." He was married to a Mexican girl named Vickie. They had four children, and he had been in the army since 1941.

We sold our whiskey by the bottle. I went off base to buy some for a man. I was going to make about $15. Some of the old soldiers drank so much that they would drink up all of their money on the first of the month. They were dry immediately towards the middle of the month.

It was late at night, around 12 midnight. I put the whiskey between my pants and stomach. I had to walk up approximately 20 steps. All of a sudden the whiskey bottle went sliding through my pants. It hit the cement and broke. It sounded like a bomb. I stood there gazing at the loss of $15. When I got up to go to reveille, I saw all the old soldiers standing around where I had broken the bottle. They could smell the odor. They were standing in a huddle as if they were calling a play for a football game. They all had sober expressions on their faces as if at a funeral. I walked past as if I knew nothing. No one knew I was the one who broke it except the guy that I went to purchase it for.

Time was getting closer to go get Sue. I worked frantically at putting money in the bank. Before I left camp, I withdrew all of my money from the bank to get married. I got $1,000 worth of traveler's checks. When I took my money from the bank, I realized that my shoe-shine idea was a gold-mine business because no one was shining shoes. Even after I brought Sue on base, I continued my business. I purchased a round-trip ticket. I sat in the passenger car when going to get Sue. I recalled the old saying of "marrying a pig in a bag," meaning I didn't know if she was a man or a woman. We didn't have an affair. That idea played around in my head for a while, but I knew I was marrying a nice, clean lady.

I reserved a sleeping car berth for return. It took three days to get there. I didn't drink anything either on the train or in the station looking for Sue. There were so many people coming into the train station. Then it dawned on me that I had forgotten what she looked like. I was just a-walkin' and a-walkin' and a-lookin' when I saw a girl standing straight in front of me. A lot of people were all around her, moving here and there. I said, "Sue, is that you?" She said, "Gene?" I said, "Yeah," and we ran to each other. We kissed and hugged. I inquired about everyone, and she informed me that they were at the apartment.

We were supposed to get married on a Sunday. My plans were to get there on Saturday so we could go out and have fun Saturday night. I wanted to hanky panky around, but to my surprise Sue had her own organized agenda. That worked. I was tricked. Women are always two steps ahead of the men. I got my bags. I was trying to flag down a cab. She told me that we did not need a cab. We were going across the street to be married. I got nervous and I began to stutter and sweat. I looked at her in amazement. I was shocked. I began to ask questions. My speech and sentence structure were full of hesitations and stammering.

She calmly took my arm and walked with me across the street to fill out the papers at the courthouse. I followed her like a dumbbell. I was shaking so much I could hardly write my name. We got married. Everyone at the court-house was nice and smiling; they were the witnesses. I didn't have the ring — it was in my suitcase. I was so excited about getting married that I walked into a closet instead of the main door when we tried to leave.

We took a cab to her place at 461 West One Hundred and Forty-Eighth Street. Everyone was there at her apartment. I did not know they were all coming. Her mother and father came from North Carolina. The Smith family were friends of mine that I had met in Lexington, Kentucky, when I was filming *Sporting Blood*. They had kept in touch with me over the years, and had moved to New York. They operated a photography studio on One Hundred and Twenty-Fifth Street.

We had a nice small reception with family and friends. The entire family came down to the station to see us off, and we got on the train for the army base. Everyone on the train knew we were newlyweds by the way we were acting, and they were smiling at us. That night they came to fix our lower berth. I had on my best pajamas and robe, and Sue had on a pretty gown and robe. She was real nervous and scared of being with a strange man. In the middle of the night, while still asleep, she got up and started to walk off the train. I believe she was sleep-walking. The next day when we woke up everybody else was already up. I got up, looked out and saw people smiling at us. I went and washed up.

We stopped in Chicago to see Sam Lancaster, a friend of mine; and Sue's uncles, Abe Lowe and Judge Duke Slater. It was freezing. We had to take the train to my friend's place. My smile froze on my face. We had to walk many blocks to his place, and we stayed there to warm up. The next day we went on the elevated train to visit Sue's uncles. Judge Slater was a former famous foot-ball athlete and lawyer.

Wedding celebration, New York, 1945. *LEFT TO RIGHT:* Eugene's grandfather; Sue; Eugene; Sue's mother, Mrs. Watt; and the Smiths, Eugene's friends he had met while filming *Sporting Blood* (1931).

We finally headed for Fort Huachuca in December of 1945. When we arrived in Fry, Arizona, we took the bus to the camp. Sue hadn't seen the desert before. The open space and the tumbling tumbleweed caught her attention. We went to our living quarters. I had talked to a lady before I left about us staying with them. Sergeant Roy Black, a career army man, and his wife, Thelma, had a comfortable three-bedroom house and wanted some company because they had no children. The next morning I took Sue to the barracks and band room. Everyone wanted to meet her.

Sue was sweet and innocent, while Thelma was flirty. I didn't want Thelma's ways influencing Sue in any manner. I would come home in between duties as much as possible. I was in love, and I wanted to check on the home front. Being so excited about marriage made me leave home for reveille at 6:00 A.M., then shoot back to the house. I was discharged in April of 1946. Sue lived with me on base for five months. When I first arrived, I had only one suitcase. By the time I left camp, I had accumulated so much junk that we couldn't see out the back window. We hit the road from Fort Huachuca to Tucson to California.

We hit Central Avenue en route to my home on Forty-Seventh Place. I showed Sue where I had performed at the Rosebud Theater, the Gaiety, the

Lincoln Theater, the Florence Mills, the Tivoli, and the Dunbar Hotel. Freddie and Mama welcomed us. Mama had a big dinner ready when we arrived. The neighbors came to welcome us, and Mama had a reception for us once we were settled. My pastor, Reverend Rakeshaw, was present at my reception. We went to church as a family the first week home. I then took time to inform the studios and casting agents that I was back for work.

12
The Jackson Trio

Vaudeville work was slow in the city and surrounding areas. I told Freddie that we should form a trio. I found an experienced piano player by the name of Virgil Johnson, and we practiced and practiced. We were getting $21 a week for jobs, which always allowed me to obtain the cream-of-the-crop piano players. We had played the clubs; restaurants; joints; social events, like my mother's teas for her organizations; the Elks, the Masons, the Shriners; and private parties. We also played classical music, which made us popular. We were the only group performing in this style. We were unique and we knew all the old songs that were requested a lot.

In the early days of our career, we were performing at a restaurant in San Fernando. We were being paid three dollars a night and food. That job was all right until we found a roach in our spaghetti. We quit that gig! We laughed all the way home. It's memories like these that I shall never forget. When I think of them my heart is warmed.

We were getting jobs like mad. We were very versatile, practicing daily with different varieties of records and trying to master and perfect everything. Some jobs didn't pay very much a night. When gigs came in paying "good bucks," we could get any good musicians to back us up. We performed in a variety of locations. The public knew when our group was performing that they would receive their money's worth from a show full of music, dance acts, skits, laughter and gaiety. The group gained a reputation of merriment, elegance and finery.

The foundation of any musical group is a piano player who can swing freely. I learned this early in show business. Whenever I started any ensemble, my search was for someone who could make the keys sing, burn and float. The piano man was always the nucleus. During my vaudeville and trio days, I used different piano players. Without these very talented men, my group would not have been successful.

It is an honor to mention Rozell Gayle, one of the greatest piano players from Chicago. He had a lot of good musical and comedy records. Lady Will Car was a genius on the piano, though she didn't play that much with me. Monroe Tucker played with me before I went to the army. I had John Shackel-

Marquee players: The Jackson Trio.

ford, Evelyn Burrell, Kittie Martel, Nevill Godfrey, Lorenzo Flenory, Lee Wesley, Eric Henry from New York, Ashly Sails, Joe Small, Charlie Martin, Jessie Gipson and Coney Woodman. Coney came from a musical family. His father began teaching him and his brothers musical instruments when Coney was five. Coney was a jovial, pleasant type of guy who never got angry. Frank White played with me for five years. Willie McDaniel was a terrific 200-pound piano player.

Virgil Johnson was a music student from the University of Southern California. We had known his family for years. He played opera: *The Fire Dance, Flight of the Bumblebee,* and *Warsaw Concerto.* He could play the boogie woogie out of this world. Virgil also had a good singing voice. Herb Gordy played the piano and bass. I also had a man named Dozier Williams, whom I met on the road. He filled in for me when I didn't have a player.

I had a piano player by the name of Jerome Parson, but I gave him the stage name of Tyrone Parson. The name Tyrone was popular because of Tyrone Power, who was a big movie star at that time. (You didn't have too many colored people named Tyrone.) We found Tyrone working at Vina's Café, washing dishes on Western Avenue as a young kitchen boy. We took him out of the kitchen and trained him.

I had Tyrone practice the piano while standing up. That was a feature in our group: There were no other piano players standing up and playing. They were doing this back East, but not on the West Coast. Tyrone had a good voice like King Cole, and people liked him. He traveled with us back East. When we got to San Francisco, he met a girl. He fell in love and left the trio to get married. I haven't seen him since.

There were so many, but I've tried to remember all of my piano players to give them their proper respect in my book.

I was still working in the movies. While on the studio sets, I would mention that I had a group available for parties. Word of mouth brought us a great deal of work, which is how I got to play at Alan Ladd's birthday party. I was working with Alan on Paramount's *Iron Mistress*. It was the story of Jim Bowie, and I played the role of a servant. While on set, I just happened

TOP: The Jackson Trio, "a show full of music, dance acts, skits, laughter and gaiety. *BOTTOM:* The boys get ready for a gig.

Eugene Jackson (right) and brother Freddie, the dynamic duo behind the Jackson Trio.

to mention to Alan that I had a trio. I always carried my ukulele, and during break on set to pass idle time I would play and sing. This was how we started talking about my trio.

I mentioned to Alan that I had worked with his wife, Sue Carol, in the 1929 *Fox Movietone Follies*. I told him anytime he had a party to be sure and call me. It just so happened that I received a call from Sue Carol asking me to play for a surprise birthday party for Alan in Bel Air. The homes in that area were beautiful. We arrived to see fabulous mansions, and she showed us where to set up. Charlie Martin was my piano man.

There were wall-to-wall stars. We started off playing soft cocktail music. The cocktails began to season the blood, and the tempo of the music began to move with the flow of the atmosphere. We began to play songs for them to do the Bunny Hop, Ballin' the Jack and the Hokie Pokie. They all joined in for the conga, a popular dance at the time. It is funny how music can erase a color line. All those stars were just plain people, and we were all having a good time. Dick Powell asked if he could blow my sax. You know I said yes. Boy, did we have a jam session. A lot of stars sang with us.

During intermission, we started a conversation with the bartender, Pee Wee. We mentioned that we were on our way to Minneapolis to play at Augies

Eugene Jackson (far right) plays a servant and right-hand man to Alan Ladd in *Iron Mistress* (1952).

Night Club on Fifth and Hennepin. Pee Wee said he was a waiter and bartender on the train and was on his way to Chicago. When the party was over, we all sat around the pool and talked about the olden days. Alan said he was raised on the east side of Los Angeles where he went to Stanton School, a school for wayward boys. I said, "You came a long way from those days," and told him my wife's name was also Sue. Alan's wife, Sue Carol, gave us a lot of food to take home.

The next week after Alan Ladd's party we boarded the same train that Pee Wee worked on. He stopped by on his way to the diner and said, "I'll take care of you when the first meal is over." We were leaving Las Vegas when he came for Freddie and me to dine. He asked if I had my horn and I said, "Yes indeed." I also told him I had our new record releases, "Love for Christmas" and "Jingle Bell Hop." I set up my horn on a table.

Freddie had some papers on the table. With the papers and wire brushes from his drum set, he kept the beat and rhythm. Talk about creativity, we had it. Now who in this day and age would have thought of taking paper and turning it into parts of a drum? Pee Wee went through the cars yelling, "Jam session in progress in the diner!" The passengers started coming in. I was blowing my alto sax like mad, and the train was rocking at 90 miles an hour. Pee

Wee was selling drinks like they were going out of style. Freddie and I were selling our new records and making some tips. The crowd was a-hoppin' and a-jumpin'. We jammed all the way to Salt Lake City. The people said they had been to Hawaii and China, but had never had so much fun as they had with us. We said good-bye to the people and Pee Wee. We weren't able to continue this action to Minneapolis because we didn't know the waiter!

We were a big success at Augies Night Club in Minneapolis. Believe it or not, Augies is still open. Ah, if only the walls of Augies could talk. They could tell you of all the fun inside those four walls. I can't tell you all the stories that occurred in Augies; I can tell only mine. Our experiences are fresh in my memory bank as if we were setting up our group in Augies to play this very moment.

Top musical groups kept the street of Hennepin jumpin' at all times. The sounds coming from the cracks, windows and doors would ooze and ease its way out into the bodies of pedestrians walking down the street who were trying to decide which place to enter. Big Jay McNeely, the honking tenor sax from Los Angeles, was playing across the street. He was a friend of mine. We would all meet up after hours at an eating joint in the area to relax and shoot the breeze.

We went back to California to become the first colored trio at the Pioneer Room in El Monte, California. The clientele were mostly working-class people. The owner, Mr. Rogers, was from Oklahoma City. He was concerned because he had never had a colored group. I said that wherever we played the white people liked us. Sure enough, we were a big hit. Joe Small was my piano man. We heard a couple of "little nigger words," but we ignored them. We went over well. We had white girl singers in the vicinity to come up and sing with us.

The American Legions weren't far away. They had all the Western singers, Tennessee Ernie Ford and others. He would come over and catch our act after they were through. Six doors down, the club owner brought in Rozell Gayle at the piano bar.

We broke the ice in El Monte and played there for a long time. We left and went to Johnny's Café in Whittier, California, where we were a big splash. We stayed there six months and put on a dancing floor show. From there we were booked at an exclusive club in El Monte at a club called the Desert Inn. They had a sophisticated crowd.

The people in El Monte had never seen black people before — we were a novelty. They would look and stare, but they were always inviting us out to their homes. I still hear from them. That's been over 40 years or more. This just goes to show you that once people get to know you as a person, then color doesn't mean a thing. El Monte was where conservative white southerners had settled.

From the Desert Inn, we went to the Topper Club on Whittier and Lakewood

Publicity still for the Jackson Trio.

in Norwalk. From there it was on to the Cartwheel, also in Norwalk. We had a following, we had a mailing list, and we had standing room only. It was a big club with plenty of food. I was surprised to see the Mexican cook, Frank Gill, and his wife, who were close friends of mine. It was like a family reunion. We are still friends today. Lau, the owner, had just gotten out of the navy.

Lau didn't know much about the nightclub business, so we helped him since we had the know and the how of running a club. He left and went on vacation for six weeks and left us in charge. (People will trust you regardless of color if you demonstrate good character.) We packed that club.

When Lau returned, we had increased his revenue considerably. He was surprised, delighted and pleased. He brought in Lincoln Perry, better known as Stepin Fetchit, for two weeks. I made Stepin Fetchit remember me from when I starred with him as a child in *Hearts in Dixie*. He was elated to see me and was glad to see that I was doing well with my trio. He did his stand-up comedy act. The public may not be aware of the fact that Stepin Fetchit was highly educated and religious. He had a degree and was a Catholic. He was very smart. He knew what the white folks liked and wanted and he always capitalized on it, which made him a lot of money.

Lau began to change. He had become arrogant and didn't want to give us a raise, so we left to play at the Dragon Den in Bellflower. The owner was Johnny Woo, and they served both Chinese and American food. We would put on a floor show and they had different guest stars — sometimes Fayard Nicholas would come out and perform. Nevill Godrey was my piano player. His wife had seen me playing some place and told me her husband played the piano. He was a concert pianist and an outstanding musician. He went with us to Cherry's Can Can, then to Cock of the North, and then to a club in Signal Hill. He stayed with me for three years. He also played with us at the Club Seville in Huntington Park. After his wife passed, he remarried and soon left the group.

We played clubs many times because of our popularity. Sometimes it would be different piano players, but the crowd wouldn't know the difference because I made sure our piano players could play anything. We played a floor show in Tony's Tavern at 1105 West Pico in Los Angeles, with Ashly Sails on piano. We were in demand everywhere. We were then booked, now with Virgil Johnson, at the Florentine Gardens in the Zanzibar Room at 5955 Hollywood.

The Florentine Gardens was a big spot on Hollywood Boulevard where all the stars played, people like Pinky Lee, Sofie Tucker and Ted Lewis. Pinky Lee was a comedian and Sofie Tucker, the last of the red hot mamas, was a singer. Ted Lewis became famous by saying, "Is everybody happy?" We were there with Sofie Tucker.

I will never forget the owner of the Florentine Gardens. His name was Mr. Bruno, a well-dressed, short, Italian man around 30, with a pleasing personality. He wore his hair in a thick pompadour, and both his gait and speech were rapid. His speech was full of idioms from the Italian culture, and he had a thick accent. His hands and body were always full of movement and helped him communicate.

I guess the Florentine Gardens had a lot of bad business. It pays to pay your bills. Mr. Bruno bought this club by being a supplier of linen to the Florentine Gardens. The bill got so high that the owner wasn't able to pay. That must have been a hell of a bill. Therefore, Mr. Bruno became the new owner. Before he could get himself straight, Sofie Tucker came in selling her life story

The Jackson Trio plays the Florentine Gardens: (*LEFT TO RIGHT*) Virgil Johnson on piano, Eugene Jackson on Saxophone, and Freddie Baker on drums.

in her act, which bankrupted the place. People would spend their money to come in, and she would sell her book for $50 or $100. This drained the club and killed the business. She was about on her last leg and she was there long enough to close the club.

Another hot spot that we played was the Tailspin Hollywood on Cahuenga. We did the Elks' Christmas, Golden West, Lodge Number 86 and Number 91 for charity dances. We played at Johnny's Café in Whittier, and Virgil played with us at the Boulevard Stop along with the Mosette Dancers. The building still stands, but it isn't famous like it used to be. When a group performed at the Boulevard Stop, it meant they had a first-class act. Only the best played there.

We played the Boulevard Stop with Tyrone the second time around. We did our jubilee singing and floor show. Our act consisted of jubilee, and black-outs containing skits and the trio. (Blackout was a short comedy skit with the lights being darkened after the punch line.) We sang a cappella songs like "Dry Bones" and "Little Liza I Love You." We also had the Mosette Dancers, which consisted of three beautiful, high-society girls: Juanita Moore, Lucy Battle and Myrtle Fortune. They were three ex–chorus girls who would open up with their number of dancing and singing. Then Freddie would come out and sing.

Next would come the blackout burlesque acting skits. In these skits, Juanita Moore was more involved with her acting than the other girls. She would put more into her work because she always wanted to be an actress. This was the beginning of her career. She, Freddie and I would do a skit, the scene from Shakespeare's *Antony and Cleopatra* with the snake and the dagger. We had a lot of fun doing this. All this was done in a little nightclub and inspired Juanita to go into acting. Juanita Moore is remembered for her role as the maid in *Imitation of Life*; she was nominated for an Academy Award.

We left there taking the entire show to the Dixie Castle in Santa Ana. We were there for six months. It was a family club, and the owners were Joe Dombroski and Jack Bell, along with Jack's mother, father, brothers, and two sisters, Viv and Dorothy. Viv was married to Joe. Our show was something different for that area. It was a nice, big club. We had a lot of fun. We put on our floor show and our blackout bits with Freddie, Juanita and myself. We changed every week.

When a song came out called "Mule Train," by Frankie Laine, I got an idea. I made up a "Mule Train" skit, pretending I had a mule to go with the song as we played it. I told Joe to get me a mule, and one night when we came to work Joe told me he had found a donkey for me. I said, "You are kidding." I began training that old donkey by talking in his ear. When I talked in his ears, they would shoot up. I would jump on his back, and he would stand there. I was lookin' for him to buck, but he never did.

We practiced and practiced, with Freddie pullin' him out on the dance floor. We had to rehearse so that old mule knew what to do. He would come on the floor and stand while I would go through the whole bit of singing "Mule Train." After the song was over, I would take off. The whole act had gotten so popular that people would come from miles around to see the show with this gentle old mule.

The old mule knew the act so well that all I would have to do was talk in his ear. He would walk out on his own and wait for me to get on and perform. It was fantastic. This went on for a couple of months — we did our routine one night. The mule had it down pat in his mind. One night we did our routine as usual. We had completed the act when all of a sudden some people arrived from San Diego. They had driven in especially for the "Mule Train" skit, but they missed it. I said, "Oh, okay," and went back and got the animal. I said to the mule, "Look mule, we got to do it again," but he didn't want to go out. He was trained to do it once a night. In his mind, he was through acting for the night. He was a stubborn, one-shot actor.

I asked Freddie to pull him out in the middle of the floor, and the music started. I started to sing "Mule Train," making the sound "clickity clack, clickity clack," to try and make him go. He just stood there. I didn't know the sucker was mad. I said "Mule Train!" with excitement and vigor in my voice. All of a sudden his back legs went apart, and he poo-poohed on the floor. The audience erupted in laughter. For months we had been lookin' for him to do this, but he hadn't.

The bosses, Jack and Joe, came running up with mops. That was the mule's way of saying, "I told you I've done my act already. I'm through." That was funny. He was actin' just like his true name: a jackass. He had come from a field in Santa Ana, which was underdeveloped. This was one time I didn't use my brain. I should have bought that old mule from Joe — he probably would have given me the mule. It may not have worked, though, because I lived in the city on Forty-Eighth Street. I had no place to keep him.

Blacks were allowed to come and sit and enjoy the show because Joe and Jack were good people. Some of our guests would come and get special seating close to us, like Mr. and Mrs. Benjamin, who were the cleaners on Central. Mrs. Fannie Benjamin was the organist and singer of a large church in Los Angeles. Mr. Fisher, who was Jewish, owned the pharmacy on Fifty-Fourth and Central. They would all come out. I introduced Mr. Fisher to Lil Cumber, who is now a famous black talent agent. (They ended up getting married.) All nationalities were welcomed at the Dixie Castle.

Another incident at this club involved my piano player, Lee Wesley, who had a jealous girlfriend. One night we were getting ready to go to work. I was driving my car, and Lee was going to ride with me. I looked at the time, saw it was late, and decided to go. I went to my car and to my surprise, I saw Lee running down the street telling me to start the car. I looked behind him and there was some chick chasing him. He jumped on the hood and I began to drive. He held on to the hood until I got to the corner where I stopped. He jumped in the car huffing and puffing, saying that woman was crazy. I told him he should get rid of her.

We got to work and were playing some groovy music when this woman burst into the club with a knife in her hand. She had driven 35 miles to Santa Ana. Lee saw her coming and immediately got up and jumped off the bandstand. He began to run, and she chased him around the club. It was terrible. Security had to be called. I had to let Lee go because he couldn't control his personal life. (A word of advice to upcoming young stars: Don't let anything interfere with your road to success. Make sure you have complete control of your life in a positive manner. My friend didn't have control of his life, which hindered his career.) Joe did very well financially with that club. In his office he would have stacks of money.

At night the fog was thick driving home. It was hazardous and nerve-racking. We left our friends and were booked at Tony's again. Tony was an Italian with a warm heart and a good sense of humor. He was around 5'8" and approximately 30 years old. He spoke with a heavy Italian accent. His hair was thinning in front and was on the sides of his ears. When he smiled, his mustache would move up and down. At this time I had a piano player by the name of Ashly Sails, a big old kid who was always falling asleep at the piano while playing. Tony decided to play a joke on him. He took some paper and balled it up and put it in a pot. He struck a match to it and put the pot under Ashly's seat while he was sleeping. Ashly woke up jumping and screaming, "What the hell?" He didn't sleep any more after that! We all laughed. We then played at the Taddle House. It was not a big club, but all the top trios and quartets played there.

Our next gig was in Laguna Beach at the Broiler Room, right on the pike. The owner of the Broiler Room ended up giving us a little apartment as a place to stay overnight. There weren't many Negroes in Laguna Beach; they were only servants. Virgil was now my piano man, but he had a drinking problem. I remember one night he got drunk. (It was embarrassing because musicians are viewed as always being involved with drinking or smoking marijuana.) When Virgil would drink, he couldn't hold his liquor. He was like a wild man. The drive coming into Los Angeles was especially hard with a drunk. I had to hit and knock him in the seat to control him, but the next day he would be like a lamb. He continued to get drunk. We played there all summer, then I let him go. I got tired of his actions. My next piano player was Eric Henry from New York. We did a good one-night gig in which we were flown first class to Sacramento to play at a private social event. During this time, I was making the movie *Scudda Hoo! Scudda Hay!* (1948).

Upon completion of this movie, I began working the CHI CHI circuit. We made an appointment for an interview with Mr. Shuman. The circuit, which was very hard to get into, consisted of Hollywood, Long Beach, Riverside, San Diego and Palm Springs. I knew Mr. Shuman was a millionaire, a very classy dresser who always wore white pants with a blue serge jacket. He was a Jewish man with a pleasant personality. He was honest and strictly business. He was a big wheel. I was determined to do things right, and I wanted everybody perfect. We had our audition at the CHI CHI in Hollywood. Mr. Shuman saw our act and said he wanted to sign us, so we were hired. I was elated to get this job. My piano player was Willie McDaniel. The contract read, "Play forty-five minutes with a fifteen-minute break." Willie said he had to have 20 minutes. I said, "Willie, I don't want to mess up this gig. I'm sorry, I will have to get someone else."

When we opened in Long Beach with Evelyn Burrell (who could play the piano, but not like Willie), Mr. Shuman had a fit. I didn't know that he liked Willie, who could play and looked good while he did it. Mr. Shuman hadn't seen us since he picked us, and when he looked up and didn't see "that big, fat, black man" playing he hit the roof. He asked, "Where is he?" I said, "Oh God Mr. Shuman, he didn't want to go with the intermission bit. I knew you were pretty strict." He said, "Okay," so we left there and went to San Diego.

Evelyn was always bitchin' about this and that, and Shuman heard her talking about people. We played one more club, then he walked up on her while she was bitchin'. Without batting an eye, he did not renew our contract for the next circuit. I should have gotten rid of her as soon as I found out that she was not flexible. This taught me the old cliche of "the slip of the lip can

Eugene Jackson, song and dance man, gets caught in the act.

sink a ship," which is exactly what happened. Mr. Shuman had so many clubs that he was hard to catch. I tried to find him to tell him that I would ditch her, but he was uncatchable. I should have kept Willie. Shuman would have gone along with Willie taking a 20-minute break because he liked Willie.

We began working at the Miami Lounge to great reviews. We went on to play in West Covina at a club called the Next Time. The owner of the club was a lady by the name of Lynn. She was a skating waitress at the Dragon Den who had saved her money and got a good deal on the club. She did so well that she bought the place next door and knocked a whole wall down to make the club bigger. She knew our music, so she hired us. We packed the place and were doing real great. A lot of fans who knew us from El Monte came to see us.

All of a sudden, things got a little slow because western music was coming on the scene, and the people in that area liked it. Country-western started getting into clubs in that area. Business fell off. We dropped from five nights to three nights, and then began cutting the band down. I started doing a one-man show, while Freddie and the piano player went out on their own. We all had to survive. Lynn brought in a western group, and I was incorporated into their act. I would open up with a dance routine and then play the sax. I stayed there until she went strictly western. She finally sold the place and totally retired from the business. She liked me as a personal friend, and we still keep in contact with each other. I call her once in a while to check on her.

I can remember all of my fights during my show business life, though I never had many because I was a likeable guy. I had a strong belief that people, friends and other minorities should be able to see us perform. I was always standing up for my people's right to enter clubs and see us entertain. We always had strong, loyal fans and friends who followed us wherever we went. Color meant nothing to me. One time we were playing at the Bridle Club, which was located at 115 East Valley Boulevard in San Gabriel, California. They hadn't had many colored entertainers. The manager came to see me and said there was a friend of mine who wanted to see me at the door. I went to see, and to my delight and surprise it was a Mexican friend of mine who had driven from El Monte just to see me. But the manager said he couldn't come in. The place was packed and was jumping, and he and I got into a fight. That 200-pounder from Texas hauled off and hit me. He knocked me out and made me see stars. After that, I decided to stop fighting when they wouldn't let blacks and Mexicans in. I was just plain tired, and I decided that it was the owner's establishment.

We had played every place, so I suggested we go on the road. We traveled from 1946 to 1953, playing some places twice. We were booked all over the United States and we met a lot of lovely people of different nationalities, from all walks of life, who have continued to visit and keep in touch over the years. We used different piano players throughout my tour, which began at Frank Oliver's Melody Club in San Jose. There was a jazz club at the Melody where all the top entertainers played. We were booked with Tyrone as my piano player. Mainly college kids would come in to this jumpin' club. We went over great. My wife Sue and son Little Gene were now traveling with us. When we began our tour, we only had one child. As time went on, we had another child. They would sometimes travel with us. When Sue and the children became tired, they would return home or visit her parents.

We were playing in a hotel in San Jose. Sue had put Little Gene to bed so we could go out dancing. He was about three years old. We were getting in the car, when down the stairs came Gene in his pajamas. He was on his way out the door behind us. Tyrone just happened to be sitting in the lobby. He spotted Gene coming down the stairs, picked him up, and followed us to the car. Tyrone was shouting and pointing, and had a smile on his face. That scared and shocked us, and quickly ended our night on the town.

From there we went to San Francisco, where we had an old army friend. We rented from him and played at the Say When Club. When we arrived, Slim Gaillard was performing. He was famous for a song called "Cement Mixer," a song that was popular because it had crazy lyrics of "cement mixer, pu-ti, pu-ti, put-ti, o'vooty." It was something different, which made it such a hit that people could barely move around in the club. The atmosphere in San Francisco was like New York.

We left the Say When and went to the House of Blue Lights, which was in the international settlement in San Francisco. After playing at the Irish Club, we played San Francisco and twice in Las Vegas. Eric Henry had replaced Virgil on piano. Eric was cool, a nontalker. He didn't have much personality, but when he played he looked good.

One night in Vegas, on our night off, we decided to go out on the town and play the slot machines. We were living in the colored section on the north side. Sue and I picked up Eric to go with us. He didn't have any spending money, and we dropped him off at a club. We stopped back by the club and saw that he was winning. Elated for him because he had been broke, we told him to give us some of the money so we could stash it for him. He had silver dollars stacked high, but he said no. When we came back by, he had lost every penny. He needed that money because he didn't even have enough to get his clothes cleaned. He was totally broke. We were so disgusted with him.

Eric completed our act in Vegas with us at the club, but then I ditched him and got Charlie Martin. I had to let Eric go because he was a leaner, an irresponsible, immature person. I could not be bothered with that type of individual. Charlie and I grew up together. He was a talented musician. He had studied music at Jordan High School. I, on the other hand, had a gift from God of being able to play by ear. Freddie, my brother, had the gift of playing drums, singing and dancing.

When we went to Medford, Oregon, we played at the Medford Club. It was a big club. They hadn't seen or heard a trio like the Jackson Trio. We had our good name and a reputation for music and an outstanding floor show. We were the first colored trio that had ever played there. The Bowler Club in Walla Walla, Washington, was our next stop. We broke all their records by being the first Negro trio, and we were treated grand by all. We then went back to Vegas.

The manager of a club from Lewiston, Idaho, was driving down the strip with some friends in Las Vegas. We had played at his club before, and he saw "the Jackson Trio" in bold print on the marquee. They made a U-turn in the street and ran in to catch our show. Afterwards, we greeted each other, and decided to do into the bar for a drink. The bartender said he could serve our white friends, but not us. We all said, "What do you mean, you can't serve us?" He said, "You heard what I said, didn't you?" I said, "I heard you," but before I could say more, our friend the manager asked, "What do you mean?" They just got finished working for me in Idaho. Why can't you give them a drink?" The bartender answered, "I just can't serve them." The manager said, "These are my friends." Freddie shot back, "If you don't serve us, I'm going to come behind that bar and beat your ass." Freddie didn't take any mess from anyone. We almost got into a big fight. This was very embarrassing because we had just left the club in Idaho where we were welcomed all over. It was very

Eugene in the middle of a swinging, midair saxophone riff.

difficult to return to the stage and perform with smiles after an incident like this. We were working under a serious strain.

The next night we were getting ready to perform. The manager, who was an Italian entertainer and comedian from San Francisco, came in with a pretentious smile, shuffling his feet and pretending to be tapping. We all knew where he was coming from before he even opened his mouth. We could read his mind before he spoke. We all looked at each other with suspicion and calmly waited for his speech. He began with "I heard you had a misunderstanding at the bar" and a fake chuckle in his voice. I looked him straight in the eyes with no laughter and said, "Yeah, we had some friends come down. They wanted to buy us a drink." My tone was solid and firm, my body poised in a serious manner. I said, "That sucker wouldn't even serve us. We weren't sitting at a damn table." He answered, "Oh well, you know how it is." He tapped a shuffle and tried to mellow the mood, but the gravity of the problem was not to be dealt with in a light way.

I had experienced this problem throughout show business, just as many other colored stars had. Whenever incidents like this occurred, I met them head on. It was not an issue to be played around with. These types of incidents seemed to say, "You are not my equal," and every colored person hated them. This has been our fight all of our lives — it could not be swept under the rug. I said, "Oh come on." He said, "Look, we've got chorus girls. Let them go and get your drinks." He called himself smoothing the surface. He shuffled on out, and we all looked at each other. This also happened to Nat King Cole at the El Rancho. That same night, Sammy Davis, Jr., was performing at another club and had a similar experience. Rumor of this incident hit the boulevard quickly.

Bill "Bojangles" Robinson had the same problem when he was appearing at the Flamingo. They wanted him to stay with a colored person who rented rooms. He put up a fuss and said no way, so they decided to let him stay in the cottage behind the hotel. (Bill had changed tremendously since the last time I had seen him. He was friendlier and had remarried a lady by the name of Elaine. He had become religious and mellow. He was easier to talk to.) No colored entertainer was spared this degradation.

This is why it is so important to remember your roots and to have love in your heart for all. One should never believe that, just because he has become a successful person, he has no ties to other blacks who are not as financially stable. Your color dictates this bond. It will always associate you with your African heritage. Try to help our African American people in whatever manner you can, no matter how small the gesture may be. Love all mankind and try to find similarities and positive distinctions to learn and grow. Never hate anyone. Always look at each individual and situation separately. Hatred destroys, but love builds strong foundations for the reality of dreams. If one looks at a people's history, especially the African American history, success can be seen against all odds for it is the individual that counts. That one person is the one who can make a difference. It is good if a group of people are on the same wavelength, but it is not necessary. It is distinguishing, inevitable difference in a person that will form a strong, peaceful tomorrow.

In the past, it was rough for blacks. The ability to go as one pleases was not available to us. Segregation was a known practice throughout the United States, and Las Vegas was no exception. A perfect example is a club in Vegas that was built especially for blacks on the north side called the Moulin Rouge. Things were going great at the Moulin Rouge. Even the whites visited the club. When the establishment saw this, the strip was opened to blacks. They did not want to lose any money on the strip, so they decided that everybody's money was green. This is a commonality that should have been used throughout all areas, but it was not.

When I was performing at the Kit Carson, Bill "Bojangles" Robinson came in and sat right up front to catch our show. After the show, we went to dinner. I told him I had my wife and son with me. He invited us to his cottage the next morning for breakfast. Bill was crazy about little Gene and took him into the Flamingo. People tried to give Gene money, but he wouldn't accept it. We all laughed and teased Gene. When we returned to Los Angeles, we invited Elaine and Bill to our home. They came in a large limo.

We were scheduled for back East. Al Devaron, our agent, booked us from Chicago to Lorraine, Ohio. We played at a club and bar with complimentary food. We went over great making friends. People would have us over for dinner. Freddie and his wife, Marsha, were staying in a hotel, but I was trying to save money. Sobel, a friend of mine, owned the jewelry store downstairs next to the club. He had apartments upstairs and a room that was the width and length of the building. It was dark and open, with no dividers for rooms. I told him I needed a place to stay and he gave me the room free of charge, with a cot and some blankets.

After the show, lovely people would converse with us and ask where we were staying. Freddie would openly state his residence. I would calmly and randomly point in an undetermined direction saying, "Oh, over there." They would always be so interested in my background that my lodging would never become the focus of the conversation. Because I was a big-shot Hollywood personality, I knew that people expected me to stay at a hotel. In the eyes of my public, my lodging would be unfitting for me. But from my view, a buck saved was a buck earned. I had to chuckle and laugh to myself because being a star is a state of mind. (We are all stars. If mankind would treat each other kindly and with respect, the world would be a more pleasant place. Everyone should be placed on a pedestal. We are all flesh; no one is better than another. We are all equal.)

We returned to Los Angeles to meet Joe Irwin, a fast-talking Irish record promoter. Joe was around 32 or 33 years old with a receding hairline. He was tall and slender, smoked cigarettes and had a handlebar mustache. He persuaded us to go with him to Midway, Utah. To get there, we had to go up in the mountains on a winding road two miles up. Joe was one of those high-speed drivers who looked at you while driving the curves. He scared us so that we would say, "Don't talk, just drive."

We were relieved to reach our destination, and each person was letting out sighs of relief upon arrival. Joe, on the other hand, not knowing he had scared us to death, was relaxed and jovial. He was whistling and calmly walking around. We were acting as if we had just gotten off a roller coaster, and that was exactly how we felt. The things we went through were unbelievable, but that was show biz. We played a Midway Booster Club for the Harvest Ball and got good reviews from our performances at the Scera Theater. He took us down to Provost, then to Mid City.

We went back to California, but I decided to drive. Upon arrival, we immediately and happily parted with Joe. We hooked up with Charlie Martin, the piano player. We had been asked to return to Lorraine, Ohio. Charlie began the drive from Los Angeles to Ohio by bragging of his judo and karate skills he acquired during his military days. He was proud to inform us that he left with the rank of sergeant in the army. Ben Hart, an ex–car salesman and Italian hustler with involvement in the rackets, booked us in a club on the east side of Cleveland on our night off to make some extra money. It was a section of town that was real shady, where no blacks lived or visited. Charlie had met a girl in Lorraine, and she told him to come down to see her. Charlie left early to visit.

When we got to the club, Charlie wasn't there. We began setting up our bandstand of drums and horns. To pass time away I had been talking to a Jewish man, at least 6'5", who was a Cleveland talent agent. As time neared to go on stage, I sat there wringing my hands, displaying my uneasiness and unaware of the reason for Charlie's tardiness. It was 9:00 P.M. and showtime. Charlie was nowhere to be seen. The Jackson Trio had a record of professionalism. Our name was at stake. Punctuality was a top priority of my group, and I was strictly business. Not knowing Charlie's whereabouts worried me. I didn't know if something had happened to him or what.

Charlie arrived an hour late. We began playing immediately without an explanation from him because of the time factor. I was blowing my horns with enthusiasm to release my tension and anger towards Charlie, eyeing him from the corner of my eyes every chance I got. I was doing my best to make up for the delay in the time. I was trying to make sure the audience received their money's worth for entertainment by making my show as full of vim and vitality as possible. Deep down inside, I had made up my mind to rid the trio of Charlie. I would not tolerate this.

Break time was upon us. We took it and returned to work. I was cool and said nothing to Charlie. His actions had shown how much he valued his job. Near closing time was our second intermission. I was sitting talking to the agent when all of a sudden the owner of the club came up to me asking what the hell I was sitting down for. I stated I was taking my intermission. What followed was totally unnecessary and shocking. Out of his mouth came words I didn't say. He ordered my "motherfuckin' black ass on the stage." Luckily, the club was only semi-full since many patrons had left because of the time.

Dirty talk was heard in clubs and taverns, but I never used bad language. I was a gentleman, but I stooped to his level by responding with, "What did you say, motherfucker?" My motto has always been that if people can't be civil, they should vacate the premises. I began packing my horns. I did something I shouldn't have, but when you are upset you sometimes let your guard down. I turned my back to pack my horns when I felt and heard that son of a gun hit me. Everything happened so fast that Freddie was unable to help. He tried to stop it, but was stunned by the actions. Charlie was bigger than I, and he was the reason for the disturbance. He was so scared that he was curled up in the corner like a frightened cat. He didn't get hurt because he didn't try to lend a hand.

My watch was knocked off, the horns were bent and my suit was torn. I was shaking. The bartender of the club broke up the fight saying, "You black motherfucker. If you don't get up on that stage to play, you won't leave here alive." I said, "Ain't this a shame." I was so upset. I picked up my bent horns and tried to blow for ten minutes, but nothing would come out. The crowd was in shock. They wouldn't dance out of fear. People began to ease out of the club tiptoeing. The bartender said, "Pack up and get your ass out of here. Your pay will be waiting for you at the door when you leave." I began to search for my watch and put my horns away. While we were putting our equipment away, the owner who started the fight came over crying, "Jackson, I'm sorry," explaining that he had had too much to drink. He said he didn't know what had gotten into him.

Thirty-five miles back to Lorraine was long and painful. While sitting in pain, I recalled Charlie's boasting of his strenuous self-defense training. I realized that he was full of hot air. I woke up the next morning with a swollen lip looking like a Ubangi. I couldn't believe my disfigured face in the mirror. I traveled the back streets of the town to get the horns fixed, not wanting anyone to see my face. It was pure punishment that night on stage, but I made it through with my swollen lips.

The next morning my tongue was swollen, which prompted me to go to the doctor. I told him I felt like the phantom of the opera, but he couldn't find anything wrong with me. We closed that town with everyone going their separate ways. I left by plane to see Sue's sister Jan, who was convalescing in the hospital from an accident. I also had plans to see my Aunt Lula, who was in a nursing home. Freddie and Charlie drove back to Los Angeles.

I searched around and found my Aunt Lula's facility in New York. She was in the Village. I woke up the next morning with a swollen foot. It was difficult getting around. My first thought was, "Lord, ain't this a mess. I'd better get out of here before I get sick. I won't be able to move." I secured Jan's apartment and limped around to catch a cab to the airport. I believe I was walking a little better and that the swelling of my face had gone down. I was relieved to be on the plane. All of a sudden, my ring finger began to swell like a balloon. It was so noticeable that the people around me became concerned. They tried to offer assistance. They called the stewardess for help in cutting off the ring, but we were unsuccessful. The aching got worse, and the hostess tried to comfort me to Los Angeles by putting my finger in ice cubes and water.

Sue met me at the airport. Seeing my condition, she called our nurse friend Helen LaMar, who worked at St. Francis Hospital. We asked her to come to our home, and she came over to give me a shot. This took the swelling down. She was a lifesaver. I went to the hospital to see if I had any types of allergies.

Eugene Jackson and Freddie Baker, comedy recording artists for dooto Records.

Pins were stuck in me, but I was fine: It was all a nervous reaction to the episode in Cleveland. Helen kept a close watch on me because from time to time my hands would swell. I started on stress pills after this for a while, until the condition totally subsided.

OUR RECORDS

Freddie and I wrote records that could have been hits, but the songs during that period were "pay-o-las": One had to pay for their songs to receive air time, which was quite expensive. We didn't have that type of money, nor did we have a financial backer to help in this business venture. A person had to have a lot of money to promote his songs. The way we would make our money back from the cost of our songs was to buy at cost and sell over the bandstand when we performed in public. Some guys were making money by the thousands. We never made any big money from our tunes of "Voote"; our ballads of "You're My Breakdown" and "I Want Love for Christmas"; "Without Sin," "Let Me Love You Tonight," "Let's Kiss Hello Again," "Jivarama Hop," "Mad About You," "Hound Dog" and "Jingle Bell Hop."

We knew two Negro men who made it big in the record business. One was Dolfin of Hollywood, who cut records and owned his own record shop on Central and Vernon. He was a very smart, demanding businessman. He was also shifty and arrogant, which led to his demise. He was his own worst enemy because of his personality. He was shot by one of his employees for not paying him. His wife is now the proprietor.

The other was Dootsie Williams, a trumpet player. He was an intelligent businessman, who had a knack for recording. His place was on Central and Ninety-Eighth Street in Watts. He made his money with Redd Foxx, Billie Mitchell, Slappy White and Gladys Bently. The records were called "off color party records" and were full of jokes. Party records were very popular in those days. Dootsie produced our party records. They were called "Night Court." Our party records were cute but were not as dirty as Redd Foxx's. We did three sessions with Dootsie.

While we were making records, I was still active in films. In 1955 *Artists and Models* was produced, starring Dean Martin, Jerry Lewis, Shirley MacLaine and Dorothy Malone. Jerry and Dean played struggling roommates. Martin was an artist. Jerry had funny dreams that Dean was able to develop in his drawings. They were able to cash in on the money from his dreams. The guys developed an interest in the two young ladies, who aspired to be models. This was a comedy where I danced in a street scene with a group of other people.

13
Amos 'n' Andy
and Elvis

AMOS 'N' ANDY

In the television version of *Amos 'n' Andy*, I played a Western Union messenger boy. I was in a total of three episodes: One was shot in 1951, and the other two were shot in 1952. These were situation comedies that had started out on radio with white actors speaking in black dialect. This show had a large radio audience, which was why it was brought to television in June 1951. Freeman Gosden and Charles Correll produced and acted in the radio cast. When it was decided to air on television, a search began for the right characters to fit the voices that had been heard on radio. The director and producers of CBS searched long and hard for the actors — it took four years to find the right people.

The only people from radio to be used on television were Ernestine Wade, who played Sapphire Stevens, and Amanda Randolph, who played Sapphire's mama. The television cast included Horace Stewart (known to many as Nick Stewart), who played Lightnin'. Nick now owns a theater in Los Angeles called the Ebony Showcase Theater.

The setting was in Harlem, and George was always trying to make a fast buck. He was active in an organization called the Mystic Knights of the Sea Lodge. His title in the lodge was "Kingfish." Because George was president, he was always trying to involve his lodge brothers in his plot to make money. This would anger his wife and mother-in-law, who did not trust his ways. Most episodes centered around George. He had the heavy roles. Andy Brown was an easygoing, naive type of fella. He was a mild-mannered, sincere, loyal lodge member who would do anything to benefit the lodge and its body. The stories were always told by Amos, the wise cab driver. He had a girlfriend named Madame Queen. Nick Stewart portrayed a slow, not-too-intelligent janitor at the lodge.

Many civil rights groups did not like the stereotypical characters, but CBS continued to air the program for two years because it had a large successful following. The reason for the popularity with blacks may have been because there were so few shows on television showing people of color. We watched for the joy of being able to see our people on television. *Amos 'n' Andy* hit the tube in June 1951 and ran solid on Thursday evenings from 8:30 to 9:00. If white people watched *Amos 'n' Andy*, and I'm sure some did, they may have been watching for different reasons than black people. We were starved for black talent on television.

The show ran in reruns all over the United States on different stations for at least ten years. The reason we no longer see it on television is because CBS sold the series to two African countries. When the Kenyan government bought the show, they made a public statement around 1963 that Kenya would not show the episodes. Their reasons were the same as those of the NAACP and other black-consciousness organizations: *Amos 'n' Andy* showed African Americans as being sly, shifty and conniving. It also showed blacks as business people and property owners.

Because there wasn't a balance of shows about blacks showing African Americans in different walks of life, people of different races may think *Amos 'n' Andy*'s main plot of shifty blacks was true. This strong theme, seen on weekly television, was what the Negro groups had trouble with. The message, which was very clear and apparent, disturbed some people. Many people believe what they see on television. The media is very powerful and suggestive. This is why it is difficult for blacks to move into white neighborhoods without the neighbors moving out. The fear of some whites toward African Americans, along with their portrayal in the media, has made integration in neighborhoods difficult.

In 1964, a Chicago station was going to show the reruns of *Amos 'n' Andy*. This was totally unacceptable during this time period, with all the marching and sit-ins for justice. People throughout the world were trying to love and understand each other. No way was *Amos 'n' Andy* going to flash across the tube again. Black consciousness and pride were at an all-time high. Around 1966, CBS discovered that there was not a market for *Amos 'n' Andy*. During this time period blacks were very articulate about their needs and desires. In the sixties, some found it degrading to hear a black person on television say "Holy mackerel" and "dis heah ding." However, if you remember JJ on *Good Times*, he would always say "Dyn-o-mite!" and "dis heah ding." Some blacks watched and enjoyed this program, and some didn't.

I also want to point out that after *Amos 'n' Andy* was taken off television in 1953, Freeman Gosden and Charles Correll came up with a cartoon program called *Calvin and the Colonel* in which they were able to use a similar plot with their voices. They used the same black English that they used on radio when they played *Amos 'n' Andy*. Freeman and Charles were still able to make money by using animals that spoke in a black dialect. This passed right by the black organizations and Negro public. The Negro actors were banned from making any more money on *Amos 'n' Andy*, whereas the whites moved on to higher ground.

More avenues are opened to white actors than blacks. This is why so many black actors die penniless. Acting may be all that person knows; if he can't get another job soon or become employed for a long period of time, hard times may seep into the life of the actor. A hole may be dug so deep that the Negro actor may not be able to dig his way out. This is why I try to be as open as I can in the field of entertainment, because it isn't easy to survive and maintain a certain standard of living.

Calvin and the Colonel aired on ABC from October 1961 through September 1962. The plot was about the bad treatment or exploitation of some animals from the south. There was a sly fox, known as the Colonel, and Calvin, a kind, sweet bear who wasn't smart but was very dependable. Other members were the weasel Oliver Wendell Clutch, who was a lawyer; the Colonel's wife Maggie Belle; and Sister Sue, Maggie Belle's sister. Similar to the history of African Americans, the animals had migrated from the south to the north.

ELVIS, THE KING OF ROCK 'N' ROLL

In 1958 Elvis starred in *King Creole*, a film that has been considered by some critics as autobiographical of Elvis's musical foundation. He played Danny Fisher, a high school kid with a love for music, from Bourbon Street in Louisiana's French Quarter. He sang black people's music with a Dixieland-style band. I played in the band at the King Creole Club. Our scene was full of "calls and responses," rendering a stimulating floor show. The movie was lively, with a lot of good music and songs. Several blacks played street vendors and sang a song called "Crawfish." This film paid homage to the influence of black culture on Elvis. During intermission on the set, Elvis would come over to our band and hang out with us. We would shoot the breeze and play our instruments. We were all relaxed and worked as a team.

14
My Family

MAMA LIL

Mama was a servant to all mankind, even her country. She had a high, piercing, pleasing soprano voice. Her sound was unique. She was only 4'10"— this is where I got my stature. She was a very spiritual person, religious, but not overly religious. She believed in God and carried her burdens to the Lord. She was instrumental in helping many. I guess that's where I also got my generosity. She was my heart and inspiration. Her spirit and drive will always be with me. I pray to her every night asking her for guidance.

We were her beloved "Big Head" and "Fatty": I was her "Big Head," and Freddie was her "Fatty." We were members of the Wesley Methodist Church and attended church and Sunday School regularly. We didn't stay home on Sunday like some of the kids today. She instilled morals and values in us. We were active in all church functions and were always in programs. We would walk to church as a family, along with people from the neighborhood. When we moved to Fifteenth Street, Frank Williams and his sister would stop by for us. We would all walk together to Sunday School on Eighth Street and San Julian.

Mama learned to drive when I was 13 years old. She drove until we had an accident. A woman ran into us on the side while we were on our way to Hollywood. After this we would use the streetcar, and I would drive when I became of age. Mama started singing in the church in Houston, Texas, when she was a young girl. She continued to sing in the adult choir at Wesley Chapel in Los Angeles for 30 years. Her voice stood out over the whole choir. You knew when she was singing and when she wasn't. Later, when she became ill, her voice was missed.

The church was originally on Eighth and San Julian, with Bishop Shaw being the first pastor. The Reverend Rakeshaw was the minister after Bishop Shaw retired. They sold that building and moved to Vernon, between Central and McKinley. They began a fund-raising drive to build Wesley on Fifty-Second and Main Street. This gigantic structure is now the church's permanent home.

Our minister, the Reverend Rakeshaw, had a large family. In those days the family and the church were the center of people's lives. The men of the church were strong male role models. If some family didn't have a father, the church had plenty of men willing to fill in. There was always a feeling of camaraderie. We, as a people, had better get back in the church in order for us to become strong and solid.

I remember Mr. Murdock, who was a postman. He was our Sunday School teacher, and his class consisted of Freddie and myself; Francis Bowden and her brother James; Yvonne Alera; Frank Williams; Gerard and James Longrish; and Dorothy Mackey. Mr. Murdock was 103 when he died. We were all very close friends. Our church was central, a focal point where people came because of its programs.

When Bill "Bojangles" Robinson would visit our church, he would put a sizeable contribution in the collection basket. My favorite church was Independent, a nondenominational church on Eighteenth and Paloma. I was the first kid to tap dance in the pulpit at age ten, on the boys' day program.

After the Reverend Graves left, the Reverend Brown became pastor. The Reverend Clayton Russell was the assistant minister for the youth. This church was youth-oriented. Children were always on program, and there would be contests between girls and boys on programs that would bring out the best in everyone. Excitement would be high on the day of events. Wendell Franklin, a friend of mine, attended this church. He ate dinner at our house frequently. He is now a big casting director. The church, along with strong families, helped to mold young men and women into productive citizens.

On Sundays and holidays, Freddie and I would be dressed sharp. Between Mama and Auntie, we were the best-dressed kids on the avenue. One Easter, Mama dressed us in creamy white pants, sport coats with red, white and blue stripes, and straw hats. We were dressed to a T walking down

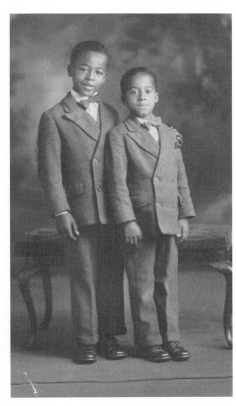

Mama Lil's boys: "Big Head" Eugene (left) and "Fatty" Freddie.

Central Avenue. Cars would slow down and people would look at us. We weren't dressed up every day, only on Sunday and special events. We always had our corduroy pants and overalls. Because I was in the movies, a lot of people may have thought I would be dressed up daily. No, that wasn't me. Mama was very practical and down to earth. She knew how to stretch and hold onto a dollar. Her inner strength came from her dad. She had perseverance and motherly wit and sense.

Mama was a good cook. She was also very neat. She loved hats and high heels. She would put on her high heels, gloves and a hat tilted to the side of her head. Mama would look like a million dollars. It seemed that Mama's little legs and the high curbs just couldn't get along. She was always falling. The kids in the neighborhood would jokingly say, " I saw Mrs. Baker getting off the ground," or "I saw Mrs. Baker down there on the ground."

She had many gifts from God. Her voice and the gift of giving were blessings from our spiritual father. She was a person who lived the word of the Bible in her actions. Children were always around our house, and everyone was welcome. We had dancers, musicians, all types at our home. Mama fed a lot of children. Thomas Boon came to our house from the South. She fed and took care of him. He went into the CCC Camp. Later, he went into the army and made something of himself. He was just one of the kids Mama helped. She assisted so many that I can't remember their names. In today's society, we have gotten away from helping people. Our extended family is gone. We must bring this back.

Mama was active in church, civic and social organizations. She was an active member of 16 organizations, including Deborah Chapter Number 13, Order of Eastern Star; Prince Hall of Adoption; Imperial Council; Imperial Court Daughter of Isis; Golden State Grand Chapter; California State Association of Colored Women's Club, Inc. Southern Section; and Communication Corps of United States, Certificate of Service. She was faithful to them all.

When we went into the army, Mama joined the War Mothers. She was a captain and visited our base for three or four days with the War Mothers. We included her in our USO act, which was our vaudeville routine. We sang so beautifully on "River Stay Away from My Door." The troops found her so charming, they made her sweetheart of the camp. When I became an adult, I saw how hard Mama worked in her clubs. Her organizations kept her busy. She would be out late at night, which would make me so angry. Sometimes they would bring her home, and sometimes they wouldn't.

I was involved, also. I joined the Mason's Garrison 45 in 1941. I took my third degree in Monrovia. I went into the Royal Arch, and from there to Knights of Templars, the Shriners, the York Rite and the Scottish Rite.

Mama didn't have much luck with men; she had a few friends who liked her. We realized that she had to have companionship when she went to social functions — she didn't go out much. She was home with her family. Some of

Mama Lil, War Mothers captain, and her sons Freddie (left) and Eugene.

these men wanted money, but she was no fool. She kept them at a distance, and they did not know our private financial affairs. She was a smart lady.

Once there was a gentleman by the name of Foster Dillingham, who worked for the post office. He was muscular, with light brown skin. He was a nice-looking fellow, but he was very mean and jealous and would jump on Mama. As children, Freddie and I would holler at him to make him stop. We went through that bit until Mama finally quit him.

The last friend in her life was a man named Miller, an attractive man around six feet tall. He didn't work much. He would work around the house, scrubbing and cleaning. I never saw him with any big money, but she liked him. He was like a gigolo. One day, when I was older, he started hitting and slapping her. Man, I got a broomstick and beat him out of the house. I cut his arm and wrist with the broom, and he never returned. Mama's male friends were few. She was an honest, sincere and sensitive person who had difficulty finding true love in men, but she never let this get her down. The ones she did have were a bunch of phonies, and I protected her.

Freddie had gotten married right after high school against the wishes of both families. He was too young to know that he was experiencing puppy love — he divorced at age 22. Mama took the kids, who were ages three, four and five. She raised them, giving them the same love and nurturing that she gave us. They all took piano lessons, but Jeanette mastered it best.

Auntie helped raise the girls. They grew to be lovely young ladies and turned out to be very successful. Jeanette is a top entertainer, an accomplished pianist and singer who has been around the world twice. She's well-liked in show business. When she was starting out, she and Oscar McLollie wrote a song called "Hey Girl, Hey Boy." It was a big hit, but they didn't realize their potential as a duo. They had the combined talent to be big stars, but they couldn't get along and would fuss. (They could have been a Marilyn McCoo and Billy Davis.) Rosina has a travel agency and Ferda is an actress and works for the Big Brother organization.

When Jeanette had a child in St. Louis, she was young. Mama and I went to get the child. I really wanted Mama and me to raise him because he was a boy, but Auntie didn't have any children, so I convinced Mama to let Auntie raise him. They had been arguing over who would raise him. (Just think, years ago families were having disputes over who would raise a child with love. Nowadays, people throw kids to orphanages or in garbage cans. We have truly changed. We no longer value life.)

Mama was watching over me like a hawk when it came to the girls. She didn't want what happened to Freddie to happen to me. I had sweethearts, but no one serious. I had been in the service for three years before I got married, so I was more mature. I liked a girl name Juanita Favor, who had been married before, but Mama didn't want me to marry a girl who had been married. Juanita didn't have children, and some guy had done her wrong. I cared for her, but Mama broke that up.

I felt Mama had paid her dues to society, so I stopped her from working. She was now free to do what she wanted. Mama didn't have to worry about a thing. I was her sole support. I saw that she had clothes. Anything she wanted, I did for her. After I got out of the service, Mama wanted to travel and see the world. I gave her trips around the United States on the bus. She also went to

Honolulu. Whatever she wanted to do, wherever she wanted to go, I took care of her. I loved my mother. I was blessed, and felt good that I was able to do things for her. The house at 1161 East Forty-Seventh Place was for Mama.

Mama was always running, running, running. This would nerve me up. When she got sick with cancer, she kept it to herself. She kept her burdens within, never wanting to worry her family about anything that was affecting her. She continued to go in and out of General Hospital. I was working on *Daktari*, a television series in Soledad Canyon, and every day I would drive in from the studios. This went on for some time. She would tell me how she didn't like the cobalt treatments, that they would burn. The last time I saw her she told me of her painful treatment. I gave her a hug and a kiss and told her to take it easy.

I went to work the next day. On my way in from the studio to the hospital was a music store on Ninth Street. I usually went directly from the studio to the hospital, but on this particular day I turned off the freeway to the music store to buy something. It was closed, so I switched over to the streets leading to the hospital. I parked the car and walked upstairs to her floor. I told the nurse I was there to see my mother. The nurse said, "Haven't you heard?" I said, "No. I just arrived from the studios." She said, "Your mother has expired." "What? When?" I asked. She answered, "About 15 or 20 minutes ago." I said, "Doggone. Had I not gone to the music store, I would have been here when she passed."

She was lying in the bed. I gently kissed her. Her face had gotten cold. I called my brother, Freddie. As I look back, I remember that he wasn't working. He could have gone by more than I did because he was free. He could have made it a daily routine, as I had done. When Freddie arrived, we had her body taken to Angelus Mortuary. Mama was 71 years old.

The funeral was at our family church, Wesley Methodist. The Reverend Rakeshaw was the presiding minister. I was very disappointed with the low attendance. Mama had been active in so many organizations. People use you for whatever they can, but Mama gave freely from her heart. For all the people she helped, there should have been standing room only. It seems that when you die, people forget you. We put her away nicely. She was laid to rest, with a lovely tombstone, at Evergreen Cemetery. I used to go out regularly, but the traffic has gotten so rough that it hinders me. I still go to place flowers and pray. Mama loved life, but she made sure her soul was ready for her creator.

My Brother, Casanova Freddie

Freddie was born December 25, 1919, at 12 midnight. I was born on the same day in 1916 at 1:00 in the afternoon. Freddie's father was a Creole. (A Creole is someone who is of mixed Negro, French and Spanish descent.) At the age of three, Freddie already had a flair for girls. They loved him, spoiled him, and chased him. He was a ladies' man. They would go crazy over him throughout his life. He was very good-looking. He had his way with the girls, but not with Mama. She was determined that he would carry his weight in the family, and he did. He and I never gave Mama a bit of trouble. He went to the same elementary schools as I did, and she kept us busy and involved.

I taught Freddie to tap. He was also very talented. He played the drums, danced, tapped and sang. He had a voice like Billy Eckstine, Arthur Prysock and Herb Jeffrey. He would sound so similar to Herb Jeffrey when he would sing "Flamingo." He was very creative in music and writing. He wrote a movie as a young adult. His hobby as a child was making miniature stages and props.

Freddie met his first wife, Catherine, at the Lincoln Theater. She had a twin, Constance, who was still in high school. They wanted to take tap dancing from us. We began teaching, and then began to date them. Constance and I broke up, but Freddie continued to date Catherine. They married after he finished high school, but they were too young. Catherine still looks the same. She has kept herself up and is a dance instructor at a senior citizens home in downtown Los Angeles.

Freddie's second wife, Kitty, was a stripper. He met her while playing in a nightclub. His third wife was named Marsha, and they had one daughter, named Lorraine. His last wife, Anne, he had met in a club as well. All of his wives were white except Catherine.

He has four daughters, and two are in the entertainment industry. Jeanette became an experienced pianist and singer and is known professionally as Miss B. She performed with Freddie and me, making us a true family trio. We were proud of her, for she was an accomplished artist. However, she was inexperienced in the area of drinking. Uncle Gene, as she called me, had to show her the ropes of survival in the entertainment industry.

Customers enjoy buying musicians drinks, but a good musician cannot stay on top by drinking. The trick of the trade is to take a sip just before intermission, then walk off the stage with it in your hand and pour it in a bottle to carry home. This keeps the home stocked with the highest quality of liquor. I learned this the hard way by driving home high as a kite in the fog and rain — receiving tickets, raising my car insurance, and angering my wife.

But with maturity I discovered that I didn't have to drink to get in the groove. I decided to rely on my natural talents in order to preserve them. I didn't know the club manager was behind me as I was passing this wisdom on to Jeanette during an intermission in our dressing room. I referred to Jeanette as being a big dummy for not knowing to pour the drinks into a bottle to supply your cabinet at home. Freddie and Jeanette tried to get my attention by pointing and making faces toward the door, but I continued to talk. Finally, I turned around to see the red, blushing face of the manager. I was just as embarrassed as he was, but smoothed it over by saying to him, "Ain't

Freddie Baker (second from left) and brother Eugene Jackson (far right) in *Harlem Tuff Kids.*

that right?" He said, "Yeah," and quickly walked away. We laughed all the way home.

Freddie's other daughter, Lorraine, writes plays for productions and is employed by Big Brothers of America. Another daughter, Constance, owns Tom's Travel Agency in Hollywood. Ferda is the proprietor of a school for the handicapped in Los Angeles.

Freddie wrote many of the songs that we recorded, but he never made it big in the movies like I did because of his color. They wanted children with a dark complexion at that time. However, he did manage to get some starring roles. At age four, he played an Italian kid in *Little Annie Rooney*, starring Mary Pickford. He was in *East Side Kids* with Jackie Cooper. He also did *Harlem Tuff Kids*, a Million Dollar production with an all-black cast which was a takeoff on *Dead End Kids*, which was a white production. Freddie and I played gang members in *Harlem Tuff Kids*. He also did *Take My Life*, with Louise Beavers, Monte Hawley, Reginald Fenderson and DeForest Covan. He was the star, with Eddie Lynn and Nina Mae McKinney. (Nina McKinney's first big movie was *Hallelujah*. She was a beauty and a big star at MGM, but she pulled herself down. She went from MGM to the smaller Million Dollar production company.)

Freddie played in *Boys of the Streets*, with Jackie Cooper, and in *Double Deal*, which was an Argus production. He played the role of Tommy McCoy.

Eugene (center) explains the situation, while brother Freddie Baker (second from left) and the other Harlem Tuff Kids look on, in *Reform School* (1939).

He was also in *Reform School*. Later in adult life, Freddie did extra work in movies. He would do silent bits with some of the stars. Silent bits are non-speaking roles, but you get paid more than extras. He worked in television on *Taxi*. On the intermission of some of the shows, Freddie and I would entertain the stars and crew by tapping and performing. When we would receive our check, we would have extra money. That extra money was called a "bump" in show business. Anytime you made more money than you were supposed to, it was called a bump.

Freddie loved cars. He had a sports car called a Cord that was made in the United States. He had three cars. Also, since Mama taught us how to budget, Freddie's house was paid for. He lived in Los Angeles on Ninth Avenue. He died in April 1995.

SUE, MY BELOVED WIFE

I had lots of sweethearts, but no one special. Mama was very protective. I'm glad, for I would never have met the love of my life, Sue. Mama knew the kind of girl I needed. Sue was that girl. She fit perfectly into my life. Sue was the baby in her family. Jan, Sue's older sister, did everything for her. We got married on December 14, 1945. Sue is a kind, sincere person, and has always been supportive of my career. She is beautiful and charming, a first-class lady who has held the family together. She handled both roles in the family because of the type of job I had. She's an ideal wife, mother and grandmother.

When we came home from the service, we stayed with Mama at 1161 East Forty-Seventh Place. I bought a house around the corner at 1236 East Forty-Eighth Street, and Mama was over every day. All the kids were born there. We lived there for ten years. We moved to Compton when Sue Carol was two. When we moved to Compton in 1956, I was working at the Dragon Den and became friends with a truck driver named Bill Slater. I told Bill that I was going to move from Los Angeles to Compton. He and his family were crazy about me. He told me that he would help me move with his truck.

Sue and I had our close friends help us pack, and we had our clothes ready. Bill came up with this big rig truck that blocked off the whole street. This gave us privacy, so I decided to turn it into a block party. I brought out drinks, and everyone was partying and working together. We were moving a six-room house, so we had a lot of furniture. I kept the house on Forty-Eighth Street for ten years.

Some advice to newlyweds: the first five years of marriage is about learning each other. The second ten, you are getting to know each other. At fifteen, it's going nice — you got it made. You know each other. At twenty, you will have ups and downs. You will have snags, the same hits and bumps as before. At twenty-five, if you don't know each other by now, you ain't going to learn each other. At thirty years, you're better at understanding. At thirty-five years, you argue, walk away, come back and make up. The best advice I can give someone is to never stop speaking and talking. One must give in. I'll say, "Oh, what the heck, let's kiss and make up." At fifty years, thank God we made it. Let's make the best of everything. We've been together so long that when we go in stores people think we look alike.

FATHERHOOD

When Gene was born I was so happy, jumping for joy to have a son. I went up and down Central Avenue giving out cigars and saying, "We just had our first child, and it is a boy." When I would give out the cigars, I would have the people sign the cigar box. People did that in those days. Gene was born at the black hospital, named King Hospital, near our home on Hooper and Vernon. It was a private hospital run by Dr. King and his wife. He was the doctor, and she was the nurse.

Hazel and Sue Carol were born at White Memorial in Los Angeles. Because I was so busy in show business, I never got to spend the time I would have

Eugene Jackson and his son, Eugene Jackson III ("Little Gene").

liked to with the children. I was always on the road. Sue was an excellent caretaker, and she filled both roles of mother and father. I didn't get to go camping and hunting with my son. When I looked up he was 19, in college, and then married. I was a good provider, but the next thing I knew he was out of the house and grown. Sue saw to it that the girls were little ladies. They married successfully.

CHILDREN AND GRANDCHILDREN

My first child was a boy, born on January 9, 1947. We named him Eugene W. Jackson III. Daughter Hazel Lee was born September 8, 1948. She was named after my Aunt Hazel and Sue's mother, Eugenia Lee Watt. Another daughter, Sue Carol, was born May 17, 1954. She was named after Sue and Alan Ladd's wife Sue Carol. All of the children were born in Los Angeles. Our children never gave us a bit of trouble. Our kids were normal children like all the other children on the block. They played and went to school with the kids in Compton public schools.

I started teaching Gene at a very early age to tap dance and sing. I made sure he was versatile, and it paid off many times. I received a call from Central Casting for four boys to dance. They told me it was going to be a big movie. I had no idea that it was the famous *Porgy and Bess*, which would introduce the boys to many top entertainers. Gene was dancing quite well. I knew he would pass the audition with no problem. Then I thought of the two Stokes brothers. Also, I had been teaching tap to Dickie, the kid across the street. I put all the boys together and taught them a routine. The routine consisted of the boys dancing together, with one coming out in front to tap while the others remained in the rear clapping.

I knew I would have some stiff competition with Willie Covan's dancers. He had some good boy dancers. By the time we got there, Willie's boys had already danced. Our boys had to tap with no music. They had to clap and stomp, then go into a time step one at a time. Each would go in front and do a little routine, then go back in line and tap with the others. They picked my boys along with the Covans, but they only picked one of the Stokes boys because one was so small that he wouldn't be seen.

The group consisted of three Covans: Little Frankie, Ken Ball, Eddie Graves; and three from my group, Gene, Dickie and the Stokes boy. They went to Stockton to film. I was elated that they had chosen my boys from Compton. They trained in my garage. It didn't matter where they had practiced and what city they had come from because they had talent. It's what you have to offer — that's what counts. These boys carried the name of Compton behind them with pride. They respected themselves and others, which brought respect back to them.

One of my good friends, Bobby Johnson, was at the audition. Bobby knew the dance director and was able to dance in the movie. (There was always — and still is — a clique in show business.) He could have told me about that so I would have been able to perform in it. To dance with my son in a movie would have been very special to me. But I didn't let it get me down because I was involved in another project. Sue was the guardian of the boys, and she traveled with them.

On the set we saw Nichelle Nichols (later to "star" in *Star Trek*). She ran up and kissed me. She asked if I remembered her from Michigan, and I assured her that I did. Dorothy Dandridge was given the role of Bess, but she had changed from when I used to showcase her. Dorothy now barely spoke to anyone. Pearl Bailey was just the opposite. She was personable. When she wasn't acting during the show, she would have everyone laughing. Ivan Dixon and Diahann Carroll were brought in from New York. Sue's sister Jan and Diahann's mother were friends. When Diahann arrived in Los Angeles, she called us. Sue went out to lunch with her, and she gave Sue one of her records.

Wesley Gale, Jack Williams and Caroline Snowden were dancers. Wesley was well-established and had played in a lot of jungle films. Caroline was a big dancing star from Sebastian's Cotton Club. My aunt, Catherine Ayres, was in the original play of 1935. She had told me years before to watch a young man by the name of Sidney Poitier. She said he was going to be a great star. He was chosen to play the part of Porgy in the movie. My aunt was absolutely correct, as we all know about Mr. Poitier.

Another break for Gene was when Central Casting called saying they needed two boys to shine shoes, tap dance and play the harmonica at Disneyland. I had taught Gene to shine, tap and pop the rag, and I found Eddie Graves to be his partner. Little Ed's dad had shined shoes before, so he was able to teach Eddie, Jr., shoe-shine, while I was able to teach him the tap routine that I had taught to Gene. We now had a team. I gave them my expertise from when I had my shoe-shine stand at Fort Huachuca. I had done a lot of shoe-shine parts in movies. Two blocks from the entrance to Disneyland, they

Eugene Jackson II, cinematographer Eugene Jackson III, and Freddie Baker.

built a two seat shoe-shine stand. The cost of a shoe-shine was ten cents. Because this was 1960, I felt that wasn't enough. After the boys began singing, dancing and tapping at the shoe-shine stand, they began to make big, big tips. They would shine shoes for international people. They were called the million-dollar shoe-shine boys by the families.

We counted the tips in bed on Sunday. We would go immediately to Coast Federal to let them count it in the machine. Gene had enough money to pay his college tuition. This shows you that it doesn't matter how much you make, it is what you do with it. He was at Disney a total of ten years. He spent five years on the shoe-shine stand; the other five years were on the Mark Twain boat as a singing and dancing waiter in the New Orleans Square.

Gene graduated from Chapman College. While at Chapman he was involved in many productions, like Shakespeare's *Much Ado About Nothing* and *Long Way from Home*. His drama teacher, Henry Kemp Blair, gave him the freedom to express himself. Henry is now deceased, but he was a strong force in Gene's life at Chapman.

Some of Gene's film credits included *Drum Beat*, with Alan Ladd; *Manhattan Towers*, with Ethel Waters; *Artists and Models*, with Dean Martin and Jerry Lewis; *Johnny Eagle*, with Kim Novak; *Jim Bowie, Porgy and Bess*, with Sammy Davis, Jr.; and the role of Gabriel in *Shenandoah*, starring Jimmy

Loving grandparents: (*CLOCK-WISE FROM TOP*) Sue holding SueAndra; Eugene and Malvin Black IV on the sax; and Eugene playing Santa for all the Jackson grandchildren.

Stewart. He was also in NBC's toast to Jerome Kern. Gene is a cinematographer for different companies. He married Bernice, a doctor. They have one daughter, Simone, and one son, Garrett.

Hazel graduated from Long Beach State College. She and her husband, Laurence, are both teachers. Their sons are Rashaan and Kareem. Sue Carol graduated from California State–Dominguez Hills. She has her own dance studio in Pasadena, California, called the Sue Carol School of Dance. She is married to a probation officer. She and Malvin III have one daughter, SueAndra, and one son, Malvin IV. The girls were trained in dancing just as Gene was. I started the New Stage Workshop in the garage of my home. I now have a school with award-winning students. We are a working family in the area of the arts. On Saturdays, Hazel and Sue Carol run my dance studio in Compton for group lessons. I offer private lessons to individuals. Most nationalities follow in their family footsteps, but not many blacks follow in their fathers' footsteps. I am very proud that my children have followed in mine.

15
My Talented Students

The black dance studios in our area in the twenties and thirties were Loretta Butler, Alma Hightower, Willie Covan, the Nash Dance Studio, and my studio. The studios were not fancy, but we taught everything a person needed. We didn't have a lot of money for frills. What we all had plenty of was talent, patience, drive and endurance. These were the makings of a good dance studio. The producers and directors knew this. When they needed talent, they knew who to call upon. I actually put out my shingle for the business of teaching tap at age 14, when I lived on 1161 East Forty-Seventh Place.

When I moved to Compton, I began teaching in my garage. My first students were my kids. My fee for the public was one or two dollars an hour. One dollar was my group rate, and two dollars was my individual rate. Word of mouth brought me students from around the United States, like Darlene Gist of New York. She started out, I believe, with my good friend Fayard Nicholas of the Nicholas Brothers. He referred her to me. I took her under my wing and groomed her so well that she was able to join the well-known Lindy Hop Dancers.

I've taught so many students that I can't remember all of their names. I kept good records of names and schedules, but because of my move from one home to the next those records have been misplaced. I worked hard with all of my students because they represented me — my work, my craft, my art. I've worked with each of my students individually, and then by putting them in groups to form teams. I'm pleased with all of my students, even the hones that chose not to go into the arts. I'm glad I was able to touch their lives and help mold them into successful human beings. Dance has helped them become diligent in their tasks and professions.

I would test my talent in competitions like "I Love Dance" in Las Vegas, where we would place first and second. We have put on shows at various theaters such as the Wilshire Ebell, Paris, Riverside, Biltmore, and Elks. My troupe would perform at banquets, parties, socials and colleges. We've put on and participated in talent shows. Many of my students, like Chester Whitmore, have gone on to successful careers in the arts. Chester is a world-renowned dance choreographer who travels around the world. The Williams Brothers also trained with me. They moved from Los Angeles to Compton and have traveled abroad to Japan and China.

I feel fortunate to have come in contact with my students' parents and family members. Grandparents have sent their grandchildren to help channel energies into positive attitudes and outlooks. Each of my students possessed his or her own style and uniqueness. I formed personal relationships with every one of my students. One of my students, Zaiid Leflore, and my grandson Malvin were at age five known as "The Little Step." They were taught the routine that the Nicholas Brothers did in the movie *Stormy Weather*. They performed it in the presence of Fayard Nicholas at the Wilshire Ebell. He was flattered and honored that someone thought enough of his style to teach it for preservation. To look on stage and see young tappers brought back special memories so dear to his heart. This dance routine gave "The Little Step" a measure of fame. They were sought after by Vegas, and performed at Caesar's Palace, the MGM Grand, the *Queen Mary*, the *Spruce Goose* in Long Beach, California, and the NAACP Image Awards filmed in Pasadena and the Robert Townsend Television Production.

As time went by, I was able to buy a building, down the street on the same block from my house, where I could open my tap school. I named it the New Stage Workshop and equipped it with mirrors, bars for the students to hold on to for practice, and a piano. I had everything necessary for a tap, jazz and ballet school. My enrollment expanded, and now I had more space. I continued to nurture my business on the side while still working in the industry. I'm proud of all my students, even the ones that chose not to go into the arts, like Wendy James and Michael Craig. Dance has helped them become successful in other areas. One students, Pat Gray, had the desire, determinism and savvy to launch her own dance school after completing my program. I'm glad I was able to touch the lives of my students to help mold them into successful human beings.

Nothing makes me happier than when I'm in public and a student of mine comes up to me and says hello. They always want to know if I remember them. Most of my students usually make a reference to how hard I trained them. Some would want to know if I still had my pointer — my stick that I used when teaching. We would chuckle and part with a hug.

16
Calls, Letters and Visits

Throughout my life in show business, I've had loyal fans. I've been very fortunate. Because I started this business at such an early age, I'm called on for information from people in all walks of life from around the world. I'm used and consulted as a historian. I've been approached by people with such questions as, "Who was the first this and that? Who was the first Negro agent in the industry? What was it like back then?" Lester Salone came all the way from England to interview me about the past. I'm always delighted to talk about how it was because it's an era that can never be imitated.

When I receive a letter or call, it lets me know that these are people interested in the industry when it was in its earliest period of development. I've received calls from many places: Wales; Athens; Australia; Canada; Miami, Florida; Minnesota; and Texas are just a few that stand out in my mind. A young lad from Europe came to visit me. His first name was John. For the life of me I cannot recall his last name, but I remember the joy in his eyes and voice while he interviewed me. He told me that I had a following in Europe because of my work in vaudeville. He asked me numerous questions that I was able to answer. He was thrilled that I was able to give him details of certain events.

I've been the guest on college campuses to discuss the past. I love going to the different Hollywood film-buff events. I meet such wonderful, interesting and sincere people. Whenever I'm asked, I still do live performances. It was an honor and a delight to participate in the Egyptian Temple Number 5 Nobles of the Mystic Shrine. I'm a proud member of the International Hoofers Club. The Sons of the Desert is an outstanding organization that has a newsletter and various activities for actors and actresses from the early era of show business. My wife and I enjoy being members of Sons of the Desert and attending their events.

It feels great to see some of the old actors and actresses at reunions. We hug and kiss each other. We sit and discuss the past, present, our children and

TOP: The Jackson Trio plays a gig for the Egyptian Temple Number 5 Nobles of the Mystic Shrine. *BOTTOM:* Eugene Jackson (right) and tap legend Stepin Fetchit at Oakland's 1991 Black Film Festival.

grandchildren. We are family that mourns the passing of each member, for we know that once we are gone there are no replacements for us. We are valuable, worth more than any rare coins, gold or silver. Always proud to know that some of us are still performing, we love to know and feel that our style and craft are wanted and respected.

It is always special when young people recognize your accomplishments. When the Oakland Black Film Festival honored me and other African American entertainers with the NAACP African American Heritage Awards, I was filled with high spirits of joy. We felt that our contributions were appreciated. Since I'm still healthy, I do a lot of volunteering in my community in the parks and recreation department and at schools, which led to my nomination for the Kool Achiever awards for outstanding work in cities.

I have so many plaques and awards from various organizations that I'm running out of places to put them. This makes me feel good to know that people respect my craft. I participate in trade shows and film festivals around the world. Being a part of the Hollywood Collector's Show is also fun; I always meet interesting people. My heart is warmed when fans care enough to call and write. When they call I'm always cordial, and I have tried to answer every letter. I also travel to perform and lecture around the United States. It feels good to be internationally known and appreciated.

17
Tap

In my opinion the greatest tap dancer that ever lived was Bill "Bojangles" Robinson, known to all as Mr. Bojangles. I really don't know why this name was pinned to him; I only know that a friend gave it to him. Eleanor Powell, who danced with him, referred to him as being "King of the Tap Dancers." He tapped in a relaxed, assured manner. Bojangles had style and class. He did tapping in a slow, confident manner. His tap was intimate. Freddie and I, along with others, loved him. No one could top his technique. Not only was his tap clean, but so was his dress. He'd have on his "top hat, white tie and tails." One couldn't help but to always call him Mr. Bill Robinson.

Everything about him was special. He was a first-class gentleman, and we could only admire and respect his craft. His tap had a joyousness, a carefree dancing style that could make people forget about their problems while he was performing. Bojangles coined the name "copasetic" to refer to his style of dance and feeling of pleasure when he tapped. Tapping brought him joy.

As a tribute to Bill Robinson upon his death in 1949, a group of professional tappers formed the Copasetics. The men in the group had backgrounds similar to Bill: They had danced on the road in vaude, minstrels and traveling tent shows. So many people were overwhelmed by his death. Forty-five thousand people stood in line to view his body. His funeral route from Times Square to Harlem was lined with more than one-and-a-half million people. The Palace Theater draped a banner that read "So Long, Bill Robinson. His Dancing Feet Brought Joy to the World."

In Times Square, a 30-piece band played "Give My Regards to Broadway." I believe New York's Mayor O'Dwyer summed up Bill Robinson's life when he said, "Without money, just good manners and decency, Bill Robinson got into places no money can buy. He got into the hearts of all Americans." This statement exemplifies how Bill had touched everyone and how powerful his style of tap was.

Though Bill was a true dancer, actor and humanitarian, his life wasn't all roses. Eleanor Powell, who danced with him, saw firsthand what being black was like in 1928. Bill was so popular back then that he performed at private parties sponsored by such rich people as the Rockefellers and the Vanderbilts.

170

He was making $500 a night, but he still couldn't ride in the front elevator. Bill said that Eleanor would ride in the service elevators with him after they would finish their routine. Because Eleanor was white, after she performed the butlers and maids would ask her if she wanted something to drink — Bill would be totally ignored. Bill said Eleanor would always kindly say, "Only if Mr. Robinson can have one also." Bill would then be given a glass.

It was a ritual with Bill that after he drank his liquid, he politely broke the crystal glass. He would pay for it. Eleanor didn't understand why he broke it every time no matter where they were. Bill explained to her that he was just beating them to the punch. This is what we went through. I'm not asking for pity because I know it was rough for all African Americans. I'm asking that you understand, accept and acknowledge us.

I want the world to know that Bill "Bojangles" Robinson gave to the causes of trying to help uplift the Negro race. He actually gave away millions of dollars to organizations and individuals for worthy causes. He was a very generous man. Bill wasn't a vocal man, one to stand up openly and state what he had done for people. What he did, he did silently. He gave from his heart. He wasn't one to debate issues and causes.

Believe me when I say that Bill "Bojangles" Robinson knew and cared what his people were going through. Just because he was famous didn't mean that he escaped unkind, degrading things. He didn't, but he continued to stand and walk tall. He never resorted to anything negative and he carried himself like a man, a black man who was proud of his craft and people. He never tried to be anything else but himself. He knew what color he was, and he never forgot his past. He openly stated that he shelled peas for a living before becoming famous. He knew his roots. Bill knew the needs of our people, and he never forgot them or their needs.

Bill had his way of introducing new tap routines to the public that would go over great with all. In *Blackbirds of 1928* he mesmerized us with "Doin' the New Low-Down." Because of his talent and style, he transcended the black vaudeville market and moved on to mainstream with no problem. He was a big star in both theater and films. Some of his films included *Dixiana* (1930), *The Little Colonel* (1935), *The Littlest Rebel* (1935), *Dimples* (1936) and *Rebecca of Sunnybrook Farm* (1938). The teaming of Bill and Shirley Temple in *The Little Colonel* was a master stroke. This was his most famous film for 20th Century–Fox. The two of them tap dancing the stairs is memorable to film fans. When Bill explains to her that all she has to do is listen with her feet, he won the hearts of everyone.

So many times the black public doesn't understand life in the shoes of a Negro entertainer. We were criticized for our roles and dance, but had we not done them we wouldn't have been following our dreams. Dreams are like goals. They must be fulfilled, for an unfulfilled dream is like a broken promise to oneself. Always follow your dreams — don't break promises to yourself by

Las Vegas, 1949: Bill "Bojangles" Robinson plays with Eugene's 12-month-old son, Eugene III. Eugene and Bill were both playing in Vegas at the time, but in different clubs.

letting someone stop you. By following our dreams, we were able to make money to help our people. It takes money to help, and we made money. We gave back to our people and our community to try to make things better, though we couldn't please everyone.

When you hear the statement that black people live in two worlds, that is true. We live in the large part, the masses, but then we also live in our own world, our culture. As entertainers, we have three worlds to balance. We dance and perform in the public world of entertainment, then we have the large world to cope with, and then we have our black world. A black person in show business must be very strong to survive all of this. When I hear of a star committing suicide, especially a black star, I sometimes wonder if the above had anything to do with it. This is why I'm so glad that the black culture is now surfacing so that all cultures can learn about us.

We always knew the culture at large because we worked for them and lived with them. However, they knew nothing of our culture because of segregation. The new trend of today of multiculturalism is the best way to live. People are able to learn and understand each other. We will be able to get along better when we know about each other's heritage. We will be able to accept people because we've been around them. Fear, which is a great deal of the world's problem now, will be eliminated. This will be a union and all people will be respected, which is one of the goals of the black man.

We were doing a job. We were entertainers. You don't tap with a frown on your face. You should tap with rhythm and use your whole body. The sounds of tap bring a natural smile to both the tapper and his audience. Tap is natural and speaks for itself. It's a rhythm of the feet that looks easy but takes hard work and practice.

Great tappers — Honi Coles; Sammy Davis, Jr.; Jimmy Payne; the Hines Kids; the Cook and Brown team act; the Nicholas Brothers; Buck and Bubbles; the High Hatters; Stepin Fetchit; Hermes Pan; Louis DaPron; Willie Covan; George Murphy; Leonard Reed; Peg Leg Bates; Fred Astaire; George Murphy; Ralph Brown; Bunny Briggs; Eddie Brown; and Maceo Anderson — made the art of tap vibrant and alive. We had some great female hoofers — I don't want to leave them out. People may not know it, but Pearl Bailey was a tapper at first, before she ventured into other areas. I remember Ruby Keeler, Jan Withers, Jeni LeGon, Shirley Temple, Peggy Ryan, Ann Miller and Frances Nealy.

There are many more hoofers that I failed to mention. Their steps aren't forgotten, for their taps are ignited and interwoven into ours. Through long hours of practice, these people developed routines that made their feet oscillate and pulsate to the different syncopations of tap. Each tapper had his or her own technique of sole and heels to create rhythm for tap. The legendary Charles "Cookie" Cook of the Copasetic Dance Group would do sequences of tap routines that would leave the crowd spellbound.

We all admired Bill "Bojangles" Robinson. Freddie and I would watch and study every move he made on stage. His act was breathtaking. He was smooth, he danced with grace, and he made tap look fun. With his wooden-soled shoes, he was the master of tap. When Bojangles was in town, if people — especially tappers — couldn't get in to see him, they'd hide under the steps of the building just to hear him. We didn't have to see him to enjoy him. Just to hear the sounds of the tap was pleasing to a tapper. Even Cookie admitted that he sat under the steps of the Cotton Club in New York just to hear Bill tap. When Bojangles was on the bill, no one wanted to follow him. His act and routine couldn't be matched.

The old-timers of tap didn't learn tap in school. Our creations were picked up on street corners, stages, and from watching others tap and perform. The audience was our teacher. From the audience responses, we knew what was enjoyable to them. In rehearsal we would remember the applause from a certain routine and expand on it more. When we appeared again on stage, sometimes in front of the same audience, our routine would have more to it. We would have taken one basic, simple routine and moved it to a higher level. The audience wouldn't recognize any of our basic steps because the steps had been mixed in with our new ones.

In tap it is good to have a mentor. Bill was one to me and many other tappers. A tapper needs someone to watch, someone to hold on to, someone to show new routines and steps to. I was happy to learn that Gregory Hines respected Cookie enough to sit under the stage of the Apollo Theater to listen to the sounds of Charles Cook, the legendary copasetic tap dancer. I will always love tap, and I respect anyone that taps. Tappers don't ever want the art of taping to die. This is why we teach it to anyone, especially the young.

In order to be a great tapper like Bill "Bojangles" Robinson, don't drink or do drugs. Stay physically fit and healthy. Bill didn't smoke or drink alcohol, and was alert in his sixties. When he was 62, he tapped 52 blocks down Broadway in New York. What an entertainer!

We're hoofers from our hearts, and we'll go to our grave tapping.

18
Theater, Film and Television

I participated in many theater productions, and my television and film works are numerous. I've done bit parts, extra work, talking roles and stand-ins. You name it, I've done it. My résumé lists me as an actor, comic, singer, dancer and musician. I am a versatile individual. I've trained and worked with some of the greatest stars on earth, and I feel blessed to live to tell my story. Below I've highlighted some of my films, theater and television credits. (And the end of the book you'll find a more complete filmography.)

As an adult, I continued to work in films and theater. In 1962, I was in *Forty Pounds of Trouble* with Tony Curtis, Phil Silvers and Suzanne Pleshette. It was great to dance with Gene Kelly in *Forty Carats* in 1973. For atmosphere dancing around him, we did "Trucking," "Boogie Woogie," "Suzy Q" and "Shim, Sham, Shimmy." He respected the black dancers and enjoyed being in our company. A funny incident happened on the set of that picture. One day we were on the set talking; I knew who Gene was, but a colored girl didn't really know who he was. She asked him if he could dance. He responded with, "Can I dance?" and began to do a few steps and fell right on his face. We all laughed. The conditions on our set were warm and relaxed.

I did more work in film than theater, but whenever I wasn't busy in the movies I would act on stage. As long as I was in front of the public bringing joy to the hearts of mankind, I believed that I was doing my job. I am blessed to be able to do a job that I love. I've done it all, which has allowed me to pick and choose parts that I want to perform.

A production company went all over the United States to cast roles for *The Last Minstrel Show*, which was the story of Black Patti. Della Reese and I were the only West Coast actors chosen. I signed my contract to do this show on February 17, 1978. We rehearsed for five weeks in New York at the Mintzkoff building, where all the big shows rehearsed. It was an honor to be in this true, historical play. Gregory Hines was also in it. It was an all-male minstrel show except for Black Patti, who was played by Della Reese.

Black Patti was a very smart business lady. She went to the cotton fields for her talented dancers, singers and musicians. She took the show on the road. When she took her production to Chicago, she was picketed by blacks. They didn't like blacks doing minstrels. What they didn't understand was that the whites were making money doing the same thing that she was doing. They did not understand the business. The same thing goes on today. We were in Delaware for ten days and had to cut the play down because it was three hours long. We were well-received by the public, and I met a lot of brother Masons and Shriners.

Next was two weeks in Philadelphia, where we had some young black critics and journalists write that they felt we were "tommin'." ("Tommin'" means sucking up to white folks, not being proud of your black culture.) They didn't know their own history, for Black Patti truly existed. Her real name was Matilda Sissieretta Joyner, and she married a man by the name of Richard Jones. One of the first African American opera singers, she was given the name Black Patti because her vocal ability was compared to the "Italian prima donna Adelina Patti." We showed that all the young minstrel dancers left her because of the pressure from the community and the press. The only ones that stayed with her were her two old minstrel dancers. I played one of the old dancers that stayed with her, and the show ended like that.

When white writers write stories, plays or books about their race, they are not attacked by the press as being unloyal to their ethnic background. *Tobacco Road*, *Hee-Haw* and Archie Bunker of *All in the Family* were huge successes that were able to laugh at themselves. We must be able to do the same. I know we don't have a true balance of our actual lives portrayed in the media, but history is history. When something actually existed, it should be shown as factually as possible. Black Patti should not be forgotten. She was our past. Young black writers should research their history before taking a pen to paper to be critical of something they know nothing about.

We had fine tuned parts of *The Last Minstrel Show*. It was tight, as we say in show business, and was ready for the Helen Hayes Theater on Broadway. To our disadvantage, the financial supporter decided to withdraw the funds for the production, which killed the play. This is why it is so important to save the money one makes in show business, because one never knows what tomorrow may bring. Show business is unstable. It has its ups and downs like a seesaw, but I have always loved it. It's a seesaw that, if balanced properly, can be very good to you.

I've had my share of the ups and downs just as any entertainer has, but it goes with the job. I've always been able to swim and ride the waves when they were rough or calm. I worked with the Lafayette Players West in *A Slice of Life* at the Coronet Theater in Los Angeles. This play was produced by Virginia Capers. I also had time in my schedule to do *The Way That Seemeth Right*, written by Dolores Crenshaw.

Eugene and Judy the Chimp have a clarinet duet on the set of *Daktari* (1965).

First assistant Johnny Wilson called me and said he knew I did parts, but that he had some steady extra work for about three years. Johnny convinced me because he said I would be working every day. He suggested that I accept this opportunity. The show was *Daktari*, and it worked out well for me. I sat back and watched black stars come in from New York. They would make about $500, but that would be the end of their pay. I, on the other hand, had a regular pay check. I played an Askari African. I drove the Jeep, and worked with Clarence the Cross-Eyed Lion and Judy the Chimp. Judy was like a human

Eugene appeared as Uncle Lou in a few episodes of *Julia* (1968).

being. We were bused from CBS to Soledad Canyon, where they turned part of the canyon into a set called "U.S. Africa."

In *Julia* I played Uncle Lou, Marc Copage's ex-entertainer uncle from Kansas City. It was a perfect role that matched my personal life. I was in a couple of shows, but that was it. The role was never written in as a regular part. This could have been a real break for me. It would have brought my face to the screen on a regular basis.

One day I received a call from my agent for a part on *Sanford and Son* for 4 P.M. the next day. I was reluctant to accept the part because I had another casting call for earlier the same day. My agent convinced me to accept because she thought I could make both tapings in the same day. My first would be completed by 12 noon, which would give me time to get to NBC in Burbank. I had no idea that I would be in a secured area of the airport. No one was allowed to leave until the entire shoot was complete. By the time I got to NBC they had rehearsed, and my part was cut because I wasn't present. I was disappointed because this position paid more and had residuals. I was sick. I'm still sick, but that's the breaks in our business. One must be able to take the bitter with the sweet. Accept it and learn from it. My word of advice is to never overbook yourself in one day.

On *Frank's Place* I played the dead man. I teased the people on set by saying, "Don't forget I'm alive!" We all laughed. I was so relaxed, warm and snug that I had the nerve to go to sleep in the casket during rehearsal. We all had a good time laughing at that. It wasn't easy playing a dead man because your body must be limp — no body movement whatsoever is allowed. I couldn't blink or scratch throughout my taping. I had to have mind over body for control. I had a talking part in *The Day After* (1983), a movie about the end of the world, starring Jason Robards. I played a hospital patient who has just had surgery.

In 1963 I was working at Warner Bros. with the Rat Pack — Sammy Davis, Jr., Frank Sinatra and Dean Martin in *Robin and the Seven Hoods*. About 40 of us were rehearsing on the lot when all of a sudden some girls came running in, crying and screaming that President Kennedy had been assassinated. We all ran out of the rehearsal hall to a car that was parked on the studio lot. We turned on the radio to listen, and we all started crying. Sinatra then sent word out for everybody to go home. I cried all the way home from Burbank to Compton. I couldn't do a thing when I got home. My body was lifeless. I watched television from my bed and saw when Lee Harvey Oswald was shot. It was like a nightmare. That whole day was upsetting to the entire world.

I was asked to stand in for Sammy and said I would. I wasn't too big to stand in for him. The crew gave me the same respect as they were giving Sammy. As always, I put my heart and soul into the part. The staff observed my talent and told me that I should have been cast in that part, which made me feel great. Sammy invited me to a party that he was having. I thanked him, but explained to him that I was playing at Johnny's Café in Whittier. I would have loved to be able to attend his party. He then left the set for home in order to get ready for his party.

On my way to the parking lot, I noticed people having a ball to the sound of a band. They were having a studio party on Stage 26. I got my horn from my car and got in the groove with the band members. I was playing my head

Top: Eugene (far right) and a 1965 gathering of friends at Universal Pictures. Jimmy Stewart is playing the piano, while Eugene III (center) plays the trumpet. *Bottom:* Eugene appeared in *Five Days from Home* (1978) with director and star George Peppard (center).

off, and we were all jammin'. All the producers and directors were present. Everyone was impressed, when all of a sudden up pops Sammy Davis, Jr. I was just getting my points in with the producers and directors when in walked Sammy. He took over, and of course all the attention turned toward him. He jumped on stage and began to sing. I backed him with my horn and said to myself, "Where did he come from?" I thought he had left.

I went in as an extra for *Swing Shift* (1984), starring Goldie Hawn. They had a five-piece colored band, and I just happened to have my horn behind the bar. I took my horn out and began jamming with the band between scenes. I got down. When they returned from lunch, the assistant director said, "Gene, get your horn. You are going to be in the scene." This upgraded my status to SAG pay. About two months later, I was working on *Splash* when I got a call to report back to *Swing Shift* immediately. I told them I was working and couldn't. They told me to report the next day because they had written in a scene for me: I would be blowing my horn in the back seat of a car. I hustled this part from my previous performance with the band. Don't let opportunities pass you by. Jump on it — show everything that you can do. This part came about because people had noticed my skills as a multi-talented performer.

In *The Blue Knight* I had a tap dance shoe-shine stand in the police station where I shined shoes for the officers. On *Webster* and Marla Gibbs's *227*, I danced and played my sax. In 1986 I did two commercials, one for the Bank of America and the other for General Telephone Company. On January 30, 1992, I did a Taco Bell commercial. My most recent film was *The Addams Family*. I played the one-armed bass player. There was a cattle call, and there were only two black men in the entire audition. When the director asked if anybody could play the bass, about three or four hands went up. I raised my hand and was picked. I had to wear a prosthesis and had to have two fittings made of clay, molded to look just like my other arm.

Eugene as the one-armed bass player in *The Addams Family* (1991).

THE [FRANK] SINATRA STORY

I was picked to play the part of a sideline musician, a piano player, in *The Sinatra Story*. I had to return three times for the audition. Contracts had been signed, and we were to begin shooting at a country club that had been rented in Encino, California. I got up early that morning to beat the traffic and drive all the way from Compton to Encino so I could check out the setting and the scene. (When I perform, I like to get there early to practice by myself.) I got there to practice and sat at the piano. In previous movies that I had worked in, and in most movies, a piano player doesn't actually play. The piano is "padded," as we say in show biz. The term "sideline musician" means that the player is faking: The sound is piped in while the piano player pretends to be playing.

I was sitting at the piano when in walked the musical director with another black man. I could see and hear them talking to the director. The musical director asked the producer who I was, and he was told that I had been picked to act as the sideline musician. He said abruptly, "Oh, no. I've chosen this man." He pointed to the man standing next to him. He had picked that man without the knowledge of anyone on the team. I was totally shocked and upset. It was a drag. I had beat out everyone, then along comes someone who had his favorite. I was pushed aside and was not given the fees of my actual contract. I could not believe that my agent did not fight for my true rights. Had Mama been my manager, they would have upheld the contract because she was honest and straightforward. Mama didn't settle for deals that would shortchange me.

As you can see, sometimes agents work for your benefit and sometimes they don't. You must be knowledgeable and be able to fend for yourself. It is always wise never to overspend and live big. In this industry you are big and receiving good pay one day, and the next you are forgotten and not making a dime or a penny. So look out for yourself and always be business-minded. Save and invest in yourself. Don't expect to stay on top as a star. Have something to fall back on to support yourself. Always trust and depend on yourself and God.

YOU BET YOUR LIFE

My coauthor saw in the February 26, 1992, issue of the *Compton Bulletin* newspaper a story about Bill Cosby's search for people to appear on a '90s remake of *You Bet Your Life*. It was a Carsey-Werner Production. (For my readers that are too young to be familiar with this show, *You Bet Your Life* was a game show hosted by comedian Groucho Marx. The show dealt with people who had interesting backgrounds.) Bill Cosby had just completed *The Cosby*

Show. The production company had set up offices in Los Angeles, New York, Atlanta and Philadelphia, and was conducting a national search for 1,000 people with unique experiences. Bill was going to be the host, and contestants would be on the show.

My writer called the production company to tell them about me, and they were interested. I was chosen because of my background in both *Our Gang* and vaudeville, and the fact that I had been stationed with the Buffalo Soldiers. It seemed that everyone loved the *Our Gang* comedies. When I did my taping in March, the contestant coordinator, Covese Silken, was very excited about meeting me. Before taping, Covese interviewed me by asking many questions for the show. She was thrilled to learn about my army days with the Buffalo Soldiers. We were both delighted and surprised to find out that Covese had gone to school with my son, Gene.

In between taping, the people from the audience would ask me questions about a certain star that I had worked with. One of the production crew wanted to know what Clark Gable was like. Also on the show was Lou Rawls's mother. On a previous taping Michael Jordan's dad, James Jordan, had appeared on the show. It was quite an enjoyable taping. Afterward, we had a good time relaxing and talking about the past.

19
The Golden Years

In honor of our 50 years of marriage, Sue and I received awards, proclamations and best wishes from President Bill and Hillary Clinton, Governor Pete Wilson; Mayor Omar Bradley of Compton; Mayor Richard J. Riordan of Los Angeles; and President Carl E. Robinson, Sr., of Compton Community College. The citations mentioned my contributions to the entertainment industry. The Sons of the Desert, an organization dedicated to preserving the memories of actors and actresses from long ago, gave us a lovely plaque. They sponsor various functions for members of the Sons of the Desert, and Sue and I participated in one of their cruises.

The renewal of vows was lovely. Our son, Eugene III, escorted Sue down the aisle. Sue Carol was the mistress of the ceremony, and Hazel did an inspirational modern dance to the tune of "Silver and Gold." The expression on my wife's face told me how proud she was of her daughter. I thought to myself that she was dancing as if she were an angel. I was so glad within that I had taught my children how to dance.

Sue at the 50th wedding anniversary celebration, December 1995.

Our toast to forever love and cherish each other meant the same in 1995 as it did in 1945. Cherish your years with your loved ones, for they go fast. Our hearts and minds are more understanding. We can truly enjoy, relax and entertain each other. We are at peace with each other and with God. Our moments are precious, and we treasure everything. We've been able to laugh and smile with such deep affection, sometimes

TOP: Eugene and Sue with the grandchildren at their 50th wedding anniversary celebration.
BOTTOM: Eugene and Sue with their children at the anniversary celebration.

without a word. It is as if we read each other's minds. We've been through a lot together, and we've learned to compromise. We're blessed to have each other. I look after Sue and she looks after me.

We've had an interesting, exciting life with each other. Being the wife of an entertainer isn't easy for any woman. She was sometimes left being the mother and father while Dad was away. They wear many hats in this business, and Sue has always been my backbone. She has been understanding, kind and unselfish. These last years of our lives will be spent making each other comfortable in life, enjoying our family and friends, traveling and staying close to our creator. Ah, those Golden Years!

Mr. J. and Me
by Gwendolyn Sides St. Julian

I pinned the name "Mr. J." on Mr. Jackson many years ago, and the name has stuck. I was around 24 when I gave him that name. I even refer to his loving wife as Mrs. J. I first met Mr. J. when I was in my early twenties. I had just finished graduate school in Cedar Falls, Iowa, at the University of Northern Iowa. My roommate, Jeanette Joeblakley, and I were living in Long Beach, California, by the beach. She saw an ad in the newspaper stating that models were needed to be instructors at the Barbizon International School of modeling in Los Alamitos and Anaheim, California. I sent in a small wallet photo and was later accepted and trained by their top modeling staff.

At the same time, I acquired a Beverly Hills talent agent. When he met me, he looked across his desk and asked what else I could do besides sit and look like I was 16. Not wanting to lose this agent, because I knew how hard agents were to get, I immediately arched my back and sat straight up in my chair. Raising my eyebrows, I informed him I could tap, do ballet and modern dancing. I told him I played the piano and played several musical instruments. I told him I had done small parts in radio, television and theater while in college. He told me to stay as active as I could in all areas, then gave me the names of surrounding black theater companies in Compton and Los Angeles.

I decided to drive home through Compton and stop off at the Paul Robeson Theater on Bradfield. The director gave me the number of Mr. Jackson because I wanted to improve my tap skills. I called, and on the other end I heard an alert voice full of vigor. He scheduled me to begin individual lessons the following week. What started out as a business venture would soon turn into a family affair. Again, I heard the question of my age. I politely stated that I was 23 years old. Mr. J. was sitting at the piano, in his tap shoes and with his pointer to his side. He said, "So you want to tap, eh?" I said, "Yes sir." "All right, let's get busy," he said. He rose from the bench and proceeded to teach me my time step.

I was never his best tap student. In fact, I was probably his worst. I

GWENDOLYN ST. JULIAN

Coauthor of the Eugene "Pineapple" Jackson story.

somehow added an extra step to the time step, which is still with me to this day. Mr. J. and Mrs. J. knew that I was far away from home without any family. He was always counseling me about life, always warning me that show business was tough. He was my guardian angel from the start. I was accepted into the family by their children. My age is close to their daughter Sue Carol.

Over the years Mr. J. got me small parts on television. I couldn't do a lot because I was under contract with the Los Angeles school system as a speech pathologist, plus I was teaching modeling for Barbizon. I was also teaching a night class in the adult school for the Long Beach unified school system. I was very busy.

I might have decided to leave the teaching field had it not been for a couple of near–casting couch advances toward me. This scared the daylights out of me. I was a small town girl from Cape Girardeau, Missouri. When the approaches were made, I handled it very professionally. Deep down inside, I was shocked. I realized that show business was just what Mr. J. had told me. It was tough, too tough for me.

I decided to try to write for television and screen, though none of my work was ever accepted. Somehow, Mr. J. had faith in me and asked me to write his life story. It took us a long time to complete it because he has remained active. Over the course of this book, Mr. J. has watched me get married, have a baby, move to the Midwest and get a divorce. He taught my only child, Dedrick, Jr., how to tap.

I've enjoyed every aspect of this project. Listening to Mr. J. tell his story, I would sometimes be put to sleep and would awake to find a blanket thrown over me. We would begin again or sometimes schedule for the next day. But there was never anything dull about his life. When I would listen, it would be like I was hearing an Aesop fable because his life was so full of valuable lessons he had learned.

I learned so much oral history, which led to my research in books. In completing my work, I realized that this was a worthwhile book when dance librarian Bob Sloane said he had enjoyed helping me on this project and had learned

TOP: Eugene "Pineapple" Jackson and coauthor Gwendolyn Sides St. Julian. *BOTTOM:* Eugene
with Gwendolyn's son, Dedrick, Jr.

a great deal. I knew then that if I had taught something to a librarian, whom I have the highest degree of respect for, then this endeavor was definitely a manuscript full of pertinent and vital information for all.

Writing a book isn't easy, especially when two people are involved. Time and schedules are always of the extreme importance. I had to dig and listen at all times for information from all sources. My son actually grew up with this book. When I moved to Chicago in 1988 for him to attend the Marva Collins Westside Preparatory School, he was only six years old. He and I would go to the main library every day after school. We went so much that we had our own table.

At the public libraries there are people who are considered regulars. If you missed a day, when you returned you would hear a kind whisper of "we missed you" from some of the regulars. I would return a kind smile.

The regulars became involved in my research. Different patrons brought me articles and clippings on *Our Gang*. All the regulars and librarians at various libraries around the United States are excited about this book because it is a part of them. It is a part of Mr. J. and me as well.

Epilogue

From the bottom of my heart, I hope you enjoyed reading my book. It wasn't easy to write. My coauthor, Gwendolyn Sides St. Julian, had to pin me down to tell my story, and it took seventeen years. It's a book full of history, the story of a black man who began his entertainment career in the early years of the twentieth century. The book preserves the history of that era. We were always using our head to make an honest dollar. I felt I had to write this book because I had such an exciting, fulfilling life, and I wanted it to be accurately documented. Many times a line or two would be written about me in someone else's book, but my life has been more than one line. I wanted my rightful place in history. I also wanted to share my life in entertainment, before the industry was revolutionized by modern technology. I enjoyed watching all the changes in the business. It's been great to train and work with some of the grandest stars of all time.

My message to the parents is to walk, talk, interact, stay close to your children, molding them into productive citizens for tomorrow. Never give up on them. Use your Bible as a guide for raising the children. Use your faith and prayers to God for strength. To all I say, never give up on a goal. Work diligently to the end, even if you must take a break and then return to the task. Remember that everyone has a God-given talent. It is up to the individual to polish, sculpt and fine-tune the gift. It is up to us to use our inner spirit and strength to better our lives, the lives of others and the world.

A note to the young drug dealers on the corner: Take your entrepreneurial skills and sell something positive. Turn your life around to promote your talent. Work hard at your task to mold it into a skill for profit, but don't expect it to be easy. Don't expect anyone to give you anything because no one owes you anything, not one red cent, not one iota. No one gave me anything — I made my own way. I always used my head to think in terms of the future.

Your mind is the most precious gift from God. Don't put anything in your mind to alter it. Keep it open for creativity to flow freely. You can carve your own way by cutting corners, maneuvering here and there. Nothing in life is

TOP LEFT: Eugene Jackson, one-man band. TOP RIGHT: Eugene plays an old man for a *Sanford and Son* appearance. BOTTOM: An *Our Gang* reunion in Sherman Oaks, California. Eugene (middle row, fourth from left) is standing directly behind Ernest "Sunshine Sammy" Morrison, who is seated next to *Our Gang* creator Hal Roach.

smooth sailing. You can be what you want to be. Should you decide to enter the field of entertainment, your road will be a little less bumpy because I experienced the bruises, scratches, scrapes, thorns, pain and joy first. You won't escape all the bruises, but the big hurdles have been cleared by me, and other entertainers of an earlier era.

I don't have big money, no big estate to leave, but I've left a rich trail of history — my history, our history, a history of dance and entertainment, of how things used to be when the show had to go on no matter how you felt.

This book tells of a time when timing meant everything, or when you could miss your punch line or cue, your train or your bus. We made a mark that should never be forgotten or erased from anyone's memory, for we were "the salt of the earth," the ones who endured the pleasant and not so pleasant all for the spirit and flavor of show business.

The people in today's industry could never feel our moments or walk in our shoes. The prints of our shoes would be too big. The load and cargo would be too heavy. We were

Recent publicity photo of Eugene W. Jackson.

raised differently, which was how we were able to withstand the demanding schedules. I'm proof of all that, for I'm still living. Remember my time, remember my kind, and remember my story.

Filmography

I started in the movies in the early 1920s, 1923 to be exact. I believe I have appeared in about 500 motion pictures, television segments and commercials. To gather all of this information is almost an impossible job because, like I told you earlier in the book, many times dancers and musicians were not listed in the credits. Before I became a featured player, I must have appeared in about 100 films as an extra, in bit parts, or as a part of the atmosphere. There is no way I can find the titles of those films. I relied on my memory, my fans' memories and my scrapbooks to aid in compiling the filmography.

My scrapbooks were full of clippings from around the United States. I had been keeping a journal of about 200 films listing the producers, directors, casts and dates, but it was lost in our move from Los Angeles to Compton. In order to complete this filmography, my coauthor used the library's reference books. I have told my story using the dates that I *worked* on the films. This will clarify possible differences between dates in my story and the original release dates. (Remember, it took a long time to produce a film back then.) We have tried, though, to list film release dates to coincide with the Library of Congress listings.

In writing this book, my coauthor combed through old books, newspapers, writings and letters for a total of 17 years' worth of research. When the exact date cannot be pinpointed for parts, such as television shows, the air-date years for my appearances are listed. For instance, I was a regular part of the atmosphere on *Days of Our Lives* from 1965–1986. I could not trace the exact dates of my appearances; therefore, the entry is listed as 1965–1986.

My files from my agent's office were unavailable to me because my agent had retired. When I could remember what kind of scene I was in to help identify me, the scene or part is listed. This was the best I could do, but I think that's pretty good memory for a man my age. Otherwise, each entry includes, in order (and where appropriate): date, title, distributor, studio, producer, director, and partial cast. To prevent redundancy, my name is omitted from the casts.

1923

Her Reputation. Thomas H. Ince Corp. **Dist.:** Associated First National Pictures. **Director:** John Griffith. **Cast:** May McAvoy, Lloyd Hughes, James Corrigan, Casson Ferguson, Eric Mayne, Winter Hall, Louise Lester, Brinsley Shaw, George Larkin, Eugenie Besserer, Jane Miller, Jane Wray, Gus Leonard, Charlie the Monkey.

Penrod and Sam. J.K. McDonald. **Dist.:** Associated First National Pictures. **Director:** William Beaudine. **Cast:** Ben Alexander, Joe Butterworth, Buddy Messinger, Newton Hall, Gertrude Messinger, Joe McGray, Rockliffe Fellowes, Gladys Brockwell, Mary Philbin, Gareth Hughes, William V. Mong, Martha Mattox, Vic Potel, Bobby Gordon, Cameo the Dog.

Boy of Mine. J.K. McDonald. **Dist.:** Associated First National Pictures. **Director:** William Beaudine. **Cast:** Ben Alexander, Rockliffe Fellowes, Henry B. Walthall, Irene Rich, Dot Farley, Lawrence Licalzi.

1924–1928

Black Casting Agency, run by Jimmy Smith and Charles Butler on Twelfth and Central. Jasper Weldon took over and ran it from his apartment on Fifty-Second Street between Hooper and Central.

1924–1980

Central Casting. I received major roles, bit parts, extra parts, stand-ins and atmosphere work.

1924

December 14. *Our Gang:* "The Mysterious Mystery." Pathé Exchange. **Producer:** Hal Roach. **Director:** Robert F. McGowan. **Cast:** Mickey Daniels, Jackie Condon, Joe Cobb, Andy Samuels, Allen "Farina" Hoskins, William Gillespie, Sam Lufkin, Dick Gilbert, Charles Bachman, Allen Cavan, Charley Young.

1925

January 11. *Our Gang:* "The Big Town." Pathé Exchange. **Producer:** Hal Roach. **Director:** Robert McGowan. **Cast:** Mickey Daniels, Mary Kornman, Joe Cobb, Jackie Condon, Allen Hoskins, Gus Leonard, William Gillespie, Helen Gilmore, Lyle Tayo, Jack Gavin.

February 8. *Our Gang:* "Circus Fever." Pathé Exchange. **Producer:** Hal Roach. **Director:** Robert McGowan. **Cast:** Mickey Daniels, Mary Kornman, Joe Cobb, Allen Hoskins, Jackie Condon, Johnny Downs, Peggy Ahearn, Wadell Carter, Ernie Morrison, Sr., Charley Young.

March 8. *Our Gang:* "Dog Days." Pathé Exchange. **Producer:** Hal Roach. **Director:** Robert F. McGowan. **Cast:** Mickey Daniels, Joe Cobb, Allen Hoskins, Mary Kornman, Jackie Condon.

April 5. *Our Gang:* "The Love Bug." Pathé Exchange. **Producer:** Hal Roach. **Director:** Robert F. McGowan. **Cast:** Mickey Daniels, Mary Kornman, Joe Cobb, Jackie Condon, Allen Hoskins, Johnny Downs, Peggy Ahearn, Wadell Carter, William Gillespie, Ernie Morrison, Sr.

May 3. *Our Gang:* "Shootin' Injuns." Pathé Exchange. **Producer:** Hal Roach. **Director:** Robert McGowan. **Cast:** Mickey Daniels, Jackie Condon, Allen Hoskins, Joe Cobb, Johnny Downs, W.R. Jones, Richard Daniels, Martin Wolfkeil, Jack Gavin, William Gillespie.

Thief of Baghdad. **Director:** Raoul Walsh. **Partial Cast:** Douglas Fairbanks, Snitz Edwards, Charles Belcher, Julanne Johnston, Anna May Wong, Winter-Blossom, Etta Lee, Brandon Hurst, Noble Johnson, Charles Stevens, Sam Baker, Jess Weldon, Scotty Mattraw, Charles Sylvester.

Little Annie Rooney. Mary Pickford Co. **Dist.:** United Artists. **Director:** William Beaudine. **Partial Cast:** Mary Pickford, William Haines, Walter James,

Gordon Griffith, Carlo Schipa, Spec O'Donnell, Hugh Fay, Vola Vale, Joe Butterworth, Oscar Rudolph.

1926–27

Buster Brown and Mary Jane comedies. Directors of comedies on the lot: Al Herman, Charles Lamont, Jess Robbins. Cast: Arthur Trimble, Doreen Turner, and Tige the Dog.

Century comedies (Boy Scouts). Producer: Julius Stern. Directors: Alf Goulding and Fred Fishback. These men did some work with child actors at Century Productions.

Mack Sennett comedies. Producer-Director: Mack Sennett. Fred Fishback was the director for a while. Associated with Pathé 1923–28.

Uncle Tom's Cabin. Universal Pictures. Director: Harry Pollard. Partial Cast: James Lowe, Virginia Grey, George Siegmann, Margarita Fisher, Eulalie Jensen, Jack Mower, Vivian Oakland, J. Gordon Russell, Skipper Zeliff, Lassie Lou Ahern, Mona Ray, Aileen Manning, Gertrude Howard.

The Jazz Singer. Director: Alan Crosland. Partial Cast: Al Jolson, May McAvoy, Warner Oland, Eugenie Besserer, Bobby Gordon, Otto Lederer, Cantor Josef Rosenblatt.

1929

Hearts in Dixie. Fox Film Corp. Producer: William Fox. Director: Paul Sloane. Cast: Clarence Muse, Stepin Fetchit, Bernice Pilot, Clifford Ingram, Mildred Washington, Dorothy Morrison, Vivian Smith, Robert Brooks, A.C. Billbrew, Richard Carlyle.

Fox Movietone Follies of 1929. Fox Film Corp. Producer: William Fox. Director: David Butler. Partial Cast: John Breeden, Lola Lane, De Witt Jennings, Sharon Lynn, Arthur Stone, Stepin Fetchit, John Griffith, Sue Carol, Dixie Lee, Jeanette Dancey.

It's a Great Life. MGM. Director: Sam Wood. Cast: Rosetta Duncan, Vivian Duncan, Lawrence Gray, Jed Prouty, Benny Rubin.

1930

Cameo Kirby. Fox Film Corp. Producer: William Fox. Director: Irving Cummings. Cast: J. Harold Murray, Norma Terris, Douglas Gilmore, Robert Edeson, Myrna Loy, Charles Morton, Stepin Fetchit, George MacFarlane, John Hyams, Madame Daumery, Beulah Hall Jones.

Dixiana. RKO Productions. Producer: William LeBaron. Director: Luther Reed. Cast: Bebe Daniels, Everett Marshall, Bert Wheeler, Robert Woolsey, Joseph Cawthorn, Jobyna Howland, Dorothy Lee, Ralf Harolde, Edward Chandler, George Herman, Raymond Maurel, Bruce Covington, Bill Robinson.

The Big Trail. Fox Film Corp. Director: Raoul Walsh. Partial Cast: John Wayne, Marguerite Churchill, Tully Marshall, Tyrone Power, David Rollins, Ian Keith, Frederick Burton, Russ Powell.

1931

Cimarron. An Academy Award–winning film. RKO. Producer: William LeBaron. Director: Wesley Ruggles. Partial Cast: Richard Dix, Irene Dunne, Estelle Taylor, Nance O'Neil, William Collier, Jr., Roscoe Ates, George E. Stone.

Sporting Blood. MGM. Director: Charles Brabin. Cast: Clark Gable, Ernest Torrence, Madge Evans, Lew Cody, Marie Prevost, Harry Holman, Hallam Cooley, J. Farrell MacDonald, John Larkin, Tommy Boy the Horse.

Secret Service. Dist.: RKO Radio Pictures. Producer: William LeBaron. Director: J. Walter Ruben. Cast: Richard Dix, William Post, Jr., Shirley Grey, Nance O'Neil, Harold Kinney, Gavin Gordon, Florence Lake, Frederick Burton, Clarence Muse, Fred Warren Virginia Sale, Carl Gerard, Gertrude Howard.

Sporting Chance. Peerless. Independent Film. **Producer and Director:** Albert Herman. **Cast:** Buster Collier, Jr., Claudia Dell, James Hall, Joseph Levering, Henry Roquemore, Hedwiga Reicher, Mahlon Hamilton.

1933

King of the Jungle. Paramount Productions, Inc. **Associate Producer:** E. Lloyd Sheldon. **Director:** H. Bruce Humberstone. **Partial Cast:** Buster Crabbe, Frances Dee, Sidney Toler, Nydia Westman, Robert Barrat, Irving Pichel, Douglass Dumbrille, Sam Baker, Patricia Farley, Ronnie Cosbey.

1935

Ladies Crave Excitement. Mascot Pictures Corp. **Producer:** Nat Levine. **Director:** Nick Grinde. **Partial Cast:** Norman Foster, Evalyn Knapp, Eric Linden, Esther Ralston, Purnell Pratt, Irene Franklin, Emma Dunn, Gilbert Emery, Russell Hicks, Christian Rub, Francis McDonald, Matt McHugh, Jason Robards, Syd Saylor, George Hayes.

Cheers of the Crowd. **Dist.:** Monogram Pictures Corp. **Producer:** Trem Carr. **Director:** Vin Moore. **Cast:** Russell Hopton, Irene Ware, Harry Holman, Bradley Page, John Quillan, Wade Boteler, John H. Dilson, Roberta Gale, Betty Blythe.

Tumbling Tumbleweeds. Republic Pictures Corp. **Producer:** Nat Levine. **Director:** Joseph Kane. **Partial Cast:** Gene Autry, Smiley Burnette, Lucille Browne, George Hayes, Norma Taylor, Edward Hearn, Jack Rockwell, George Chesebro, Frankie Marvin.

1936

Lonely Trail. Republic Pictures Corp. **Producer:** Nat Levine. **Director:** Joseph Kane. **Partial Cast:** John Wayne, Ann Rutherford, Cy Kendall, Bob Kortman, Sam Flint, Denny Meadows, Jim Tony, Etta McDaniels, Jack Ingram.

Red River Valley. **Dist.:** Republic Pictures Corp. **Director:** B. Reeves Eason. **Partial Cast:** Gene Autry, Smiley Burnette, Frances Grant, Boothe Howard, Jack Kennedy, Sam Flint, George Chesebro, Ken Cooper.

The Singing Kid. Warner Bros. Pictures, Inc. A First National Picture. **Producer:** Robert Lord. **Director:** William Keighley. **Partial Cast:** Al Jolson, Sybil Jason, Beverly Roberts, Edward Everett Horton, Hattie McDaniel.

Guns and Guitars. **Dist.:** Republic Pictures Corp. **Producer:** Nat Levine. **Director:** Joseph Kane. **Partial Cast:** Gene Autry, Smiley Burnette, Dorothy Dix, Earl Hodgins, J.P. McGowan, Ken Cooper, Tracy Layne.

Hearts in Bondage. **Dist.:** Republic Pictures Corp. **Producer:** Nat Levine. **Director:** Lew Ayres. **Partial Cast:** James Dunn, Mae Clarke, David Manners, Charlotte Henry, Henry B. Walthall.

Born to Dance. MGM. **Producer:** Jack Cummings. **Rec. Director:** Roy Del Ruth. **Partial Cast:** Eleanor Powell, James Stewart, Virginia Bruce, Una Merkel, Sid Silvers, Buddy Ebsen, Juanita Quigley.

1937

It Can't Last Forever. **Dist.:** Columbia Pictures Corp. **Producer:** Irving Briskin. **Director:** Hamilton MacFadden. **Partial Cast:** Ralph Bellamy, Betty Furness, Robert Armstrong, Raymond Walburn, Thurston Hall, Wade Boteler, Charles Judels, Barbara Burbank.

Midnight Court. **Dist.:** Warner Bros. Pictures. **Producer:** Bryan Foy. **Director:** Frank McDonald. **Partial Cast:** Ann Dvorak, John Litel, Carlyle Moore, Jr., Joseph Crehan, William Davidson, Stanley Fields, Walter Miller, Lyle Moraine, Joan Woodbury.

Blonde Trouble. **Dist.:** Paramount Pictures, Inc. **Producer:** Paul Jones. **Director:** George Archainbaud. **Partial Cast:** Eleanore Whitney, Johnny Downs, Lynne

Overman, Terry Walker, Benny Baker, William Demarest, John Patterson, El Brendel, Spec O'Donnell.

***Wine, Women and Horses.* Dist.:** Warner Bros. Pictures, Inc. **Producer:** Jack L. Warner and Hal B. Wallis. **Director:** Louis King. **Cast:** Barton MacLane, Ann Sheridan, Dick Purcell, Peggy Bates, Walter Cassell, Lottie Williams, Kenneth Harlan, Charles Foy, James Robbins.

1938

Rhythm Rodeo. Million Dollar Productions. **Producers:** Harry and Leo Popkin. **Director:** George Randol. **Cast:** Troy Brown, The Four Tones, Freddie Baker, Rosa Lee Lincoln, Jim Davis.

***The Buccaneer.* Dist.:** Paramount Pictures, Inc. A Cecil B. De Mille Production. **Director:** Cecil B. De Mille. **Partial Cast:** Fredric March, Franciska Gaal, Akim Tamiroff, Margot Grahame, Walter Brennan, Spring Byington, Douglass Dumbrille.

***You Can't Take It with You.* Dist.:** Columbia Pictures Corp. of California. **Producer-Director:** Frank Capra. **Partial Cast:** Jean Arthur, Lionel Barrymore, James Stewart, Edward Arnold, Mischa Auer, Ann Miller, Spring Byington, Donald Meek.

***Arrest Bulldog Drummond.* Dist.:** Paramount Pictures, Inc. **Producer:** William LeBaron. **Director:** James Hogan. **Partial Cast:** John Howard, Heather Angel, H.B. Warner, Reginald Denny, Jean Fenwick.

***Tom Sawyer, Detective.* Dist.:** Paramount Pictures, Inc. **Associate Producer:** Edward T. Lowe. **Director:** Louis King. **Partial Cast:** Billy Cook, Donald O'Connor, Porter Hall, Phillip Warren, Janet Waldo, Howard Mitchell, Elisabeth Risdon, Edward Pawley.

***Kentucky.* Dist.:** 20th Century–Fox Film Corp. **Associate Producer:** Gene Markey. **Director:** David Butler. **Partial**

Cast: Loretta Young, Richard Greene, Walter Brennan, Douglass Dumbrille, Karen Morley, Cliff Clark, Stymie Beard, Bernice Pilot.

1939

Harlem Tuff Kids. This was a takeoff of the white *The Dead End Kids.* The Gold Seal Company, under the Million Dollar name. Released by Sack–Million Dollar international circuit. **Cast:** Freddie Baker, Paul White, DeForest Covan, Eddie Lynn.

Reform School (Harlem Tuff Kids). Million Dollar Productions. **Cast:** Louise Beavers, Reginald Fenderson, Monte Hawley, Maceo B. Sheffield, Jess Lee Brooks, Vernon McCalla, Freddie Baker, Paul White, DeForest Covan, Eddie Lynn, Bob Simmons.

***Boy Friend.* Dist.:** 20th Century–Fox Film Corp. **Associate Producer:** John Stone. **Director:** James Tinling. **Partial Cast:** Jane Withers, Arleen Whelan, George Ernest, Richard Bond, Douglas Fowley, Warren Hymer, Robert Kellard, Minor Watson, Myra Marsh, Ted Pearson, Robert Shaw.

***The Lady's from Kentucky.* Dist.:** Paramount Pictures, Inc. **Producer:** Jeff Lazarus. **Director:** Alexander Hall. **Partial Cast:** George Raft, Ellen Drew, Hugh Herbert, ZaSu Pitts, Louise Beavers, Lew Payton, Forrester Harvey, Harry Tyler, Edward J. Pawley, Gilbert Emery.

***Television Spy.* Dist.:** Paramount Pictures, Inc. **Producer:** William LeBaron. **Director:** Edward Dmytryk. **Partial Cast:** William Henry, Judith Barrett, William Collier, Sr., Richard Denning, John Eldredge, Minor Watson.

At the Circus. MGM Corp. **Dist.:** Loew's Inc. **Producer:** Mervyn LeRoy. **Director:** Edward Buzzell. **Partial Cast:** Groucho Marx, Chico Marx, Harpo Marx, Kenny Baker, Florence Rice, Eve Arden, Margaret Dumont, Nat Pendleton, 30 circus performers from the Hagenbeck–Wallace Circus.

The Honeymoon's Over. **Dist.:** 20th Century–Fox Film Corp. **Producer:** Sol M. Wurtzel. **Directors:** Eugene Forde and William Beaudine. **Partial Cast:** Stuart Erwin, Marjorie Weaver, Patric Knowles, Russell Hicks, Jack Carson, Hobart Cavanaugh, June Gale.

1940

Seventeen. **Dist.:** Paramount Pictures, Inc. **Producer:** William LeBaron. **Director:** Louis King. **Partial Cast:** Jackie Cooper, Betty Field, Otto Kruger, Ann Shoemaker, Norma Nelson, Betty Moran, Thomas Ross, Peter Hayes, Buddy Pepper, Donald Haines, Richard Denning.

1941

Dumbo. Walt Disney. **Director:** Ben Sharpsteen. **Voices:** Edward Brophy, Herman Bing, Verna Felton, Sterling Holloway, Cliff Edwards.

Unfinished Business. Universal. **Producer-Director:** Gregory La Cava. **Partial Cast:** Irene Dunne, Robert Montgomery, Preston Foster, Eugene Pallette, Dick Foran, Esther Dale, Walter Catlett, Richard Davies, Kathryn Adams, Samuel S. Hinds.

1942

Reap the Wild Wind. Paramount. **Producer-Director:** Cecil B. De Mille. **Partial Cast:** Ray Milland, John Wayne, Paulette Goddard, Raymond Massey, Robert Preston, Lynne Overman, Susan Hayward, George Reed, Hedda Hopper, Ben Carter, Davison Clark, Milburn Stone.

Take My Life (Harlem Tuff Kids). Toddy-Consolidated. **Producer-Director:** Harry M. Popkin. **Cast:** Freddie Baker, Paul White, Eddie Lynn, DeForest Covan, Monte Hawley, Jeni LeGon, Lovey Lane, Robert Webb, Jack Carr, Harry Leverette, Guernsey Morrow, Herbert Skinner, Arthur Ray.

1943

Moo Cow Boogie. Sack Amusement Enterprises. **Cast:** Dorothy Dandridge, Stepin Fetchit, Troy Brown.

Reveille with Beverly. Columbia Pictures. **Producer:** Sam White. **Director:** Charles Barton. **Partial Cast:** Ann Miller, William Wright, Dick Purcell, Franklin Pangborn, Tim Ryan, Larry Parks, Adele Mara, Walter Sande, Wally Vernon, Barbara Brown, Andrew Tombes.

What's Buzzin' Cousin? Columbia. **Producer:** Jack Fier. **Director:** Charles Barton. **Cast:** Ann Miller, John Hubbard, Eddie Anderson, Leslie Brooks, Jeff Donnell.

1946

Lady Luck. RKO. **Producer:** Warren Duff. **Director:** Edwin L. Mann. **Partial Cast:** Robert Young, Barbara Hale, Frank Morgan, James Gleason, Don Rice, Harry Davenport, Lloyd Corrigan, Teddy Hart, Douglas Morrow, Frank Dae, Nancy Saunders, Jack Norton.

1948

Scudda Hoo! Scudda Hay! Fox. **Director:** Hugh Herbert. **Cast:** June Haver, Lon McCallister, Walter Brennan, Anne Revere, Natalie Wood, Robert Karnes, Marilyn Monroe, Henry Hull, Tom Tully.

1951–53

Amos 'n' Andy. **Producers:** Freeman Gosden and Charles Correll. Television. CBS situation comedy. I played a Western Union messenger boy. **Cast:** Alvin Childress, Spencer Williams, Jr., Tim Moore, Johnny Lee, Ernestine Wade, Horace "Nick" Stewart, Ramona Smith, Amanda Randolph, Lillian Randolph.

1954

Drum Beat. Warner Bros. **Producer:** Alan Ladd. **Director:** Delmer Daves. **Partial Cast:** Alan Ladd, Audrey Dalton, Marisa Pavan, Robert Keith, Rodolfo

Acosta, Charles Bronson, Warner Anderson, Elisha Cook, Jr., Perry Lopez, Richard Gaines, Frank De Kova, Pat Lawless, George Lewis.

1955

Artists and Models. Paramount. **Producer:** Hal B. Wallis. **Director:** Frank Tashlin. **Partial Cast:** Dean Martin, Jerry Lewis, Shirley MacLaine, Dorothy Malone, Eddie Mayehoff, Eva Gabor, Anita Ekberg, George Winslow, Jack Elam, Herbert Rudley, Richard Shannon, Richard Webb, Alan Lee, Kathleen Freeman, Art Baker, Carleton Young, Nick Castle.

1957

Jeanne Eagels. Columbia. **Producer-Director:** George Sidney. **Partial Cast:** Kim Novak, Jeff Chandler, Agnes Moorehead, Charles Drake, Larry Gates, Virginia Grey, Gene Lockhart, Lowell Gilmore, Leon Tyler, Lee Trent, Jack Ano.

1958

King Creole. Paramount. **Producer:** Hal B. Wallis. **Director:** Michael Curtiz. **Partial Cast:** Elvis Presley, Carolyn Jones, Dolores Hart, Dean Jagger, Liliane Montevecchi, Walter Matthau, Jan Shepard, Paul Stewart, Vic Morrow, Brian Hutton, Jack Grinnage, Dick Winslow, Raymond Bailey, Ziva Rodann, Hazel Boyne.

The Long Hot Summer. Fox. **Producer:** Jerry Wald. **Director:** Martin Ritt. **Partial Cast:** Paul Newman, Joanne Woodward, Orson Welles, Lee Remick, Angela Lansbury, Richard Anderson, Sarah Marshall, William Walker, Ralph Reed, Jim Brandt.

1959

The Gene Kelly Pontiac Special. CBS. **Partial Cast:** Claude Bussy, Cherylene Lee, Liza Minnelli, Carl Sandburg.

1963

Forty Pounds of Trouble. Curtis Enterprises. **Dist.:** Universal Pictures. **Producer:** Stan Margulies. **Director:** Norman Jewison. **Partial Cast:** Tony Curtis, Suzanne Pleshette, Phil Silvers, Claire Wilcox, Larry Storch, Howard Morris, Edward Andrews, Stubby Kaye, David Allen, Sharon Farrell, Tom Reese.

1964

Robin and the Seven Hoods. **Dist.:** Warner Bros. Pictures. **Producer:** Frank Sinatra. **Director:** Gordon Douglas. **Partial Cast:** Frank Sinatra, Sammy Davis, Jr., Bing Crosby, Dean Martin, Barbara Rush, Peter Falk, Edward G. Robinson, Victor Buono, Barry Kelley, Hank Henry, Robert Carricart.

1964–65

The Tycoon. Television. ABC. This was a situation comedy. I played a barber and had a shoe-shine stand in an episode. **Partial Cast:** Walter Brennan, Van Williams.

1965–1987

Days of Our Lives. Television. NBC soap opera. I did atmosphere work on this soap during this time period. Trivia: The Fifth Dimension's Marilyn McCoo joined the soap in 1986 when she came to sing at Marlena's wedding. Tonya Boyd (Celeste) sang backup for Lou Rawls, Anita Baker and Natalie Cole.

1966–69

Daktari. Television. CBS. I drove the jeep in every scene. Trivia: Clarence the lion had starred in an Ivan Tors movie called *Clarence the Cross-Eyed Lion* before coming to *Daktari.*

1968–71

Julia. Television. CBS. I played Uncle Lou, who would visit periodically. **Partial Cast:** Diahann Carroll, Lloyd Nolan, Betty Beaird, Marc Copage. Trivia: Singer Diahann was the first black woman to star in her own comedy series in a "prestige" part. She was not a maid; she was a professional nurse. The show had an integrated cast. The network executives were delighted that *Julia* was accepted into all households — they had been very nervous about the airing of this show.

1969–72

The Merv Griffin Show. Television. CBS. In one of his segments, I was in a dance group routine. Trivia: Merv was a former band singer. He created *Wheel of Fortune* and *Jeopardy*, creations that made him a wealthy man.

1970

The Great White Hope. **Dist.:** 20th Century–Fox Film Corp. **Producer:** Lawrence Turman. **Director:** Martin Ritt. **Partial Cast:** James Earl Jones, Jane Alexander, Lou Gilbert, Joel Fluellen, Chester Morris, Robert Webber, Scatman Crothers, Bill Walker, Roy Glenn.

1971

Support Your Local Gunfighter. **Director:** Burt Kennedy. **Cast:** James Garner, Suzanne Pleshette, Jack Elam, Harry Morgan, John Dehner, Joan Blondell, Dub Taylor, Ellen Corby, Henry Jones, Marie Windsor, Dick Curtis, Chuck Connors, Grady Sutton.

1971–76

Cannon. Television. CBS. In different segments I did extra and bit parts. William Conrad was the star.

1972–77

Sanford and Son. Television. NBC. In many segments I played one of Fred's cronies. **Partial Cast:** Redd Foxx, Demond Wilson, Slappy White, Whitman Mayo, Hal Williams, LaWanda Page, Beah Richards.

1973–88

Police Story. Television. NBC and ABC. I did extra and bit parts on different segments.

1973

Forty Carats. Columbia Pictures. **Producer:** M.J. Frankovich. **Director:** Milton Katselas. **Partial Cast:** Liv Ullman, Edward Albert, Gene Kelly, Binnie Barnes, Deborah Raffin, Billy Green Bush, Nancy Walker.

1973–90

Kojak. Television. CBS and ABC. I did atmosphere work throughout. Telly Savalas was the star.

1974

Mame. Warner Bros. **Producers:** Robert Fryer and James Cresson. **Director:** Gene Saks. **Partial Cast:** Lucille Ball, Robert Preston, Beatrice Arthur, Bruce Davison, Joyce Van Patten, Don Porter.

1975–76

The Cop and the Kid. Television. NBC. I had a part in several segments. This was a show about an Irish policeman having custoy of a black youth. **Partial Cast:** Charles Durning, Tierre Turner, Sharon Spelman, Eric Laneuville.

1975–76

The Blue Knight. Television. CBS. During this series, I had a shoe-shine stand. **Cast:** George Kennedy, Phillip Pine, Charles Siebert, Lin McCarthy.

1975

The Friday Comedy Special. Television. CBS.

1976

Treasure of Matecumbe. Disney. **Director:** Vincent McEveety. **Cast:** Robert Foxworth, Joan Hackett, Peter Ustinov, Vic Morrow, Jane Wyatt, Johnny Doran, Billy "Pop" Attmore.

Rocky. Won Academy Award for Best Picture. **Director:** John G. Avildsen. **Cast:** Sylvester Stallone, Talia Shire, Carl

Weathers, Burt Young, Burgess Meredith, Thayer David.

All the President's Men. Warner Bros. **Producer:** Walter Coblenz. **Director:** Alan J. Pakula. **Partial Cast:** Dustin Hoffman, Robert Redford, Bob Woodward, Carl Bernstein.

1976–77

Serpico. Television. NBC. I did bit parts throughout this series. **Cast:** David Birney, Tom Atkins.

1977

The Richard Pryor Show. Television. NBC. I was a dancer. *Partial Cast:* Richard Pryor, Tim Reid, Marsha Warfield, Robin Williams.

1977–78

Roots. Television. ABC. I was the stand-in for LeVar Burton. I wasn't chosen for a role because the producers and directors did not feel that I had African features.

1978–91

Dallas. Television. CBS. Atmosphere work. **Partial Cast:** Larry Hagman, Barbara Bel Geddes, Jim Davis, Patrick Duffy, Victoria Principal, Charlene Tilton, Linda Gray.

1978

Five Days from Home. Director: George Peppard. **Cast:** George Peppard, Neville Brand, Savannah Smith, Sherry Boucher, Victor Campos, Robert Donner.

1979–81

Roots: The Next Generations. Television, ABC. Stand-in for stars.

1979

What's Happening Now. Television. Syndicated. I had a role in one of the segments.

Escape from Alcatraz. Director: Donald Siegel. I was a prisoner with a band behind bars. **Partial Cast:** Clint Eastwood, Patrick McGoohan, Roberts Blossom, Jack Thibeau, Fred Ward, Paul Benjamin.

1980

Joni. Director: James F. Collier. **Cast:** Joni Eareckson, Bert Remsen, Katherine De Hetre, Cooper Huckabee, John Milford, Michael Mancini, Richard Lineback. This film was financed by Billy Graham.

American Gigolo. Director: Paul Schrader. **Partial Cast:** Richard Gere, Lauren Hutton, Hector Elizondo, Nina Van Pallandt, Frances Bergen.

Popeye. Director: Robert Altman. **Cast:** Robin Williams, Shelley Duvall, Ray Walston, Paul Smith, Paul Dooley, Richard Libertini, Wesley Ivan Hurt, Linda Hurt.

1981

The Gangster Chronicles. Television. NBC. **Partial Cast:** Michael Nouri, Joe Penny, Brian Benben. E.G. Marshall was the narrator.

Simon and Simon. Television. CBS. I had a shoe-shine stand. **Partial Cast:** Jameson Parker, Gerald McRaney, Mary Carver, Jeannie Wilson.

1983–87

Webster. Television. ABC. **Partial Cast:** Emmanuel Lewis, Alex Karras, Ben Vereen, Susan Clark. Trivia: At 12 years old, Emmanuel was only 30 inches tall. He was discovered by a network executive in a Burger King commercial.

1983

The Day After. Director: Nicholas Meyer. **Cast:** Jason Robards, JoBeth Williams, Steve Guttenberg, John Cullum, John Lithgow, Bibi Besch, Amy Madigan, Jeff East.

1984

Splash. **Director:** Ron Howard. **Cast:** Daryl Hannah, Tom Hanks, John Candy, Eugene Levy, Dody Goodman, Richard B. Shull.

1984–89

Highway to Heaven. Television. NBC. **Producer-Writer:** Michael Landon. **Partial Cast:** Michael Landon, Victor French. I played a barber in a segment.

1984–91

Night Court. Television. NBC. Throughout this series, I had a shoe-shine stand. **Partial Cast:** Harry Anderson, Karen Austin, Selma Diamond.

1985–1990

227. Television. NBC. I played different roles, such as musician and dancer. **Partial Cast:** Marla Gibbs, Hal Williams, Jackee (Harry), Paul Winfield, Stoney Jackson.

1986

Bank of America commercial.

G.T.E. Telephone commercial.

The Redd Foxx Show. Television. ABC. **Partial Cast:** Redd Foxx, Sinbad, Beverly Todd.

1987

Burger King commercial. April 19.

Frank's Place. Television. CBS. I played a dead man. **Partial Cast:** Tim Reid, Lincoln Kilpatrick, Daphne Reid, Virginia Capers, Tony Burton.

1990

Lotto commercial.

1992

Life Stinks. MGM-Pathé. **Producer-Director:** Mel Brooks. **Partial Cast:** Mel Brooks, Lesley Ann Warren, Jeffrey Tambor, Stuart Pankin, Howard Morris, Teddy Wilson, Rudy DeLuca.

The Addams Family. Paramount. **Director:** Barry Sonnenfeld. **Partial Cast:** Anjelica Huston, Raul Julia, Christopher Lloyd, Dan Hedaya, Elizabeth Wilson, Judith Malina.

You Bet Your Life. **Host:** Bill Cosby. Carsey–Werner Company.

Taco Bell commercial.

1993

Picket Fences. Television. CBS. **Partial Cast:** Tom Skerritt, Kathy Baker.

Year Unknown

Romance Theater: The Heiress. Television. ABC Special. The production company was from San Diego. Virginia Capers was the star. I called her to see if she could remember anything, but she could not. No one can seem to find the year that we did this special. Perhaps a television buff can contact us with some information.

Bibliography

Books

Baer, D. Richard. *Harrison Reports and Film Reviews 1947–1949*. Vols. 8–10. Hollywood: Hollywood Film Archives, 1992.

Bogle, Donald. 1989. Reprint. *Blacks in American Films and Television: An Encyclopedia*. New York: Simon and Schuster. Original edition, New York: Garland, 1988.

Bond, Tommy, and Ron Genini. *Darn Right It's Butch: Memories of* Our Gang. Wayne, Pa.: Morgin Press, 1994.

Brooks, Tim, and Earle Marsh. *The Complete Directory to Prime Time Network Television Shows, 1946–Present*. New York: Ballantine Books, 1992.

Brown, Gene. *The New York Times Encyclopedia of Film, 1937–40*. New York: Times Books, 1984.

Bushnell, Brooks. *Directors and Their Films: A Comprehensive Reference, 1895–1900*. Jefferson, N.C.: McFarland, 1991.

Carrick, Peter. *A Tribute to Fred Astaire*. Salem, N.H.: Salem House, 1984.

Cary, Diana Serra. *Hollywood's Children*. Boston: Houghton Mifflin, 1979.

Cary, Diana Serra. *What Ever Happened to Baby Peggy?* New York: St. Martin's, 1996.

Case, Patricia Ann. *How to Write Your Autobiography*. Santa Barbara, Calif.: 1977.

Coghlan, Frank. *They Still Call Me Junior*. Jefferson, N.C.: McFarland, 1993.

Conners, Martin, and Julian Furtaw. *Video Hound's Golden Movie Retriever*. Detroit: Visible Ink, 1991.

Dawson, Jim. *Nervous Man: Nervous Big Jim McNeely and the Rise of the Honking Tenor Sax*. Milford, N.H.: Big Nickel Publications, 1994.

Diawara, Manthia. *Black American Cinema*. Routledge, N.Y., and London: American Film Institute, 1993.

Dye, David. *Child and Youth Actors: Filmographies of Their Entire Careers*. Jefferson, N.C.: McFarland, 1988.

Edgar, Kathleen. *Contemporary Theater, Film and Television*. Vol. 16. Detroit: Gale Research, 1997.

Evans, Glen. *The Complete Guide to Writing Nonfiction by the American Society of Journalists and Authors*. New York: Harper and Row, 1988.

Frank, Rusty E. *The Greatest Tap Dance Stars and Their Stories 1900–1955*. New York: William Morrow, 1990.

Gilbert, Douglas. 1963. Reprint. *American Vaudeville: Its Life and Times*. New York: Dover. Original edition, New York: Whitlesey House, 1940.

Halliwell, Leslie. *The Filmgoer's Companion*. Sixth Edition. New York: Hill and Wang, 1977.

Halliwell, Leslie. *The Filmgoer's Companion*. Eighth Edition. New York: Scribner's, 1984.

Hanson, Patricia King, and Alan Gevinson. *The American Film Institute Catalog Feature Films, 1911–1920*. Los Angeles: University of California Press, 1988.

Hanson, Patricia King, and Alan Gevinson. *The American Film Institute Catalog of Motion Pictures Produced in the United States: Feature Films, 1931–1940*. 2 vols. Los Angeles: University of California Press, 1993.

Haynes, Elizabeth Ross. *Unsung Heroes: The Black Boy of Atlanta: Negroes in Domestic Service in the United States*. New York and London: Prentice Hall International, 1997.

Jones, G. William. *Black Cinema Treasures Lost and Found*. Denton: University of North Texas Press, 1991.

Katz, Ephraim. *The Film Encyclopedia*. New York: Perennial Library, 1990.

Kernfeld, Barry. 1994. Reprint. *The New Grove Dictionary of Jazz*. New York: St. Martin's Press. Original edition, New York: Macmillan, 1988.

Kimes, Beverly. *Standard Catalog of American Cars, 1805–1942*. Iola Wis.: Krause, 1985.

Kinkle, Roger D. *The Complete Encyclopedia of Popular Music and Jazz, 1900–1950*. New Rochelle, N.Y.: Arlington House, 1974.

Korn, Jerry. *This Fabulous Century 1930–1940*. Vol. IV. New York: Time-Life Books, 1971.

Krafsur, Richard P. *The American Film Institute Catalog of Motion Pictures Feature Films, 1961–1970*. New York and London: R.R. Bowker Company, 1996.

Lamparski, Richard. *Whatever Became of...?* Ninth Series. New York: Crown, 1985.

_____. *Whatever Became of...?* Tenth Series. New York: Crown, 1986.

Larkin, Colin. *The Guiness Encyclopedia of Popular Music*. New York: Stockton Press, 1995.

McMurray, Emily. *Contemporary Theater Film and Television*. Vol. 12. Detroit: Gale Research, Inc.

McNeil, Barbara. *Performing Arts Biography Master Index*. Detroit, Mich.: Gale Research Company, 1982.

Magill, Frank. *Magill's Survey of Cinema English Language Films, First Series*. Vol. 4. Englewood Cliffs, N.J.: Salem Press, 1980.

Maltin, Leonard. 1982. Updated edition. *The Great Movie Comedians: From Charlie Chapin to Woody Allen*. New York: Harmony Books, 1982. Original editions, New York: Crown (1978), Bell (1982).

Maltin, Leonard. *Leonard Maltin's 1997 Movie and Video Guide*. New York: Signet, 1996.

Maltin, Leonard, and Richard W. Bann. *Our Gang: The Life and Times of the Little Rascals*. New York: Crown, 1977.

Miller, Lee O. *The Great Cowboy Stars of Movies and Television*. New Rochelle, N.Y.: Arlington House, 1979.

Monush, Barry, and James Moser. *International Motion Picture Almanac*. 1996–97 edition. New York: Quigley Publishing, 1996.

Moore, William. "Legendary Copasetic Tap Dancer Dies." *Crisis*. National Association for the Advancement of Colored People: Baltimore, Md.: November 1991.

Munden, Kenneth W. *The American Film Institute Catalog Feature Films, 1921–1930*. New York and London: R.R. Bowker Company, 1971.

Nash, Jay Robert, and Stanley Ralph Ross. *The Motion Picture Guide*. Vols. 1–10. Chicago: Cinebooks, 1985.

Null, Gary. *Black Hollywood: From 1970 to Today*. Secaucus, N.J.: Carol, 1993.

Null, Gary. *Black Hollywood: The Negro in Motion Pictures*. Secaucus, N.J.: Citadel Press, 1975.

Odd, Gilbert E. *Encyclopedia of Boxing*. New York: Crescent, 1983.

Okuda, Ted. *The Columbia Comedy Shorts: Two-Reel Hollywood Film Comedies, 1933–1958*. Jefferson, N.C.: McFarland, 1986.

Parish, James Robert. *Today's Black Hollywood.* New York: Pinnacle, 1995.

Parrish, Robert. *Growing Up in Hollywood.* New York: Harcourt Brace Jovanovich, 1995.

Pickard, Roy. *A Companion to the Movies, from 1903 to the Present Day.* New York: Hippocrene Books, 1974.

Ragan, David. *Who's Who in Hollywood, 1900–76.* New Rochelle, N.Y.: Arlington House, 1976.

Rose, Phyllis. *Jazz Cleopatra: Josephine Baker in Her Time.* New York: Vintage, 1989.

Rothel, David. *The Singing Cowboys.* South Brunswick, N.J.: A.S. Barnes, 1978.

Sampson, Henry T. *Blacks in Black and White: A Source Book on Black Films.* Metuchen, N.J.: Scarecrow, 1993.

Schiffman, Jack. *Harlem Heyday: A Pictorial History of Modern Black Show Business and the Apollo Theater.* Buffalo, N.Y.: Prometheus Books, 1984.

Siegel, Scott, and Barbara Siegel. *The Encyclopedia of Hollywood.* New York: Facts on File, 1990.

Slide, Anthony. *The Encyclopedia of Vaudeville.* Westport, Conn.: Greenwood Press, 1994.

Slide, Anthony. *The Vaudevillians: A Dictionary of Vaudeville Performers.* Westport, Conn.: Arlington House, 1981.

Solomon, Aubrey, and Tony Thomas. *The Films of Twentieth Century–Fox: Fiftieth Anniversary Edition.* Secaucus: Citadel Press, 1985.

Solomon, Aubrey. *Twentieth Century–Fox: A Corporate and Financial History.* Metuchen, N.J.: Scarecrow, 1988.

Stein, Charles W. *American Vaudeville as Seen by Its Contemporaries.* New York: Knopf, 1984.

Stewart, John. *Filmarama.* Metuchen, N.J.: Scarecrow, 1975.

Terrace, Vincent. *Television Specials: 3,201 Entertainment Spectaculars, 1939–1993.* Jefferson, N.C.: McFarland, 1995.

Thomas, Bob. *Astaire: The Man, the Dancer.* New York: St. Martin's Press, 1984.

Thomas, Nicholas. *International Dictionary of Film and Filmmaker-Directors.* Second edition. Chicago and London: St. James Press, 1991.

Thomas, Tony, and Aubrey Solomon. *The Films of Twentieth Century–Fox: A Pictorial History.* Secaucus, N.J.: Citadel, 1979.

Thomson, David. *A Biographical Dictionary of Film.* Third edition. New York: Knopf, 1994.

Truitt, Evelyn. *Who Was Who on Screen.* Third edition. New York: R.R. Bowker, 1983.

Variety's Film Reviews 1983–1984. Vol. 18. New York: R.R. Bowker, 1986.

Weaver, John T. *Forty Years of Screen Credits, 1929–1969.* Metuchen, N.J.: Scarecrow, 1970.

Whiteburn, Joel. *Top Pop Singles, 1955–1993.* Menomonee Falls, Wis.: Billboard Record Research, 1994.

Zenka, Lorraine. *Days of Our Lives: The Complete Family Album.* New York: HarperCollins, 1995.

Documents

Langellier, Dr. John P. "Buffalo Soldiers." United States Postal Service. Gene Autry Western Heritage Museum, Los Angeles, Calif. 1994.

Articles

"The Arts." *Crisis* 98.10 (1991).
"Black Child Star Paved Way for New Generation." *Wave Publications.* Black History Month Special Edition. February 1992.
"Black Entertainment Legend Opens Doors." *Compton Bulletin.* July 15, 1987.
"Black Inventors and Their Inventions." The Black Museum, a Non-Profit Corporation, 1994.
The Chicago American, April 23, 1932.
Chicago Defender, June 25, 1997.
Chicago Tribune, March 26, 1993.
Classic Images, July 1, 1996.
Compton Bulletin, April 1988.
"L.A.'s Arts Festival Jammin' with the Past." *Los Angeles Times* Calendar, August 15, 1993.
"The Little Rascals." *International Photographer Film and Video Techniques.* September 1994.
Los Angeles Times, August 15, 1993.
"A New Stage in His Life." *Los Angeles Times* Southeast. December 3, 1992.
The New York Times. Theater Reviews. October 11, 1935.
"No More Bwana." *Bronze America.* 2.1 (1965). Wesley Gale.
"Walk of Fame Bid for Local Citizen." *Compton Bulletin.* January 29, 1992.

Unpublished

Wanamaker, Marc. *The Encyclopedia of American Motion Picture Studios: Century Film Company (1917–1926), Stern Film Corporation (1927–1932), Alexander Brothers (1932–1943).* Manuscript.

Index